Protesting America

The Seoul-California Series in Korean Studies is a collaboration between the University of California, Berkeley, and the Kyujanggak Institute for Korean Studies, Seoul National University. The series promotes the global dissemination of scholarship on Korea by publishing distinguished research on Korean history, society, art, and culture by scholars from across the world.

Protesting America

Democracy and the U.S.-Korea Alliance

KATHARINE H. S. MOON

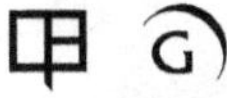

Global, Area, and International Archive
University of California Press
BERKELEY LOS ANGELES LONDON

The Global, Area, and International Archive (GAIA) is an initiative of the Institute of International Studies, University of California, Berkeley, in partnership with the University of California Press, the California Digital Library, and international research programs across the University of California system.

University of California Press, one of the most distinguished university presses in the United States, enriches lives around the world by advancing scholarship in the humanities, social sciences, and natural sciences. Its activities are supported by the UC Press Foundation and by philanthropic contributions from individuals and institutions. For more information, visit www.ucpress.edu.

University of California Press
Berkeley and Los Angeles, California

University of California Press, Ltd.
London, England

Library of Congress Cataloging-in-Publication Data

A catalog record for this book is available from the Library of Congress.

21 20 19 18 17 16 15 14 13 12
10 9 8 7 6 5 4 3 2 1

ISBN: 978-0-520-28981-9

To Daddy, Douglas Kwang Hwan Moon (1938–2001), who wished for me to serve as a bridge between America and Korea

Contents

Acknowledgments

The idea for this book was conceived in the late 1990s, and despite my yearning and good intentions to complete it sooner, the stuff of life happened. The project endured the sudden loss of my father, Douglas Kwang Hwan Moon, a week after the shock and tragedy of September 11, 2001; the death of my young cousin Jin Soo Kim; and the severe pain and grief that accompanied me for many years. My mother, Ai Ra Kim, retired from her teaching position in the midst and struggled to find a new identity, pace, and place of belonging. I learned that the strongest of people can get shaken when the foundation of one existence must transform into another. But life is generous and full of renewal. Along with the disheartening events, I witnessed the heroic efforts of my sister, Caroline Moon, who dove into medical school in her mid-thirties and now serves with devotion as a pediatrician. She gave birth to her first child in December 2010 and gave me the gift of becoming *imo* (auntie). Life also sparked new and unimagined blessings and brilliance in the love and companionship of Jeffrey Frankel, who became my husband in 2011, and his son, Evan, in whom I have a son. In known and unknown ways, these precious people, together with my close friends, saved me from the many blows and lows and enabled me to appreciate the highs of moral support, perseverance, laughter, and sheer fun (heaps of thanks to Jeff and Evan in this category).

I describe this personal context in which I have pursued this book project to highlight that just like human life, Korea is ever dynamic, wrestling with the pains and contradictions of the past, the old and the new mixing and colliding, throwing around ideas and fads, with an eye always on the future. The constant flux that makes South Korea exciting and exhausting gets reflected in its relationship with the United States. And despite the ups and downs in the bilateral alliance, the ties endure, simultaneously thickened, knotted, and frayed over sixty years. The neverending news about U.S.-Korea relations made the project more drawn out than I might have wanted. At some point, I had to decide to stop reading about the political and societal changes and the potpourri of interpretations and just "do the book."

To those who offered venues for intellectual exchange, specific comments and insights, and hearty encouragement, as well as other invaluable resources, I am sincerely grateful: David Kang, who read significant portions of the work in progress, bandied about ideas with me, and consistently cheered me on to the finishline; and Jojo Abinales, Youngshik Bong, Jae Chung, Shari Cohen, Alex Cooley, Bruce Cumings, Cynthia Enloe, Roxanne Euben, John Feffer, Stacie Goddard, Roy Grinker, Donald Gregg, Yong Chul Ha, Sung-joo Han, Kyudok Hong, Naoki Kamimura, Choi Kang, Peter Katzenstein, Bob Keohane, Byungkook Kim, Taehan Kim, Sunghan Kim, Eunmee Kim, Sam S. Kim, Joel Krieger, Insook Kwon, Geun Lee, Karin Lee, Namhee Lee, Sook-Jong Lee, Derek Mitchell, Chung-in Moon, Marianne Perlak, Wilbur Rich, Dick Samuels, Mark Selden, Gi-Wook Shin, Andre Schmid, Sheila Smith, Scott Snyder, David Steinberg, Sidney Tarrow, and Meredith Woo-Cumings. I owe very special thanks to Bob Hathaway, Asia director at the Woodrow Wilson International Center for Scholars, and Mike Mochizuki of The George Washington University, who provided good guidance and great community during my fellowship at both institutions in 2002–3. I am indebted to the Luce Foundation, who funded that year of work. I also received generous funding from the U.S. Fulbright Program and Wellesley College.

During my field work in Korea in 2001 and subsequent visits through 2009, Korean activists, academics, and government officials, as well as American Embassy (Seoul) officials and various members of the U.S. Forces, Korea (USFK) provided valuable resources and perspectives on the alliance relationship, "anti-American" sentiment among South Koreans, and civil society activism in Korea's vibrant—and chaotic—democracy. Serapina Mikyung Cha was a wealth of knowledge and insight about the politics of NGOs in Korea. She generously offered her time, observations, and friendship. Particular thanks go to Sunghan Kim of Korea University, diplomat Changbom Kim, and other officials in the Korean Foreign Ministry's North America Division, as well as Steven Rounds and his Public Affairs staff at the U.S. Embassy in 2001–2.

Over so many years, I have had so many research assistants that I cannot name them all, but I could not have done the work without them, in particular Jeeyoung Bae, Rachel Stern, Chiaki Nishijima, Mattie Fitch,

Rakeen Mabud, Laura Stevens, Minjung Paik, GiYoon Kim, Janice Kim, and several students at the Graduate School of International Studies at Ewha University (2002). Erin Choi, who was graduated from Wellesley in 2010 and is now on her own path toward Korean studies and U.S.-Korea policy, was the most outstanding RA, especially through a critical stage of my research and writing. Special thanks also go to Ellie Choi, Ph.D. in East Asian Studies from Harvard University and now assistant professor at Cornell University, who oversaw the romanization of the Korean words in the manuscript.

Last, a word of thanks to Nathan MacBrien, my kind and patient editor, and to John Lie of the University of California, Berkeley, for encouraging me to publish in the Seoul-California series.

Portions of this book were previous published under my name in the following publications: "Resurrecting Prostitutes and Overturning Treaties: Gender Politics in the South Korean 'Anti-American' Movement," *Journal of Asian Studies* 66, no. 1 (2007); "Challenging U.S. Hegemony: Asian Nationalism and Anti-Americanism in East Asia," in *The United States and East Asia: Old Issues and New Thinking* ed. G. John Ikenberry and Chung-in Moon (Lanham, MD: Rowman & Littlefield, 2007); "Rethinking Young Anti-Americanism in South Korea" (co-authored with Youngshik Bong), in *The Anti-American Century,* ed. Allan McPherson and Ivan Krastev (Budapest and New York: Central European University Press, 2007); and "Korean Nationalism, Anti-Americanism and Democratic Consolidation," in *Korea's Democratization,* ed. Samuel S. Kim (New York: Cambridge University Press, 2003).

Introduction

In the winter of 2002–3, South Korean citizens responded en masse to the military trials and acquittals of two U.S. servicemen whose armored vehicle had run over and killed two school girls—Sim Misŏn and Sin Hyosun—that June. Demonstrations in front of the U.S. embassy and at the gates of U.S. military compounds had proliferated since the incident. In July, protesters broke through the chain-link fence at Camp Red Cloud, pelting stones at U.S. personnel. On September 15, three U.S. soldiers were assaulted and another abducted by Korean protesters. U.S. Ambassador Thomas Hubbard and Secretary of State Colin Powell, along with various officials at the Pentagon, offered various apologies for the loss of the two lives to little effect in appeasing Korean anger and grief. In December, Deputy U.S. Secretary of State Richard Armitage traveled to Seoul and delivered yet another round of apologies and hoped that his "visit will serve as an opportunity to convey to Korean people the U.S. government's respect for them again."[1]

By mid-December, 2002, more than 100,000 Koreans had gathered in Seoul to hold now-famous candlelight vigils, with thousands more in other parts of the country. They protested the acquittal; demanded a revision of the Status of Forces Agreement (SOFA),[2] believing it to undermine Korean sovereignty; and held or chanted slogans such as "Punish the Murderous GIs," "Revise the SOFA," and "Down, Down, USA," and billed the massive vigil on December 14 as the "Day of Rehabilitating Sovereignty."[3] The power of the people seemed to have the potential to undo a bilateral alliance of more than fifty years. Seung-Hwan Kim referred to the negative public sentiment as "a critical wildcard harming the future of the U.S.-Korean relationship."[4]

Observers and policymakers in the United States and Korea reacted to the demonstrations and negative public opinion polls with surprise, alarm, and even fear that something dangerous, irrational, and destabilizing was brewing among the Korean masses. In Washington, many wondered out loud, How could South Korea, a longtime ally, who had together, with Americans, shed blood against communism during the Korean War, turn so critical and ungrateful toward its benefactor?

Chung-in Moon wrote that "[c]ries of 'abandon the U.S.' are on the rise in South Korea, which have in turn precipitated . . . [American conservatives'] call for the U.S. to 'abandon South Korea.'"[5] Indeed, the conservative American analyst Nicholas Eberstadt added South Korea to the growing list of "problem nations" confronting the U.S. and blamed a resurgent nationalism, a generational gap, the rise of the left in Korean politics, and a misguided Sunshine Policy.[6] Victor Cha believed that together with the lack of future vision about the alliance, the anti-U.S. sentiments "could induce a crisis if left unaddressed."[7] The journalist Richard Halloran saw East Asia more generally as a place where "a virulent anti-Americanism rumbles just below the surface," weakening alliances with Korea and Japan and "tempting China to miscalculate in its dealings with the United States."[8] In late 2000, reporting on the Pentagon's plans to restructure (including reducing or withdrawing) U.S. forces in East Asia, Halloran stated that military officers were responding in part to "protests in Japan and Korea against the presence of US forces."[9]

DOMESTIC POLITICS AND SECURITY POLITICS

Analysts have been quick to jump on psychological explanations of South Korean society's changing regard for the alliance and the U.S. bases stationed in their country. Seung-Hwan Kim wrote that a "rise in anti-Americanism might be a component in the natural path of South Korea's graduation from a client state to a dynamic and vibrant member of the international community."[10] With rapid economic development and the successful institutionalization of democracy—marked, since the mid-1990s, by its membership in the OECD, the growth of civil society, the hosting of the 2002 World Cup, its leading role in the production and use of information technology, and the growing spread of its pop culture throughout the Asia-Pacific region—it is understandable that Koreans have come to "seek greater political and security independence from the United States; and to demand a more equal partnership and mutual respect in the bilateral relationship."[11] The Korean scholar Chaibong Hahm goes further, emphasizing that anti-Americanism "is an expression of a deep-seated sense of anxiety regarding Korean identity,"[12] a function of the recurring "clashes of civilization" that Korea gets embroiled in and the ensuing new "global standards" that Korea is forced to adopt.[13] According to Hahm, regardless of the hegemon or culture wars, whether Chinese, Japanese, or American, the "process of such fundamental and total civilizational transitions [leaves] deep psychological scars on the collective Korean psyche."[14]

This book challenges oft-repeated assumptions about "anti-Americanism,"[15] with its related nationalism and a perceived generational gap among South Koreans, in the early 2000s, and its causal role in destabilizing the U.S.–South Korea alliance and creating doubts about its sustainability and long-term future (chapter 1). It particularly rejects psychological explanations of Korean citizens' criticisms of and demands for change in managing the alliance and the presence and conduct of U.S. forces. Notions about the connections among anti-Americanism, Korean nationalism, and the generational gap have been reiterated by various writers without serious critical evaluation and analysis of alternative explanations.

By contrast, I focus on empirical transformations in Korean domestic politics that allow us to pose questions about Korean society and alliance politics differently: How did the power of the people, which has been enabled and claimed only since democratization in the late 1980s, grow so formidable by the late 1990s so as to challenge so seriously the more than half-century-old military alliance between the United States and the Republic of Korea (ROK)? How did civil society organizations (CSOs) grow in numbers and influence to become prominent political actors in alliance politics? Why did this once actively pro-U.S. ally become a poster child for anti-American protests by the early 2000s? What are the institutional and procedural changes in the relationship between state and society in Korea and among the U.S. military and the Korean state and people that might explain some of these societal attitudes, public events, and political processes?

I argue that the redistribution of power within Korea—in legal and administrative structure, normative orientation, communication channels, access to external resources, and so on—and the accompanying opportunities and constraints explain the public's responses to the United States and alliance issues, in particular, the presence and role of the U.S. Forces, Korea (USFK). I analyze the Korean civil society's development as a political actor in alliance politics in the context of democratic deepening and the decentralization of government that took place during the 1990s.

Sidney Tarrow, who has written extensively on social movements and politics, states that

> contentious politics is produced when political opportunities broaden, when they demonstrate the potential for alliances, and when they reveal the opponents' vulnerability. Contention crystallizes into a social movement when it taps embedded social networks and connective structures and produces collective action frames and supportive identities able to sustain contention with powerful opponents. By mounting familiar forms of contention, movements become focal points that transform external opportunities into resources. Repertoires of contention, social networks, and cultural frames lower the costs of bringing people into collective action, induce confidence that they are not alone, and give broader meaning to their claims.[16]

Chapter 2 focuses on the legal and structural changes in power and policymaking through decentralization that enabled the periphery—the local towns that have housed the U.S. installations—to challenge the central government's monopoly over alliance matters and claim interests and pursue policies that competed with those set by the center. Chapter 3 analyzes the composition and coalition dynamics of the *kiji undong* (bases movement),[17] a social movement to critique and challenge the U.S. bases and alliance management by national security elites. The focus on social movements includes an examination of the ways in which Korean CSO actors mobilized constituencies, exchanged information and movement tactics, and competed and collaborated with one another for influence and resources on wide-ranging issues, including the revision of the SOFA, the return of land used by U.S. forces, the relocation of installations from Seoul to other areas, the environmental impact of the U.S. bases, crimes against Korean civilians, women's rights, and local autonomy. In that chapter, I zero in on the People's Action for the Reform of the SOFA (PAR-SOFA), the first large coalition of organizations and networks, big and small, that sought to influence the negotiation and revision of the SOFA during 2000–2001. Rather than have disparate groups run around on their own raising voices and pitching protest banners on a variety of grievances toward the U.S. military, the PAR-SOFA and the related campaign for the return of land occupied by U.S. forces (Return of Land movement, or *panhwan undong*) helped consolidate various agenda issues and establish a more coherent framing of the political message.

I use key concepts from the literature on social movements to understand what I call the "political anatomy" of the CSOs that intervene in alliance politics: their, goals, leadership, framing of issues, competition for resources, coalition activities, mobilization tactics, transnational networking, and more. I highlight the structural inequalities between Seoul-based CSOs and those in the periphery or "countryside" (*chibang*) and assess the impact of these inequalities on movement cohesion, dynamics, and goals. While most Korean and American analysts have tended to view the *kiji* movement as monolithic in the background, ideology, and interests of its participants, I uncover their differences, competition, and clashes, while revealing their reasons for cooperation, compromise, and collective action. Chapter 5 concentrates on gender differences in movement goals, framing, and tactics, which led to clashes between "maximalist" and "reformist" agendas, between ideological nationalism/anti-Americanism and issue-oriented activism, and between "masculine" and "feminine" modes of activist politics.

Chapter 4 considers the regional and international context of social movement activism that helped shape the bases movement in Korea. First, civil-societal vigilance over U.S. bases and their impact on the local environment are not unique to South Korea. Rather, the Korean movement gathered momentum and learned—and taught—lessons from the larger bases movement in the Asia-Pacific, specifically, through alliances with activists in Okinawa, the Philippines, the United States, and Vieques, Puerto Rico. Second, antiglobalization and social justice protests that sprung up in various parts of the world in the late 1990s and early 2000s provided key framing devices for the Korean *kiji undong*, particularly, the emphasis on environmental concerns, local empowerment, and human rights.

Examining the *kiji undong* and other challenges to the alliance as part of a broader study of civil society and social movements helps us to avoid reducing the problem to a monolithic "anti-Americanism," psychological resentment (by Koreans) of great power dominance (*sadae chuui*), or a singular "nationalist resurgence" or ideological agenda. Rather, a social movement approach enables us to understand the challenges from the Korean civil society as a contestation of ideas, leadership, organizational influence, and resource mobilization—that is, politics—among various state and nonstate actors. Tom Berger's observation that national security involves ongoing "renegotiation," persuasion, legitimation, and institutionalization of political-military culture by competing political actors aptly applies here.[18]

In turn, we learn something about the power of civil society to claim democratic participation in what is probably the most undemocratic issue area in any democratic society: foreign policy and national security. We also learn about the limits to democratic politics in civil society—that rather than being an open marketplace for political interests and ideas, civil society has great power to decide who belongs and who does not, whose grievances and losses are worthy of collective attention, and whose case presents organizations and their leaders with enough political capital to challenge state authorities. For example, as chapter 5 shows, Korean women's organizations and transnational women's rights groups in the 1980s were the first to raise public awareness about the poor living and working conditions of militarized prostitutes/sex workers (one particular group of local Koreans whose lives have been intimately affected by the U.S. bases). However, in the 1990s and early 2000s, environmental groups and local autonomy issues eclipsed such concerns in the bases movement and in the policy arena.

As much as internal changes within Korea have challenged the rationales for the bases and the stability of the alliance, Americans also have contributed to the problems by (1) interpreting Korean civil society activism out of context, and (2) through policy blunders and institutional lags. Such shortcomings manifested themselves in the mostly ineffectual responses to the bases movement and obviated preventive action. The conclusion discusses these issues as part of a larger critique of American democracy promotion and a call for vigilance in improving civil-military relations between the USFK and the Korean society. It also discusses and assesses the steps that the USFK has taken since the death of the two girls to improve civil-military relations, particularly the Good Neighbor Program and the normalization of tours of duty for U.S. military personnel stationed in Korea. I emphasize the importance of normative, not only strategic, values and interests that a foreign military and a host society need to negotiate and adapt to in order to facilitate a sound and stable alliance relationship.

Since the mid-to-late 1990s, both state and nonstate actors in Korea have become diverse in terms of political background and experience, views, and interests, as well as sociopolitical identities and resources. They also have become more agile in commanding audiences, particularly through alternative media, both within and outside Korea. Consequently, alliance management, in particular, and bilateral relations, in general, have become more messy and complicated—there are numerous cooks stirring numerous pots. Put another way, Korean democracy holds the key to the future of the alliance, and understanding how that key turns is of critical importance.

The remainder of this introduction discusses the deterioration of alliance politics in the 2000s in brief and the important but inadequate geopolitical explanations of the decline and the rise of civil society intervention in alliance politics. It also questions whether the leadership styles and policy preferences of former presidents Roh Mu Hyun and George W. Bush serve as satisfactory explanations of alliance deterioration and citizen intervention. Finally, it emphasizes the erroneousness of nationalism as an explanation for the social and political changes in U.S.-Korea relations.

CRISIS IN THE ALLIANCE

The two girls' deaths and the acquittal of the GIs elicited the largest and most resounding public protests regarding the alliance since the permanent stationing of American troops in 1957. But they did not erupt out of thin air. Rather, they took place as part of a longer stream of public demonstrations and citizen activism critical of U.S. troops and the alliance that had persisted, albeit in private homes and in remote and restricted areas like military camp towns of the 1960s and 1970s.[19] But the period from the 1990s to the early 2000s ushered in multiple, back-to-back, and often simultaneous challenges to the alliance: the discovery and publicization of the alleged massacre at Nogunni of Korean civilians by American troops during the Korean War, bombing accidents and strafing exercises at Kunni range in Maehyangni, the murder of bar hostess Kim Sŏnghui by a U.S. corporal (and the bungled handling of his detention by U.S. officials), environmental damage in various compounds and the dumping of formaldehyde into the Han River, the proposed U.S. sale of FX fighter jets to Korea, negotiations over the revision of the SOFA, the building of a new hotel in Yongsan Garrison—the list goes on. President George W. Bush's labeling of North Korea as part of the "axis of evil" in January 2002 and the Pentagon's decision to adopt a strategy of preemptive nuclear strike against North Korea sealed the "anti-American deal" for many South Koreans. By January, 2003, "South Korea ha[d] become one of the Bush administration's biggest foreign policy problems."[20]

In 2005, the iconic "savior" of South Korea from the threat of Communism, General Douglas MacArthur, was attacked: Thousands of protesters, led by radical leaders such as Kang Sunjŏng, the former vice-chairman of an illegal pro–North Korea group (Pan-Korean Alliance for Reunification) who had been jailed for providing "national secrets" to P'yŏngyang in the mid-1990s,[21] threw rocks, bottles, and eggs at the general's statue in Inch'ŏn's Freedom Park. They also tried to topple the statue, which had been erected in 1957 by Koreans to commemorate the successful Inch'ŏn landing that reversed the early successes of the North Korean troops in the first few months of the war. The most strident of thes protests took place on September 11, 2005, which particularly offended Americans and others around the world who observed the anniversary of the September 11, 2001 terrorist attacks on the United States.

Among the motley crew of protesters, motivations ranged from lingering anger over the deaths of the two girls in 2002, general anti-(Iraq) war sentiments, the view of MacArthur as a megalomaniacal "war criminal" rather than a hero, resentment toward the United States for "dividing" the peninsula, the continued presence of U.S. troops, as well as pro-North/anti-U.S. sentiments among some radicals. The demonstrations elicited strong responses from Korean conservatives, with 10,000 such activists, including Korean Marine Corps veterans who vowed to guard the statue themselves, pouring out to counter the anti-MacArthur protesters.

The political struggle over the statue triggered anger on the part of some members of the United States Congress. Representative Henry Hyde led a group of colleagues to write a protest letter to President Roh Mu Hyun against the removal or demolition of the general's statue: The congressmen reminded Koreans that MacArthur led troops "which liberated the Republic of Korea twice" and that "(o)ur critical bilateral alliance was forged in the crucible of Inch'ŏn." Bluntly put, "Without the victory at Inch'ŏn, there would be no Republic of Korea today."[22] Even the British ambassador to Korea, Warwick Morris, took a stance in a letter to the editor of the *Chosun Ilbo:* "By attacking [MacArthur's] statue and his memory, these protestors are also denigrating ALL those foreign soldiers under the UN command, who came to fight alongside South Korea in that war. There were men and women from more than 20 nations involved, including my own."[23]

Despite the uproar on the western coast of Korea, the majority of Koreans supported the maintenance of the statue, and Inch'ŏn's city government took the responsibility of cleaning and polishing the statue for the first time since it had been erected. They were prompted by (Korean) private MacArthur supporters to restore the statue to it shiny glory.[24] And various offices of the Korean government promised to defend the statue, prompting U.S. Representative Hyde to send a letter to Rep. Yoo Jay-kun (Yu Chaegŏn), chairman of the National Assembly's National Defense Committee, in which he "expressed gratitude for efforts Yoo and his committee members have made to preserve the statue."[25]

Relations between Korea and the United States became so frayed in the first half of the 2000s that in October 2005 the Ministry of Foreign Affairs and Trade decided to hire an American "public relations" company—lobbyists—to improve Korea's image in the United States, especially among decision makers and public opinion leaders. Even Japan felt compelled to intervene, such that when a delegation of Korean legislators visited Japan, Vice-Foreign Minister Shotaro Yachi scolded Korea for "neglecting" its relationship with the United States over the North's nuclear program. He blamed the Roh administration for being on the wrong side of the team, stating that the U.S. shared important intelligence with Japan but did not trust Seoul enough to do the same.[26]

GEOPOLITICAL CHANGES IN THE REGION

Scholars of alliances generally assume that geopolitical transformations give rise to changes in the alliance structure, burden-sharing, and societal acceptance of the presence of foreign troops. Do such systemic explanations, particularly the changing power configuration in East Asia and a reduction of Korean dependence on the United States security umbrella, explain the rise of Korean citizen intervention in alliance politics? A quick answer is yes, but it is incomplete. At the close of the twentieth century and the beginning of the twenty-first, the East Asian geopolitical landscape had been changed by the end of the Cold War, Sino-Korean normalization in 1991, the "abandonment" of North Korea by Russia, the rapid economic and political rise of China, the historic June 2000 summit between the leaders of both Koreas, and September 11 and the ensuing U.S. war on terrorism. U.S. commitments to Korea and the region were in flux in the first half of the 1990s and again in the early 2000s, with the U.S.'s attention increasingly focused on China as the big competitor and the wars in Afghanistan and Iraq. Korea was left with both doubts about U.S. commitments as well as new opportunities to forge closer friendships with China and Russia.

Indeed, by 2003 China became the largest export market for South Korean products, displacing the United States (exports to China grew by 48 percent versus 2.7 percent for the U.S.), leading 63 percent of Korea's ruling party legislators in spring 2004 to "identify China as South Korea's most important partner" (versus 28 percent for the U.S.).[27] "China Fever" swept through Korea in the early 2000s, as the "Korean Wave" of pop culture (*Hallyu*) hit the streets and TV screens in China. The China scholar Jae-ho Chung emphasizes the rapid rise of people-to-people exchanges between Korea and China, with 1.6 million Koreans visiting China in 2003, up from half a million in 1996. Moreover, by 2003 46 percent of all foreign students in China originated from South Korea,[28] and the number of Chinese students interested in learning Korean had risen to more than 60,000.[29] Normalization of relations had been established only in 1992 and education exchanges in 1993, but ten years allowed a tremendous improvement in relations between the two former enemies. Indeed, Chung observed the disparity in Korea's two main bilateral relationships: "The deaths of the two schoolgirls and subsequent explosion of anti-American sentiments in South Korea in the latter half of 2002 constituted a stark contrast with high-profile celebrations of the tenth anniversary of the South Korea-China diplomatic normalization."[30]

But opportunities come with constraints and conflicts. If China holds promise as a close friend, it also promises to be a serious competitor. In 2004, Victor Cha summarized the growing economic rivalry:

> [M]any people believe that South Korea's technological lead over China has been reduced to four to five years. South Korean companies are already losing third-country market share to Chinese firms because of higher labor costs. A recent Federation of Korean Industries and Ministry of Commerce report noted China's growth rate in exports to the United States and Japan in autos, textiles, petrochemicals, and shipbuilding at 23.6 percent and 13.1 percent respectively. This rate was much higher than that of the ROK, which managed only 7.4 percent and 2.7 percent, respectively.[31]

On February 10, 2004, the *New York Times* ran a provocative article, "Koreans Look to China, Seeing a Market and a Monster," emphasizing the severe economic competition that was building up. Indeed, as soon as South Korea had outpaced Japan in 2004 as the world's leading shipbuilder (U.S.$15.09 billion), "the South Koreans [were] already looking over their shoulder at China, which ha[d] embarked on a path toward becoming the largest shipbuilder by 2015. Chinese competition, which has unnerved American manufacturers, is also putting much of Asia on edge as China rapidly narrows the technological gap with higher-wage Asian neighbors."[32] A Korean businessman who was interviewed characterized China as the "chaser," with Korea the "chased," working harder and harder to keep the lead.[33]

In another case, in early 2009, five years after the Shanghai Automotive Corporation (China's largest car manufacturer) had bought controlling stakes in Ssangyong Motor Company, "a milestone of China's rising industrial clout and South Korea's deepening economic ties with its neighbor, [was] falling apart in acrimony and criminal investigations."[34]

With declining sales and conflict with the Chinese investor, Ssangyong declared bankruptcy. According to the *New York Times*, its "combative labor unions and some South Korean commentators have vilified Shanghai Auto as an exploitative owner that siphoned off Ssangyong's technology, reneged on promises to invest, and dumped the company when the market turned sour."[35] Even though Shanghai's interpretation differed, "the collapse of the venture [was] a black eye for China."[36] Similarly, Chinese BOE Technology Group bought Hydis of South Korea in 2003 and then let it go bankrupt in 2006.

In both cases, with South Korean workers being laid off and their companies in shambles, resentment grew that China was buying up Korean companies to "steal" their technology with little or no return for Korean investors and workers. Ssangyong employees went on strike for nearly two months in 2006 as employees were being dismissed: "Workers barricaded themselves inside the factory and locked the managers out." Later in December, "union members surrounded a car carrying Shanghai Auto officials and held it hostage for seven hours outside their factory south of Seoul, accusing the executives of absconding with proprietary technology."[37] Such politicized responses and dramatic actions echo those often characterized as "anti-American."

Even when Sino-Korean relations were in their "honeymoon period," they were rife with tensions. Jae-ho Chung describes the eruption of the "garlic war" in the summer of 2000, noting that the "pace, magnitude and the aftershock of the trade dispute were felt so intensely":[38] the Koreans slapped high tariffs on Chinese imports of frozen or pickled garlic, while the Chinese took only six days to slap a complete ban on imports of important Korean industrial products, mobile handsets and polyethylene (retaliatory tariffs would have been the customary first-step response). Chung compares this bitter trade war with the toned down version of the Sino-Japanese "mushroom war" around the same time, whereby Beijing was gentler and more cautious in dealing with Tokyo. He raises the possibility that the Chinese were less concerned about resolving the matter diplomatically with Seoul and more interested in asserting power: "[D]on't mess with China."[39]

And if we add other contentious issues to the Sino-Korean pot, such as China's policy of repatriating North Korean border crossers, the trafficking of North Korean women into the PRC for sex slavery and/or forced or fraudulent marriage to Chinese farmers, as well as the increased reliance of South Korean society on Korean-Chinese migrants as low-wage workers, domestics for middle class families, and "foreign brides" for aging Korean bachelors[40]—the potential for negative, nationalistic sentiments in both countries is real. In the mid-1990s, the anthropologist Heh-Rahn Park had presciently addressed "people-to-people" tensions as consequences of Sino-Korean normalization in the early 1990s and the arrival, soon thereafter, of Chinese nationals in Korean society.[41] South Koreans oscillated back and forth between welcoming long-lost "kin" and treating them as "con men" and criminals. Park offers poignant and compelling narratives of Korean Chinese whose high hopes in coming to Korea were dashed as they experienced disappointment and hurt by the Korean society's discrimination against them. And numerous Chinese migrant workers in Korea have worked for Korean small business owners who either refused to pay them or delayed their pay, withheld their travel documents, or refused to pay for medical expenses even when workers' limbs were cut off or faces burned while on the job. Conditions and legal protections have improved since the 1990s but discrimination and exploitation continue, in addition to official threats and migrants' fears of deportation of those who are "illegal" or undocumented.[42]

Worse than any trade dispute or potential conflict over how to deal with North Koreans or Chinese nationals in South Korea has been the territorial contention over Koguryŏ. In the early 2000s, Chinese academics as well as government officials seemed intent on provoking Korean ire over its national history and territorial integrity by claiming as Chinese the Korean kingdom of Koguryŏ in what is now North Korea. One Korean academic saw sinister signs in China's strategic ambitions in East Asia: "its real objective is to establish China's pre-eminence."[43] Another academic responded more vehemently to both governments' diplomatic efforts to paper over the conflict: "This is not [the] end of the controversy. The real beginning of war is from now on. The Chinese government will not easily give up its insistence that Koguryŏ is its ancient nation."[44]

It is particularly interesting how event-driven the strength or weakness of South Korea's "China fever" can be. Before April 2004, when the Chinese Foreign Ministry deleted Koguryŏ from its official website on Korean history (and refused to respond to Seoul's requests to restore the information), a survey of Korean politicians revealed that 80 percent believed China was Korea's "most important trade and business partner."[45] But by summer 2004, a *Korea Herald* survey showed that almost 80 percent of the 237 National Assembly members (out of 299) who had responded ranked the United States as "Korea's top priority in diplomatic as well as economic issues."[46] In their scholarship on Koreans' trust or distrust of the United States, Myongsob Kim and his coauthors observe that "the growing interest in and popularity of China among South Koreans are not necessarily related to declining trust in the USA."[47] Rather, the "growing interest" between China and South Korea has endogenous limitations. The point to keep in mind is that any geopolitical shifts Korea may express toward China and the East Asian region are not linear or cumulative and cannot explain Korean civil society activism in alliance politics with the United States.

The end of the Cold War of course made both elites and masses in many places reassess security threats and readjust security commitments and expectations. This involved significant implications for the size, structure, mission, and budget requirements of military establishments, as well as the public's general tolerance for military action or intervention. The United States was no exception, with expectations of a "peace dividend," base closures, and renewed focus on domestic issues such as economic well-being and global competitiveness. It made sense that in the run-up to the 1992 presidential election, the internal motto of Bill Clinton's campaign was "It's the economy, stupid."

With respect to East Asia, the U.S. conducted debates and reviews about American strategic interests; the appropriate number, configuration, and size of overseas bases in the region; as well as burden-sharing costs with host nations. In the early 1990s, through the East Asia Strategic Initiative (EASI), the Department of Defense planned for a gradual but steady reduction of forward deployed forces. The aim was to reduce U.S. troops and costs and to increase burden-sharing by host nations and to transform their role from supporting to leading actors in the field and commands. Under Phase I of the EASI, the U.S. withdrew about 7,000 troops from Korea by 1992,[48] but escalating tensions over the North Korean nuclear program put a halt to further reductions. By 1995, the Clinton administration consolidated its priorities and approach in the East Asia Strategy Review (EASR)—or the "Nye Initiative"—which committed the United States to maintain 100,000 troops in the region. Many Korean (and Japanese) policymakers sighed a breath of relief, understanding EASR to be the clear and firm statement of U.S. intentions and commitments for which they had hoped in the aftermath of the Cold War. (But the shifting U.S. policy lines in the first half of the 1990s created conflicting and confusing expectations in Korea, abetting guesswork on the future of the U.S. bases.)

By 2000, the winds were changing again, as analysts and policymakers debated whether to reduce or withdraw some ground forces in Korea and Japan and adapt the military to smaller, more mobile and versatile units that could confront contemporary security challenges such as terrorism, peacekeeping, and humanitarian interventions and take advantage of new developments in arms technology that favor "long-range, precision-strike fighting capabilities that could fundamentally change the face of the U.S. forward presence around the world."[49] U.S. policy in the early George W. Bush years continued this erratic tendency, leading Asian policymakers and publics to be lobbed back and forth about what the new administration's intentions and commitments would be. For example, in early 2001 Secretary of State Colin Powell affirmed the continuation of Clinton's engagement policy with North Korea, building on the 1994 Agreed Framework. Later that year, President Bush backtracked and said that his administration would review rather than continue the policy. And the administration shifted gears yet again that year, re-embracing the engagement policy. The *New York Times* commented that the "frequent changes of policy have aggravated other actors in producing divisions between the United States and its Asian ally."[50]

But with terrorism hitting American soil on September 11, 2001, U.S. strategic policy—global and regional—became clear, and a militaristic worldview and strategy won the day. Hard-liners took over U.S. policy; they had very little tolerance for either North Korean nuclear saber-rattling or South Korean protests against the United States. And U.S.-Korea relations took a rapid nosedive. Since early 2002 rhetoric about the "axis of evil," the preemptive nuclear strike option, and the so-called tailored containment policy to exert political pressure and economic sanctions (aimed at stopping the North's nuclear program) thrust a heavy wrench into the new Roh Mu Hyun administration's engagement policy.[51] Additionally, advisers close to the Bush inner circle, like Richard Perle, head of the Pentagon Defense Policy Board, verbalized the unthinkable for most South Koreans, that a military option to destroy the North's nuclear facilities was on the table.[52] Both outgoing President Kim Dae Jung and incoming President Roh feared that the U.S. hard-line policy toward North Korea would derail the ROK's engagement policy toward the North and lead the U.S. toward military confrontation on the peninsula.

LEADERSHIP

Observers like to attribute the deterioration in the bilateral relationship partly to differences in policy priorities, preferences, and political styles between the conservative Bush and liberal Kim Dae Jung and Roh Mu Hyun administrations. Specific disagreements on U.S. unilateralism, hegemonic militarism, nuclear saber-rattling toward North Korea through the preemptive strike doctrine (Nuclear Strategy Review), and Kim Dae Jung's backing of then Russian President Vladmir Putin's ABM treaty are commonly known and certainly made bilateral coordination and cooperation between the U.S. and Korea difficult. Additionally, Koreans viewed Bush's treatment of Kim Dae Jung when he visited Washington in March 2001 as rude and disrespectful, and the Bush leadership was suspicious of Roh and his anti-establishment, left-leaning background and populist tendencies.

Roh Mu Hyun indeed campaigned for the presidency on what many considered an "anti-American" platform, even boasting naïvely that in contrast to his pro-American, elitist establishment opponent, Lee Hoi Chang, he was proud of never having visited the United States, and promising to raise Seoul's independence and sovereignty in its relations with Washington. But here it is important to avoid viewing the U.S-Korea relationship in a vacuum. In the first half of the 2000s, Korea was not the only ally with which the U.S. was having a hard time; it was experiencing unrequited love from Europe. A sixteen-nation survey conducted by the Pew Research Center found that by 2005, while 66 percent of Americans surveyed wanted to remain close to Europe while 28 percent wanted to seek more independence, the inverse was true for Europeans: 73 percent of French, 59 percent of Germans, and 53 percent of Britons desired more independence in security and foreign policy.[53] Yet, despite the alarm and dismay over Koreans' lost love for the United States, 37 percent of Koreans surveyed for a Chicago Council on Foreign Relations (CFR) report in 2004 preferred a strengthened alliance, while only 31 percent called for more independence; the mean response was the status quo (32 percent).[54] And interestingly, on a "thermometer" of "warm feelings" toward nations, South Koreans gave the United States a mean of 58 degrees (Great Britain topped the gauge at 62 degrees), while Americans measured South Korea at only 49 degrees, just above France, China, and Cuba.[55] Additionally, 78 percent of Koreans viewed the relationship with the U.S. as beneficial, while only 12 percent thought of the U.S. as threatening.[56] Significantly, even with the "anti-American" fervor of 2002 and 2003, the United States was Korea's preferred partner for cooperation at 53 percent, with China a distant second with 24 percent.[57]

Despite the new Korean president's rhetoric, his transformation from candidate Roh to President Roh was quite rapid and reflected the pragmatism that the public espoused about the practical need for cooperation with the United States, much more than their European counterparts. When Assistant Secretary of State for East Asian and Pacific Affairs

James Kelly went to Korea in January 2003 to check out the new "maverick" president, Roh conveyed to him: "We hope the United States will remain our ally in the future and I have consistently said that we need U.S. forces here and will continue to do so."[58] He also told Kelly "that even the candlelight vigils by young Koreans [in late 2002–early 2003] assume the continued presence of American soldiers in Korea, since they ask only for revision of the Status of Forces Agreement."[59] Roh then traveled to Washington in May 2003 with the hope of reconciling differences with the Bush administration over North Korea and to allay fears about South Korea's reliability as an ally, given the highly publicized anti-American protests of the previous winter.

Despite the aggressive protests against the United States in late 2002 and early 2003, and a public that was strongly opposed to the U.S. war in Iraq and contribution of Korean combat troops to Iraq and Afghanistan, the "anti-American" administration of President Roh and the liberal National Assembly (as of the April 2004 election) offered significant human, material, and moral support to the United States' war on terror. And contrary to common assumption, the election of the conservative Lee Myung Bak in late 2007 did not put Korea-U.S. relations on a smooth course. His near-unilateral decision to reverse import bans of American beef provoked almost a million Koreans to run out to the streets in protest in June 2008. The new president, who had been known as the "bulldozer" as mayor of Seoul, was forced to renegotiate the terms of beef imports. Chung-in Moon of Yonsei University highlighted the people's resistance to authoritarian-style governance: "The protests were seen as a stern popular warning on the Lee government's policy incompetence, one-way vertical communication, and physical repression of dissent."[60]

The geostrategic environment, ideological orientations and the leadership style of top officials, and the vagaries of public sentiments all matter in influencing policy preferences and decisions around alliances. But big geostrategic change—the end of the Cold War—and erratic U.S. policies during the decade did not eliminate support for U.S. forces in South Korea, despite the growing criticism of U.S. policies that were liberally publicized in the newly democratic society. In 1995 Joseph Nye, as U.S. assistant secretary of defense for international security affairs, stated with confidence that the alliances in Europe and East Asia were surviving the end of the Cold War with resilience: "In neither region is there a demand that the Americans go home."[61] He was proved wrong the same year in Okinawa, with the rape of a teenage girl by three U.S. marines. The intensity of citizens' anger and demands for change that followed, as well as the local government's criticism of the U.S.-Japan alliance, cannot be explained by geopolitical shifts. Domestic changes, at the national and local levels, were key to galvanizing, mobilizing, and legitimating citizen activism. The same applies to South Korea in the 2000s.

BLAME NATIONALISM

Those who study and manage the Korea-U.S. relationship have often expressed fear about how a "new nationalism" in Korea since the 1990s—a combination of "assertive nationalism" vis-à-vis the United States and "inter-Korean nationalism"[62]—has been fueling anti-Americanism.[63] That is, with newly achieved affluence and self-confidence as a successful economic power and political democracy, the younger generations in particular feel a national pride that fuels tensions with the United States. As one Korean scholar neatly put it, "Anti-Americanism in Korean society is fundamentally a generational phenomenon."[64] Assertion of new identity and power are not the only interpretations, of course. Chung Min Lee of Yonsei University takes the geostrategic context into consideration, arguing that the new nationalism includes the "desire to minimize fallout from the vestiges of great-power politics."[65] Yet, whether Korean or American, sociologist or security studies expert, liberal or conservative, resurgent nationalism has been taken for granted as a fundamental cause of the spread and intensity of anti-U.S. sentiments in Korea.

It is not surprising, then, that the sociologist Doug McAdam concluded that "[a]t the heart of the current antipathy to the United States is deep nationalist resentment at what is perceived to be the unequal nature of U.S.-South Korean relations."[66] This assumption remains one of the most oft-repeated and underexamined claims regarding changes in Korean attitudes toward the United States and tensions in the alliance. To attribute South Korean anti-American sentiments to new nationalism is to simplify cause and effect and to ignore the domestic and social movement context in which demonstrations and other collective actions take place. It overlooks a complex terrain of political alliances, interests, infighting, and goals.

Simply put, there is no monolithic South Korean nationalism, and in parallel, there is no monolithic anti-Americanism. If South Koreans share anything, it is a divided polity. Even if voices for unification with the North are blasted in the streets of Seoul and featured on front page news, there is no unified rush toward unification and willingness to sacrifice for the collective interests of Northerners. What those "interests" would and should be, how they are to be prioritized, and who is to define and develop them are all up for grabs. On national security, there are fissures not only between generations and between left and right, but also, increasingly *within* the left, right, and a growing center.

It is puzzling that so many people have repeated nationalism as a root cause of the decline in Korea-U.S. relations but have not offered new ways either to prove this nor to understand how nationalism might have been in flux since democratization. Many of these claims have cited articles in *Asian Survey* by Jinwung Kim and Gi-Wook Shin, both of which were written *before* the actual public explosion of anger and grievances against the United States in the early 2000s and were based on political observations and research data gathered in the late 1980s to 1990–91. Both Kim and Shin were early birds, recognizing, assessing, and even foretelling general undercurrents to come, but their findings do not suffice as firm foundation on which to build an understanding of Korean society and its attitudes toward the U.S. in the early decades of the twenty-first century. Two obvious missing factors, because both Kim's and Shin's articles predated the events, are the Asian financial crisis of 1997–98 and the North-South summit of 2000, which significantly reshaped Koreans' beliefs about their recent collective past and future. Another missing factor is the enormous shift in American foreign policy toward unilateralism, militarism in the Middle East, and the unilateral restructuring of U.S. forces in Korea since September 11, 2001, which was responsible in part for the growth of negative sentiments toward the United States in Korea (and elsewhere) and the tensions in the alliance.

Those who often mention Korean nationalism as a threat to the alliance need to be reminded of what leading scholars of nationalism remind us: "Nationalism is rarely the nationalism of the nation, but rather marks the site where different representations of the nation contest and negotiate with each other."[67] Prasenjit Duara, the author of this quote, as well as Rogers Brubaker and John Breuilly emphasize that people often attribute a "master identity" to nationalism, but in truth, nationalism "exists only as one among others and is changeable, interchangeable, conflicted or harmonious with them."[68] According to Breuilly, nationalist "ideology/imagery contains many different messages, and it is difficult to know which evokes a chord."[69] He continues that such ideology/imagery "can only supply the most general orientations and that the criterion of specific objectives, forms of action, and bases of support must be understood in terms other than the appeal of the proclaimed values of the nationalist movement."[70]

Such scholarship challenges the notion of nationalism as a political, social, or psychological monolith and makes room for us to explore the probability that ideas and values other than nationalism are also at play within and among seemingly nationalist actors and groups. In *Ethnic Nationalism in Korea,* Gi-Wook Shin drives home this point: "Indeed, ethnic nationalism has been combined with different forms of ideologies in modern Korea, the Left (communism) and the Right (capitalism), modern (industrialism) and antimodern (agrarianism), authoritarian and democratic politics, and local and transnational forces (globalization)."[71] And to understand how nationalism is at play, we need to ask when, why, how, and by whom events and ideas trigger or lend themselves to nationalistic thought and action. Even with respect to habituated anti-Japanese nationalism, we need to ask why, as Youngshik Bong does, both Japan and Korea "had managed the [Tŏkdo/Takeshima] island issue quite successfully since the signing of the 1965 ROK-Japanese normalization treaty"[72]—by maintaining a materialist (maritime commerce) approach—but in the late 1990s took to a collision course fueled by nationalism. In his view, the specific trigger was external to both nations: ratification of the UN Convention on the Law of the Sea.

While the analytical applicability of nationalism often is underspecified, nationalism is also overused to describe Koreans and Korean politics to the point that it can be used to explain just about any Korean phenomenon. And because in some ways, nationalism and modern Korea are practically synonymous, the explanatory power of nationalism in relation to specific events and policy issues becomes diffuse and weak. Even with regard to the arch-rivals Rhee Syngman and Kim Ilsung, Gi-Wook Shin observed "the surprising similarities of the nature of nationalist rhetoric" between them. For Kim, according to Shin, the "[n]ation, and not ideology—not even Communism—comes first."[73] It is a commonplace to emphasize that Park Chunghee's eighteen-year rule was characterized by a developmentalism based on nationalism: National security and economic development were tantamount to national survival and necessary as foundations for national reunification. In truth, every South Korean leader has waved the flag of nationalism to mobilize public support and to build political legitimacy but have had different policy trajectories and relationships with the United States and Japan.

Those who challenged the state also employed nationalism. Increasingly in the 1980s, fighting for democracy meant fighting for the moral (and political) right and authority to claim legitimate power to determine the past, present, and future of the Korean nation. With respect to the democracy movement, Sheila Miyoshi Jager observed that "people with very different political agendas often deploy[ed] [the] same narratives in a variety of ways and for very different ideological ends."[74] She explains that the nationalist "ideas or ideological concepts, whether they stem from politically 'dominant' or 'subordinate' cultures or groups, are never intrinsically oppressive or liberating in themselves."[75] I argue further that therefore, nationalist ideas or concepts can abound but with no clear or set correlation to political or policy outcomes. If South Korean nationalism has fed anti-American sentiments, it is also true that during periods of threat and fear, as in the 1950s and 1960s, it led to pro-Americanism among the general public.

Recent survey data on Korean nationalism also gives us some conflicting food for thought. The oft-cited Pew Global Attitudes survey of 2003 ranked South Korea near the top as a nation that exhibits what we might call "defensive nationalism" (way of life to be protected against foreign influence). Asked whether their way of life needs protection from foreign influence, 82 percent of Koreans and 81 percent of Filipinos said yes, compared to 51 percent of Germans, 63 percent of Japanese, and 64 percent of Americans.[76] Yet Korea is not part of the pack that exhibits the "strongest nationalist sentiment," which Pew specifies as the belief in cultural superiority, the need to protect culture from foreign influence, and the belief that their nation has a rightful claim to parts of other people's territories.[77] India, Turkey, Bangladesh, South Africa, and Pakistan top that list, but they vary in their fondness for Americans and U.S. policies.

If we compare South Korea to this roster of nations, how are we to understand the meaning of high defensive nationalism with high regard for the U.S. and Americans relative to the countries espousing the "strongest nationalist sentiment"? For example, in the summer of 2002, 53 percent of Koreans had a favorable view of the United States, compared to only 10 percent in Pakistan and 30 percent in Turkey. In 2003, 74 percent of Koreans expressed favorable views of Americans, even in the wake of widespread and vigorous anti-American protests in the winter of 2002–3, compared to 32 percent of Turks and 38 percent of Pakistanis.[78] Koreans were in agreement with Australians (74 percent), Canadians (77 percent), and Israelis (79 percent). America's "best friend" at the time, Great Britain, topped the list of those liking Americans by only six more percentage points (80 percent).[79]

If we include opposition to or rejection of the spread of American culture as part and parcel of nationalism and anti-Americanism, then almost the entire world during the early 2000s was anti-American, for most viewed "the export of American ideas and customs as a bad thing." In this regard, the anti-American trio of U.S. allies is in accord: 67 percent of Germans, 71 percent of French, and 62 percent of Koreans disliked the spread of Americana, while those who consider the spread of American culture as a good thing were definitively in the minority: 28 percent of Germans, 25 percent of French, and 30 percent of Koreans. Here it is interesting to note that the eager partners in "new Europe" that former Secretary of Defense Donald Rumsfeld touted at the start of the Iraq war shared with Koreans very similar views of American culture: only 36 percent of Bulgarians, 35 percent of Ukrainians, 34 percent of Slovakians, 34 percent of Czechs, and 31 percent of Poles had positive regard for Americana.[80]

If we make a "composite" of nationalist indicators, it is difficult to come up with a non-contradictory understanding of what nationalism is and how it works toward outside forces, namely the United States. For example, when we include views of globalization, which is often paired with nationalism as two simultaneous yet contending forces in today's world, South Korean nationalism becomes even more incoherent. Support for globalization was highest in Korea among Asian nations and second highest among the forty-four nations assessed in the Pew 2003 Global Attitudes survey. Ninety percent of South Koreans were in favor of globalization, with 77 percent surveyed remarking that they "see 'a lot' or 'somewhat' more trade and business ties between their country and other countries."[81] This is in contrast to the Filipinos, who despite similarly high levels of defensive nationalist sentiment, show low support for globalization. In Asia, Korea had the largest proportion of people saying globalization is 'very' good for the country, second to Vietnam (56 percent).[82] Therefore, nationalism is at best an elusive and at worst an erroneous explanation for the Korean public's regard for the United States and its alliance with Korea. As chapter 1 shows, there also are significant counter-nationalist trends in Korea that need to be accounted for. Nationalism is an unstable and unverifiable determinant of changing societal attitudes toward the alliance and related policies.

The politics of U.S. military bases and the relationship between local and domestic politics and foreign policy are particularly important to study, given the U.S. military's struggles in Iraq and Afghanistan to understand and operate among disparate local political actors and conditions, in addition to the national actors. In these countries as well as elsewhere around the world where the United States has military bases or access, there are struggles over the terms of basing rights, troop count and location (relocation), (cost) burden-sharing, environmental responsibilities, and juridical license and accountability, local civil-military relations, and more: witness the contention over such issues between the U.S. and Japan/Okinawa, Turkey, Kazakhstan, and Kyrgyzstan as well as South Korea in recent years and a bit further back in time in the Philippines, Italy, Portugal, and Spain.[83] Although the United States is a global actor and needs to think globally on the level of strategy, it needs to become a better local actor. In general, international relations scholars and foreign policy practitioners have had the luxury of leaving out the local in politics, but such omission comes with costs. In dynamic democracies like South Korea, the local nature of politics has become ever more salient a factor to negotiate for domestic and foreign elites alike. Citizen politics at the local and national levels need to be incorporated into future studies and policies related to the alliance.

NOTES

1. "Armitage Offers Seoul 'Sincere Apologies,'" *Korea Times*, December 10, 2002, times.hankooki.com (accessed December 12, 2002).

2. SOFA is the bilateral document that governs the terms, conditions, rights, and obligations of overseas U.S. forces and the host government of the country where the forces are stationed. For a more detailed discussion of SOFA politics, see chapter 3 in this volume.

3. *Ohmynews*, December 14, 2002, www.ohmynews.co.kr/article_view.asp?menu=0480&no=91074 (accessed December 16, 2002).

4. Seung-Hwan Kim, "Anti-Americanism in Korea," *Washington Quarterly* 26, no. 1 (2002), 109.

5. Chung-in Moon, "Changing South Korean Perception of the United States since September 11" (paper presented at the annual meeting of the Japan Association for Asian Studies, Tokyo, November 8, 2003).

6. Nicholas Eberstadt, "Our Other Korea Problem," *The National Interest*, no. 68 (fall 2002).

7. Victor D. Cha, "Focus on the Future, Not the North," *Washington Quarterly* 26, no. 1 (2002), 105.

8. Richard Halloran, "The Rising East: Anti-Americanism brews quietly in Asian societies allied to U.S.," *Honolulu Star-Bulletin*, February 24, 2002, archives.starbulletin.com/2002/02/24/editorial/halloran.html (accessed May, 23 2006).

9. Ibid.

10. Seung-Hwan Kim, 115.

11. Ibid.

12. Chaibong Hahm, "Anti-Americanism, Korean Style," in *Korean Atti-*

tudes toward the United States: Changing Dynamics," ed. David I. Steinberg (Armonk, NY: M. E. Sharpe, 2005) 229.

13. Ibid., 227–229.

14. Ibid., 228.

15. When I use the terms "anti-American" or "anti-Americanism," I am referring to a multiplicity of grievances, complaints, and demands by Korean civilians with regard to the U.S. bases. The term should not be interpreted literally as Koreans hating the United States or Americans or American values. Ideologically anti-American activists form a small minority among the coalition activists that I discuss in the book. I have described "anti-Americanism" as a "big tent" of Koreans' varied discontents in "Korean Nationalism, Anti-Americanism and Democratic Consolidation," in *Korea's Democratization,* ed. Samuel S. Kim (New York: Cambridge University Press, 2003).

16. Sidney Tarrow, *Power in Movement: Social Movements and Contentious Politics,* 2nd ed. (New York: Cambridge University Press, 1998), 23.

17. I employ the terms *kiji undong* and "bases movement" interchangeably to refer to political activism around issues regarding U.S. bases and troop conduct in Korea. *Kiji undong* is the term that the activists themselves use and can encompass a variety of views on the foreign military presence, ranging from those who want to raise concerns about local citizens' interests and rights to those who want to reform the Status of Forces Agreement, to those who seek to kick out the U.S. bases. My intention is to avoid using the term "anti-American" or "anti-base," because they are inaccurate and narrow or misdirect the political and analytical content of Korean collective action on base-related issues.

18. Thomas U. Berger, "Norms, Identity, and National Security in Germany and Japan," in *The Culture of National Security: Norms, and Identity in World Politics,* ed. Peter Katzenstein (New York: Columbia University, 1996), 326–327.

19. For a discussion of accumulated grievances and smaller eruptions of protest against U.S. troops, see Katharine H. S. Moon, "Citizen Power in Korean-American Relations," in *Korean Attitudes toward the United States: Changing Dynamics,* ed. David Steinberg (Armonk, NY: M. E. Sharpe, 2005).

20. "South Korea, Once a Solid Ally, Now Poses Problems for the U.S.," *New York Times,* January 2, 2003.

21. *Chosun Ilbo,* November 29, 2006, english.chosun.com (accessed October 15, 2009).

22. U.S. Rep. Henry Hyde, letter to President President Roh Moo Hyun, September 15, 2005, archived at www.icasinc.org/2005/2005l/2005lh2h.html (accessed July 25, 2009).

23. "Attack on MacArthur 'an Insult to All UN Soldiers,'" *Chosun Ilbo,* September 23, 2005, english.chosun.com/site/data/html_dir/2005/09/23/200509236I021.html (accessed October 16, 2009).

24. "S. Korea City Cleans Controversial MacArthur Statue," Reuters,

December 6, 2005, www.redorbit.com/news/international/321916/skorea_city_cleans_controversial_macarthur_statue/index.html (accessed October 16, 2009).

25. "Hyde Thanks Lawmakers for Statue," *Korea Times,* November 30, 2005, www.koreatimes.co.kr (accessed October 16, 2009).

26. "Korean Lawmakers Get Earful from Allied Hardliners," *Chosun Ilbo,* May 24, 2005 (accessed July 26, 2009).

27. Victor D. Cha, "South Korea in 2004: Peninsular Flux," *Asian Survey* 45, no. 1 (2004), 35.

28. Jae Ho Chung, "The Rise of China and Its Impact on South Korea's Strategic Soul-Searching," Korea Economic Institute, Joint U.S.-Korea Academic Studies, vol. 15 (2005), www.keia.org/Publications/JointAcademicStudies/2005/05JaeHo.pdf (accessed February 14, 2007).

29. "Korea-China Ties: 12 Years Mark Gains but Challenges Loom," *Korea Herald,* August 24, 2004, www.koreaherald.co.kr (accessed August 24, 2004).

30. Jae Ho Chung, "How America Views China-South Korea Bilateralism," CNAPS working paper (Washington, DC: Brookings Institution, July, 2003), 5.

31. Cha, "South Korea in 2004," 37.

32. "Korean Shipbuilders See China's Shadow," *New York Times,* January 6, 2005 (accessed October 18, 2009).

33. Ibid.

34. "In Carmaker's Collapse, a Microcosm of South Korea's Woes," *New York Times,* February 24, 2009.

35. Ibid.

36. Ibid.

37. Ibid.

38. Jae Ho Chung, "From a Special Relationship to a Normal Partnership? Interpreting the 'Garlic Battle' in Sino-South Korean Relations," *Pacific Affairs* 76, no. 4 (winter 2003/2004), 550.

39. Ibid., 558.

40. See chapter 1 for a discussion on the growing multiethnic and "multicultural" demographics of Korean society.

41. Heh-Rahn Park, "Narratives of Migration: From the Formation of Korean Chinese Nationality in the PRC to the Emergence of Korean Chinese Migrants in South Korea" (Ph.D. diss., University of Washington, 1996).

42. Katharine H. S. Moon, "Migrant Workers' Movements in Japan and South Korea," in *Egalitarian Politics in the Age of Globalization,* ed. Craig N. Murphy (New York: Palgrave, 2002), 186–188.

43. "Korea-China Ties."

44. "Goguryeo Accord Leaves Some in Doubt," *Korea Herald,* August 25, 2004 (accessed August 25, 2004).

45. "Korea-China Ties."

46. Ibid.

47. See Myongsob Kim, Suzanne L. Parker, and Jun Young Choi, "Increasing Distrust of the USA in South Korea," *International Political Science Review* 27, no. 4 (2006), 437.

48. Thomas R. Riley and Steven A. Raho, III, "Engagement and Enlargement in Korea," U.S. Army War College Fellowship research project, U.S. Army War College, Carlisle Barracks, PA, April 1996, 17.

49. Cha, "Focus on the Future, Not the North," 94.

50. "South Korea, Once a Solid Ally, Now Poses Problems for the U.S."

51. "Bush's New N.K. Policy Sparks Concern of Possible Seoul-Washington Conflict," *Korea Herald,* December 31, 2002 (accessed December 30, 2002).

52. "US Hawk Warns Not to Rule Out Military Option," *Chosun Ilbo,* December 20, 2002 (accessed December 28, 2002)

53. Pew Global Attitudes Project, "American Character Gets Mixed Reviews: U.S. Image Up Slightly, But Still Negative" (a sixteen-nation survey conducted in spring 2005), June 23, 2005, 30.

54. Chicago Council on Foreign Relations, *Global Views 2004: Comparing South Korean and American Public Opinion and Foreign Policy* (Chicago: CCFR, 2004), 18.

55. Ibid., 16.

56. Ibid., 19.

57. Ibid.

58. *Korea Herald,* January 14, 2003 (accessed January 14, 2003).

59. "Roh Reassures Kelly on Alliance," *JoongAng Daily,* January 14, 2003, joongangdaily.joins.com (accessed January 14, 2003).

60. Chung-in Moon, "South Korea in 2008: From Crisis to Crisis," *Asian Survey* 49, no. 1 (2009), 124.

61. Joseph S. Nye, "The Case for Deep Engagement," *Foreign Affairs* 74 (July-August 1995), 92.

62. Sook-Jong Lee, "Allying with the U.S.: Changing South Korean Attitudes," *Korean Journal of Defense Analysis* 17, no.1 (spring 2005): 93–94.

63. For more on nationalism as a cause of anti-Americanism, see Jiyul Kim, "Pan-Korean Nationalism, Anti-Great Power-ism and U.S.-South Korean Relations," *Policy Forum Online,* Nautilus Institute, January 4, 2006, www.nautilus.org/fora/security/0601Kim.html (accessed July 19, 2006).

64. Sook-Jong Lee, "Anti-Americanism in Korean Society: A Survey-Based Analysis," *The United States and South Korea: Reinvigorating the Partnership* 14 (Washington, DC: Korea Economic Institute), June 30, 2004.

65. Chung Min Lee, "Revamping the Korean-American Alliance," in *Korean Attitudes toward the United States,* ed. Steinberg, 175.

66. Doug McAdam, "Legacies of Anti-Americanism: A Sociological Perspective," in *Anti-Americanism in World Politics,* ed. Peter J. Katzenstein and Robert O. Keohane (Ithaca, NY: Cornell University Press, 2006), 265.

67. Presenjit Duara, *Rescuing History from the Nation: Questioning Narratives of Modern China* (Chicago: University of Chicago Press, 1995), 8.

68. Ibid. See also Rogers Brubaker, *Nationalism Reframed: Nationhood and the National Question in the New Europe* (New York: Cambridge University Press, 1996), 10.

69. John Breuilly, *Nationalism and the State*, 2nd ed. (Chicago: University of Chicago Press, 1993), 13–14.

70. Ibid., 68.

71. Gi-Wook Shin, *Ethnic Nationalism in Korea: Genealogy, Politics, and Legacy* (Stanford, CA: Stanford University Press, 2006), 15–16.

72. Youngshik Bong, "Flashpoints at Sea?: Legitimization Strategy and East Asian Island Disputes" (Ph. D. diss., University of Pennsylvania, 2002), 98.

73. Shin, *Ethnic Nationalism*, 154.

74. Sheila Miyoshi Jager, *Narratives of Nation Building in Korea: A Genealogy of Patriotism* (Armonk, NY: M. E. Sharpe, 2003), xv.

75. Ibid.

76. Pew Global Attitudes Project, *Views of a Changing World* (Washington, DC: Pew Research Center for the People and the Press, 2003), 94.

77. Ibid., 95.

78. Ibid., 21.

79. Ibid.

80. Pew Research Center, "Global Opinion: The Spread of Anti-Americanism," in *Trends 2005* (Washington, DC: Pew Research Center, 2005), 115.

81. Pew Global Attitudes Project, *Views of a Changing World*, 71.

82. Ibid.

83. Alexander Cooley, *Base Politics: Democratic Change and the U.S. Military Overseas* (Ithaca, NY: Cornell University Press, 2008).

1. Nationalism versus Alliance

"This is our land! Let's drive out U.S. troops!" shouted the approximately 100 activists and residents gathered at the Kunni bombing range to protest exercises on the U.S. base, which had led to accidents and alleged damage to local residential property and stability.[1] This demonstration, about fifty miles southwest of Seoul, was one of many that took place in South Korea in 2000. Later in downtown Seoul, the famous statue of General Yi Sunsin, nationalist hero par excellence, became the stage for the burning of an American flag by Korean youth. Indeed, there was plenty of visible and audible evidence of nationalism in the "anti-American"[2] rhetoric and protests that swept through Korea in the first half of the 2000s.

Seemingly more bizarre expressions of nationalism and anti-Americanism, at least to American eyes, have also been on display. For example, the well-known activist pastors Han Sangyŏl and Mun Chŏnghyŏn shaved off their hair in ritual protest (*sagbal sik*) against what they considered was a sham court martial and illegitimate acquittal of the two American servicemen whose armored vehicle ran over and killed Sim Misŏn and Sin Hyosun in June 2002. Han raised his fists and tearfully exclaimed:

> My entire body is shaking, not because of the cold but because of this rage that is rising up within. How can it be that the killers are declared guiltless; the killers should be punished, and U.S. troops should get out of here. . . . Through this incident, we confirm that the U.S. should leave Korea. We can't take any more of this. We'll take 1,200,000 signatures to the White House and present our petition. Bush must repent [*hoegae*]. Toward a Korea free of the U.S. military, long-live our people. We the Korean people will achieve unification on our own.[3] (author's translation)

Nationalism evokes great passions: rage, righteousness, hope, sacrifice and suffering, political demolition, and communal regeneration. Perhaps that is why it catches our attention and imagination. As the preceding discussion shows, there is good evidence of nationalistic impulses at play in Korean society and politics. Moreover, in the early 2000s there was no shortage of survey data showing high degrees of nationalist sentiment and negative attitudes toward the United States. But, as I argue below, correlation does not equal causation.

This chapter highlights specific events that fueled nationalist sentiment that snowballed and publicly shattered against the U.S. Forces, Korea (USFK) after the deaths of the two girls. The accumulated buildup of such sentiments was sometimes justifiable and yet had no particular bearing on the outcome of Korean policy toward the United States. Moreover, the chapter illustrates the "learned" traits or reiterations of nationalistic responses that have been indoctrinated into the public psyche through numerous social campaigns and political mobilizations led by the government as well as civil society actors. I emphasize that Korean nationalism—elusive and habituated—is a static, overused, and underspecified explanation for diverse political phenomena, while counternationalist trends, especially among the young, like rational self-interest, regional identification, and cosmopolitan sensibilities are often ignored or underexamined as part of the South Korean social fabric.

Alexander Cooley, who undertook extensive comparative studies of basing agreements and politics between the United States and host nations, is clear that "all basing agreements are, to some extent, a hierarchical security contract in which a base host legally cedes part of its sovereignty when it accepts a foreign military presence on its territory."[4] Since democratization in the late 1980s, South Koreans have been quick to blame the U.S.-ROK Status of Forces Agreement (SOFA) for problems related to the U.S. bases. As a matter of course, in the aftermath of the two deaths, public opinion against the United States military hardened, and demands for yet another revision of the SOFA (which had just been completed by the winter of 2000 and ratified in 2001) became more aggressive. In September, 2000, *Hankyore Sinmun* found that 85.2 percent of the 1,000 residents surveyed believed that the SOFA was unfair toward Korea and needed to be revised, and age was not a divisive factor: the totals were 88.4 percent of those in their twenties, 87.4 percent in their thirties, 86.4 percent in their forties, 81.7 percent in their fifties, and 76.2 percent sixties and older.[5] Many Koreans desired a reversal of what they believed to be a handicap for their own government in dealing with the U.S. military presence: unequal and unfavorable terms (for Korea) of the U.S. military presence. They believed that a weak SOFA abetted abuses by American personnel toward Koreans and ensured that Koreans' rights could not be fully protected by their own government.

Popular events in 2002, like the Olympics and the World Cup, also agitated nationalist sentiment and rocked Korean-American relations. The year began badly. In February, South Korean speed-skater Kim Dong Sung got stripped of his chance at an Olympic gold medal in Salt Lake City, and the American competitor, Apollo Ohno, took home the prize. Kim had reached the finish line first but was quickly disqualified for having blocked Ohno in the last lap. This was salt added to a fresh national wound—a month earlier, President George W. Bush had outraged the Korean public by labeling North Korea a part of the "Axis of Evil."

South Koreans reacted with collective resentment toward U.S. "bullying" in sports and politics. In the early months of 2002, political leaders of varying political stripes, actors and singers, intellectuals and students, the old and the young raised the volume of criticism in words and song against the United States. The *Korea Times* reported: "The overnight online hit that tapped into that exposed nerve was a headbanging tune 'F**king USA.' In the song, the singer vents his rage with lyrics like 'Mean thief that stole Olympic gold, F**king USA . . . Threatening North Korea with a war and intervening in South Korea's affairs, rogue country F**king USA.'"[6] Hanch'ŏngnyŏn, the Federation of Korean University Student Councils, the radical student group, called for an anti-U.S. boycott campaign "to restore Koreans' national pride and fortify South Korea by ridding college campuses of foods such as McDonald's and Coca Cola."[7]

Mid-year, the Korean soccer team's sudden rise in the World Cup competition both stimulated and was encouraged by an outpouring of euphoric energy by Koreans. For them, the sporting event was more than a game. It was tantamount to a celebration of Korea's miraculous accomplishments in just a few decades and a vindication of their sacrifice and suffering through decades of colonial rule by Japan, civil war, poverty, powerlessness, authoritarian abuses, and the Asian Financial Crisis. Chaibong Hahm put it aptly:

> When the national team reached the quarter finals, after having beaten in succession all "great powers" in soccer—Portugal, Spain, and Italy—Korea's improbable success provided the occasion for an outburst of national pride and solidarity never before witnessed. It was the first time in anyone's memory that Korean came together not

> to oppose someone or something, be it a dictator, the communists, or insensitive remarks by right wing Japanese politicians, but simply to celebrate Korea and being Korean. The rallying cry for this festive occasion was *Taehan-minkuk*, the official name of the country.[8]

Indeed, the Korean flag was hung, worn, plastered, painted, and pictured just about everywhere, along with variations of "Go Reds" (for the national soccer team, the Red Devils) and images of the triumphant players. The newly deified athletes and their passionate and loyal fans moved together in a synergy that many in Korea and around the world viewed with admiration. I was present in Korea during this period, and in some ways the collective outbursts of emotion and energy were akin to the collective ritual of *kut* (exorcism) central to Korean shamanism, through which spirits that haunt and frustrate are purged and the individual or family is freed from the baggage or burdens of the past. There were Koreans who celebrated the surge of nationalistic sentiment, and those who feared it. Both the conservative *Chosun Ilbo* and left-leaning *Hankyore 21* magazines cautioned that such nationalist outpourings can become dangerous if people lose their heads, even as they expressed enthusiasm for and pride in the Korean team. But do face-painted flags and disappointment at losing a gold medal amount to anti-Americanism? Was opposition to the "axis of evil" statement and the grief over two innocent deaths tantamount to nationalism and the deterioration of the alliance?

THE ACCUMULATION AND HABITUATION OF NATIONALISM

As any casual observer of Korean politics and U.S.-ROK relations knows, the Kwangju massacre/uprising of May 1980 definitively changed the bilateral dynamic. Violence erupted in the capital city of Chŏlla Province, when demonstrations by student and other democracy activists turned into bloody chaos after Chun Du Hwan deployed military troops who brutally suppressed the demonstrators and bystanders. Many Koreans had assumed that the USFK commanders could have prevented or put a stop to the Korean military's retaliation. When no American assistance was forthcoming, the Kwangju people and other Koreans blamed the United States for allegedly supporting Chun's dictatorial actions.[9] Before Kwangju, the United States was viewed by dissidents as a model for democracy rather than as a cause of military rule and political repression.

But with the deepening of Koreans' sense of abandonment and betrayal in the first half of the 1980s and the simultaneous radicalization of the student (democracy) movement, Korea's relationship—historical, military, political, and cultural—with the United States came to be regarded as fundamental to the problems of Korean political development since liberation from Japanese rule. Ideological anti-Americanism became popular among democracy activists. The statement by Koryo Theological Seminary students who had set fire to the American Cultural Center in Pusan on March 18, 1982, sums up their views of U.S. "culpability":

> The United States should not make Korea its subordinated country, but leave this land. Looking back on history from the 15 August Liberation (of 1945) until today, the United States, while providing economic aid for Korea, has closely colluded with Korean businessmen and forced us to obey its domination under the pretext of being an ally.
>
> The United States has supported the military regime which refuses democratization, social revolution and development and unification. In fact, the United States has brought about the permanent national division. We must resolve this problem for ourselves. Let us stage the anti-U.S. struggle to eliminate U.S. power which is rampant in this country.[10]

Post-Kwangju politics led to the development of an explicit and aggressive anti-American interpretation of Korean politics, contemporary history, and nationalism, with dissident intellectuals leading the way.[11] Kie-chiang Oh has remarked that "[i]n almost direct proportion to the intensifying autocratic pressures of the Chun Regime, the rhetoric of protesters became more and more extreme, radical, anti-foreign, and anti-American, such that 'Down with the Chun Dictatorship' and 'Yankee Go Home!' became the twin battle cries of demonstrators."[12] The United *Minjung* (People's) Movement for Democracy and Unification (UMDU), which had been formed in 1984 by a diverse gathering of dissidents and anti-government organizations, characterized the Chun regime as "an extreme minority of anti-democratic, anti-national and anti-people military elite."[13] The Korean military, under this "anti-nationalist" leadership, was tantamount to a "'mercenary force' for the US."[14]

Chuch'eron, a nationalist historiography that intellectuals used to critique both authoritarian rule and the role of the United States in contemporary Korean history, became the dominant discourse among dissidents and sympathizers in the 1980s. According to this line of thinking, the South Korean government had a "historically 'insidious' relationship" to the United States (and prior to that, to the Japanese colonial government) and was "nothing more than a 'puppet' regime whose primary aim was to serve foreign, not Korean, interests," in particular, U.S. imperialism.[15] Sheila Miyoshi Jager writes that *chuch'eron* celebrates the *minjung*'s (people's)[16] "struggle against adversity . . . by arguing for a vision of potential success": the "reunification of the two Koreas through active resistance to both internal *sadaejuŭi* [obedience to great powers] 'dictatorship' and external American 'imperialism.'"[17]

By 1985, the U.S. eclipsed the Chun regime as the biggest political enemy; "it was apparent that most student activists subscribed to the view that the United States was primarily responsible for the very existence of the military-authoritarian regime of President Chun Doo Hwan."[18] In April, 1986, Chamint'u (Committee for the Anti-U.S. Struggle for Independence and the Anti-Fascist Struggle for Democracy), a student organization for the explicit purpose of fighting U.S. power and influence, was established on the campuses of Seoul National University and Korea University. The dissidents asserted that they were the true advocates of the Korean nation and democracy and the rightful leaders of national redemption, freedom, and unification.

Jinwung Kim and Gi-Wook Shin have written about the correlation between nationalism and anti-Americanism in the years following the transition to democracy (1987–88).[19] However, unlike the 1980s, when leftist critiques of the United States prevailed, Shin found that "national consciousness" and "nationalist concerns" served as the primary political source of anti-Americanism in the 1990s,[20] meaning it was less about America and more about Korea. According to Shin, "Korean anti-Americanism is an expression of new nationalism" that reflects "new self-confidence which is commensurate with South Korea's growing economic power" and a desire "for a change in the U.S.-South Korea relationship from patron-client to partners."[21] Based on a major survey conducted in June 1990, Shin found that 57.8 percent of 1,523 respondents viewed the U.S. as "faithful to its own interests . . . , [and] less than a third (29.5) regarded it as helpful [to Korea]," with the majority (55 percent) wanting South Korea "to maintain the same relationship it has with other nations," and 16 percent believing "Korea should be wary of the United States."[22] Moreover, a 1991 survey of 2,016 college students by the Korea Institute of Social Studies reported that only about a quarter of the respondents or less viewed U.S. influence on economic growth, human rights, political democratization, and unification in a positive light.[23] With regard to the 2000s, Shin states: "Unlike the 1980s when perception of U.S. economic and political dominance fueled anti-American sentiment, today's resentment largely stems from Koreans' belief that the United States is increasingly going against Korea's national interests."[24]

The new democratic energy in the post-1987 period translated into new license to interpret anew—and in public—the U.S.'s role in Korean history and national development. Students, intellectuals, and the media participated in heated debate as to whether the U.S. is responsible morally and practically for many of the problems in Korean society, most notably the division of the nation and the decades of anti-Communist authoritarian rule by the military. They also challenged the legitimacy of the presence, terms, and conduct of U.S. troops. In covering a wave of strident student protests and demonstrations in the summer of 1988, the *Washington Post* stated: "South Korean students have staged violent protests that have linked the themes of reunification and anti-Americanism. In addition to blaming the partition on Washington, the students have charged that the United States has acted to prevent reunification and the flourishing of democracy."[25] Anti-Americanism was no longer a taboo subject, in contrast to the authoritarian period, when criticizing the United States, especially the bases, was deemed tantamount to being a Communist and serving North Korea's interests and therefore subject to the National Security Law (NSL) and punishment. For example, Article 7 of the 1980 NSL was "used to imprison people who have written or disseminated material about the North Korean system of government, or which criticized the South Korean Government or the presence of U.S. armed forces."[26] But increasingly, freedom of speech and thought had new legal sanction and popular support, such that the *Christian Science Monitor* remarked, "The now unfettered Korean media eagerly publicizes incidents of alleged crimes by GIs or military dependents," and while violent expressions of anti-Americanism are rejected by most Koreans, "the mood of national assertiveness cannot be ignored."[27]

Disputes over Kimch'i and Territory

Throughout the 1990s and into the 2000s, the new democratic mood fostered a freewheeling tendency to air out all sorts of discontents, both old and new, including those with nationalist edges. And events with the potential to galvanize the Korean public around nationalist themes erupted, providing a feeding frenzy for the media, which in turn served up a tempting diet of nationalist angst and rancor to the public. There is an embarrassment of riches in this regard: the "*kimch'i* war" with Japan in 1996 over Japan's proposal to make *kimuchi* (the Japanese pronunciation) an official food at the Atlanta Olympic Games, the bitter conflict over Japanese claims to Tokdo/Takeshima (reignited in the mid-1990s), opposition to revisionist textbooks released in Japan in 2001 (a decades-old conflict), and China's claim to Koguryŏ (starting in the 1990s but still emitting political steam in the early 2000s). In the same period, difficult negotiations over the U.S.-Korea SOFA, along with lingering charges of civilian massacres by U.S. troops at Nogunni, and upset over U.S. accidents and environmental damage on U.S. bases in Korea (including the dumping of formaldehyde into the Han River) flashed on television screens and Internet sites, and appeared in newspapers.

In truth, nationalistic responses on the part of the Korean public contained both emotional excess and justifiable ire. For example, although on one level, it amounted to a case of trade competition, the *kimch'i* war with Japan hit a foundational point of Korean identity and daily existence: the centrality of *kimch'i* as a national dish and the safeguarding of its authenticity. Koreans successfully submitted a petition to the Food and Agriculture Organization to have the Korean recipe (natural fermentation versus chemically induced, as in the Japanese preparation process) adopted as the standard in its Codex Alimentarius. For non-Koreans, this much ado about cabbage, garlic, and red pepper easily could be interpreted as nationalist excess; however, Korean insistence on authenticity can be viewed as comparable to the French holding strict standards for themselves and outsiders regarding the labeling of champagne and distinguishing between sparkling wine and *la méthode champenoise.*

The territorial disputes with Japan and China are more complicated, involving international law (in the case of Tokdo/Takeshima, the Law of the Sea Convention), bilateral agreements (in the case of Tokdo/Takeshima, the 1965 fishery accord), economic competition, conflicting historical claims, and more. In both cases, the responsibility for politicizing the issues as nationalistic causes lies with the Japanese and Chinese governments, in addition to their Korean counterpart. With respect to Tokdo/Takeshima, Japan's turn in 1998 toward "seizure diplomacy" (seizure of Korean fishing vessels) and its unilateral abrogation of the 1965 fishery accord, which outlined the respective exclusive economic zones (EEZ), upped the ante.[28] In his study of East Asian island disputes, Youngshik Bong blames both then-Prime Minister Ryutaro Hashimoto and President Kim Young Sam for escalating tensions by transforming "'maritime' issues into a clash of 'territorial nationalisms.'"[29]

Koreans have developed a habituated nationalism, ritualistic at times, toward Japan. But the Korea-Japan nationalism constitutes a two-way street; they fuel each other. And it is difficult to imagine nationalistic suspicions and distrust toward Japan disappearing among Koreans (or Chinese) without a genuine airing of the colonial and wartime abuses by the Japanese state and society. What this historical bottleneck does is systematically restrict smooth diplomatic relations by the two East Asian neighbors and creates a spillover of nationalist sensitivities on the part of Koreans toward foreign insults, both real and perceived.

Asian Financial Crisis

If the *kimch'i* and textbook controversies heightened Koreans' sense of injured national pride and historical victimization by a foreign power, the Asian Financial Crisis sent them over the edge. The very foundation of Koreans' newly developed pride in themselves and their country was shaken in the late 1990s when the value of the *wŏn* plummeted dramatically and the nation fell into collective economic, political, and psychological despair. Common people and analysts alike named the crisis as "one of the most pivotal events to negatively shape modern Korean perceptions, both internal and external, equal in impact to the Japanese occupation, the Korean War, and the Kwangju massacre for most Koreans."[30] As Nicholas Kristof observed in December 1997, "For an over-achiever and A-plus student like South Korea to be sent to the corner with what feels like a dunce cap is a torture more psychological than economic, and the heartbreak here on the frosty streets of Seoul is almost palpable."[31]

What was known as the Asian Financial Crisis in the West had a different name in Korea: the IMF Crisis. And the United States was perceived as the big bad bully behind the International Monetary Fund's demand for economic restructuring and liberalization in return for $58 billion in bailout funds. "To Koreans, the IMF represented quintessential economic imperialism—a group of economists sent out from Washington to tell them how to run their country."[32] The *New York Times* remarked that "many see the United States as the puppeteer behind the I.M.F.," with American and Japanese businesses poised to benefit from "unbearable market-opening measures."[33] According to the journalist Donald Kirk, author of *Korean Crisis,* even "Finance Ministry officials and chaebŏl executives alike blamed the United States for influencing the IMF to negotiate for reduction of chaebŏl power—and for foreign interests to be able to own up to 50 percent [rather than 26 percent] of stock in Korean companies."[34]

Koreans were not alone in harboring such negative sentiments toward the United States; "rumblings of resentment and the stirrings of anti-Americanism" were noted as the "most striking emotion" in the Asian region as the crisis spread.[35] The Thai daily, *Matichon*, "warned that the West is aiming at the 'intellectual colonialism' and 'economic colonialism' of Asia, and denounced the 'financial and economic wars' that it said the West had mounted to humble the region."[36] The *New Straits Times* of Malaysia warned that "Americans should not indulge in triumphalism amidst the Asian financial problems" and should be prepared for negative impacts on the U.S. economy and the rise of anti-Americanism in Asia.[37] China, which did not suffer the afflictions of its neighbors during the crisis, also regarded U.S. intentions with suspicion and at times asserted a pan-Asian united front against American power. The *People's Daily* wrote, "By giving help, it [the United States] is forcing East Asia into submission, promoting the American economic and political model and easing East Asia's threat to the American model."[38]

In many ways, Korea fared better in receiving international attention and in the speed and effectiveness of recovery than its less affluent neighbors like Thailand and Indonesia. But the publics in all three countries felt deep national embarrassment and humiliation. Economic policy, international regard, self-image, and national identity were inextricably tied. For example, Indonesians seemed less angry "about the contents of the IMF agreement as they [seemed] about the 'humiliating' image of [President] Suharto hunched at a table signing the IMF deal."[39] Similarly, for South Koreans, the economic debacle and IMF intervention became a "sting to national honor."[40] Kim Bong So, a pushcart vendor in Seoul, summed up the common sentiment: "It's a national humiliation. . . . I feel so ashamed."[41]

Koreans became engulfed by and obsessed with the IMF crisis. They conflated personal loss and grief with national humiliation and shame. They began and ended their day with the crisis on their minds. As one Korean writer explained, every conversation began with a reference to the IMF: "When people talk about good news, they begin with 'Even though the IMF . . . ' Discussion of bad news begins with 'Because of the IMF . . . ' A ten-year-old boy might say, 'Because of the IMF my parents don't have the money to buy me a toy robot.'"[42] The IMF *sidae* (era) became a way of life, even a culture, as television serial dramas and comedies depicting the impact of and adjustment to the crisis proliferated. Given that TV serials are central to Koreans' daily entertainment (families, neighbors, and friends gather in the evenings to watch them together), the IMF crisis came to life in their living rooms in addition to their workplaces, bus stations (where the unemployed gathered en masse), grocery stores, schools, banks, and elsewhere.

But the tendency to suffer losses collectively had a mirror image: collective sacrifice. Restaurants large and small put up signs that advertised slashed prices in recognition of people's tight pocketbooks. Citizens took whatever foreign currency they had to banks with the hope that small gestures would add up to help pay the nation's short-term foreign debt. People grabbed their gold jewelry and mobilized gold drives in order to donate the precious metal to the country. And many participated in or supported various frugality campaigns, assuming (incorrectly), as did Yoon Byoung Joon, a noodle shop owner, that "[r]unning a nation's economy and running a household are the same. . . . When you owe someone money you have to tighten your belt and cut your spending."[43]

A frugality campaign that already had been in place gained new momentum, taking on nationalist coloring as civic groups and citizens encouraged one another to support a "Buy Korea" campaign, essentially abetting the boycott of foreign goods, especially luxury items. For example, Koreans criticized compatriots who consumed foreign labels and traveled internationally, heckling them at airports and denouncing their unpatriotic and "selfish" behavior.[44] It made bad economic sense to undermine spending, risking further economic recession and instability. It also made for poor diplomacy with the very nations that were being counted on to resuscitate the Korean economy. For example, with the support of the United States, the European Union had brought a complaint before the World Trade Organization in February 1997, prior to the crisis, stating their objection to a frugality campaign. Specifically, they argued that the campaign "by civic society against luxury consumption was orchestrated and organized by the government to protect domestic industry and thus violated WTO rules."[45] During the crisis, private sector representatives became alarmed and dismayed by the frugality fervor. For example, Edward Yardeni, the chief economist of Deutsche Morgan Grenfell commented in the *Washington Post* that in order for Korea to get back on its economic feet, people "should stop this xenophobic backlash, because no one is going to want to lend to them."[46]

But frugality campaigns are nothing new in Korean society, and they have a long association with Confucian and Christian notions of virtue as well as nation-saving and nation-promoting ideas, which had been adopted long before Japanese colonialism and American dominance. In

Measuring Excess, Laura Nelson made the following observations about the politics and culture of Korean consumption that have resonated among Koreans since the mid-late 1980s:

> While moral constructions of appropriate and patriotic consumption can be traced back to the pre-colonial period, in recent decades frugality has been represented as a strategy for national economic development, a moral practice of cultural preservation from the corruption of luxury and modernization, and a means of defending the nation from international shame and economic ruin.[47]

Even without the insults of a colonial past, Koreans might be prone to a moralistic regard for consumption, even while indulging in it. But resistance to Japanese colonial rule fostered an immediate linkage between acts of "economic patriotism" and actions toward independence. Nelson recounts the nationalist leader Cho Mansik's rationale for establishing the Korean Products Promotion Society in 1922: "In order to promote Korean Products we must make it our aim to buy and use goods made by Koreans, and also unite to manufacture and supply those goods we need. Unless we come to our senses and exert ourselves in this way, how can we expect to maintain our livelihood and develop our society?"[48] And of course the fusion of individual economic preferences and acts and national economic development was a foundation of Park Chung Hee's modernization drive: "When a frugal spirit permeates homes, schools, and offices, making all citizens watchful against waste and loss, no matter how trivial it may be, this will display formidable power in economic construction. . . . [This spirit] will act as a 'hidden force,' benefiting not only housekeeping in individual homes but the whole national economy."[49]

Most relevant to import boycotts and frugality was the anti-consumption (*kwasobi ch'ubang*) campaign of the late 1980s and early 1990s that Laura Nelson has analyzed. Led by groups like the YMCA and later the national government and publicized widely by the media, *kwasobi ch'ubang* put the burden of Korea's economic and social problems on the shoulders of individual consumers. Individual spending on everything from weddings to extracurricular studies to cars and leisure were targeted as sources of personal immorality and weakness (and debt) in the national economy. And the public was reminded many times throughout the day—through government-commissioned posters on subways and buses, advertisements in newspapers, and private broadcasts of anti-consumerist messages via loudspeakers and billboards in public places—to practice "modesty, increased savings, and longer work hours."[50] Nelson found that many participants in the campaign had stored memories of past frugality campaigns in their heads.

However, each and every frugality campaign or boycott in contemporary Korean society does not amount to a nationalist tactic or anti-American (or -Japanese or -European) program of action. Rather, these are learned mental and social devices that often gain momentum by rote because they are readily available in the collective memory as a way to make sense of challenges. They are also easy ways for people to feel a sense of participation in a collective effort. Mobilization campaigns to inculcate personal and public virtue and to transform national life abound in the history of the Korean republic, especially under Park Chung Hee. The *Saemaul Undong* (New Village Movement) of the 1970s was emblematic of such schemes. But there were numerous miscellaneous "purification campaigns" (*chŏnghwa undong*)—against corruption, incivility (e.g., spitting in public), frugality, modesty—and of course, for anti-Communist patriotism. Even in the democratic era, Korean politics has been full of such campaigns, led by the government and/or the public. The globalization drive under Kim Young Sam is a good example, as is the push for environmental consciousness and recycling. The point to keep in mind is the cumulative effect of past mobilization campaigns on individuals and groups. Given the decades of myriad political and social campaigns and the specific highlighting of the *kwasobi ch'ubang* campaign in the early 1990s, a habituated turn toward frugality (and import boycott) by the Korean public and state should have come as no surprise.

During the initial period of the financial crisis, Korean government officials and political leaders indeed fanned the flames of nationalistic ire, and the economic crisis became a major issue in the 1997 presidential election as candidates capitalized on the crisis to gather support and deflect responsibility. The lame-duck president, Kim Young Sam (YS), under whose watch the debacle occurred, tried to show solidarity with the suffering citizenry, asking Koreans to endure "bone-carving pain," while the opposition party's candidate Kim Dae Jung (DJ) declared that YS should be impeached unless he forced economic reforms.[51] And Lee Hoi Chang, the Grand National Party candidate, "denounced the IMF demands as 'rude acts that encroach upon the autonomy of a sovereign state.'"[52]

But ultimately the Kim Young Sam government quickly had to step in to put a brake on anti-foreign sentiments and boycotts. Don Kirk observed that the YS government despaired about both growing anti-foreignism and the broken economy:

> The Blue House, sensitive to the negative impact, called on groups such as the National Alliance for the Unification of the Fatherland to tone down their language for fear of undermining efforts to bring in foreign money. Such "inflammatory" verbiage, said Ban Ki Moon, presidential assistant for international affairs, would disturb "foreign lenders and investors who may want to help."[53]

As soon as Kim Dae Jung won the election, "DJ's camp quickly forgot the campaign and about 'National Shame Day.'"[54] The realities of governance required Kim Dae Jung to step up to the IMF plate. Public outcry over national humiliation and loss of economic sovereignty abounded, but in the end it had limited effect on policy.

2000 North-South Summit

The June 2000 summit between North Korean leader Kim Jong il and South Korean president Kim Dae Jung generated a kind of euphoria (termed, e.g., "euphoric reunification fever" or "Kim Jong Il fever") among South Koreans, giving them hope and vision of a unified, proud, and strong nation in the foreseeable future.[55] The event served as a balm to soothe the shock and pain of the financial crisis. It also offered a redemptive promise of new national potential and possibility and shifted the dynamics of national identity. "That the two heads of state publicly embraced and used a complimentary vocabulary to describe each other constituted a major divergence from deeply entrenched patterns" of mutual vilification and hostility that preoccupied both Koreas during most of the Cold War period.[56] Whether one believes the summit to have been simply supreme stagecraft or a significant advancement of inter-Korean relations, it was indeed "an unprecedented event in post-war Korean history," one that the Australian scholar Andrew O'Neil described as "arguably the most anticipated bilateral leadership encounter in Asia since the Nixon-Mao Beijing meeting of 1972."[57]

As momentous as the event was at the time, there was concern that the euphoria unleashed powerful emotional forces of ethnonationalist sentiment and expectations for rapid changes in inter-Korean relations and Korea's foreign policy orientation. Lee Hoi Chang, then the leader of the conservative Grand National Party, worried that the summit would erroneously—given no substantive changes between the two Koreas—make South Koreans question the need for the U.S. forces.[58] Roland Bleiker has observed that the summit generated an "ambivalent attitude toward the North: the image of an 'enemy' prevails in realist security policy, while the image of a 'brother' dominates the more nationalistic attitudes toward unification."[59] Indeed, one South Korean who was interviewed by the *New York Times* put it bluntly: "Now, I'm not sure what to believe about North Korea, but I know that what I was told in the past is not exactly the truth."[60]

According to Victor Cha, the "Sunshine Policy had the unintended consequence of creating nationwide perceptions of the United States as an impediment to inter-Korean relations."[61] It is not by accident that "the first article of the North-South Joint Declaration of June 2000 declares 'the importance of the "independent" resolution of the unification issue.'" Less than three years later, the newly elected president Roh Moo Hyun declared that he would steer the nation toward a more independent course vis-à-vis the United States. As a reporter for *Asia Times* pointed out, "In short, the rising hostility against the United States in South Korea has been warming its ties with the North."[62] Conversely, the wider and deeper the South's ties to the North become, the harder it would be for South Korea to advocate "pro-U.S." policies, especially when distrust and hostility characterized the United States' relationship with North Korea during most of the George. W. Bush years.

However, as Bleiker states, the June summit did not undo decades of the "deeply entrenched antagonistic identity constructs" that had "penetrated virtually all aspects of [South Korean] life." "Categorizing people into friends and foes is a type of pathological illness that persists even if external images and circumstances change. It is not surprising, then, that right after the summit meeting Kim Dae-jung declared in a public statement that 'we must not let our guard down and should strengthen our defense posture. Only those who are well prepared for war can enjoy peace.'"[63] Bleiker also comments on the continued negative depictions of North Korea in a new school textbook that had been released around the time of the summit.[64] Similarly, O'Neil underscores the carrot-and-stick approach to Kim Dae Jung's sunshine policy and reminds its critics that in addition to emphasizing military preparedness, Kim reaffirmed the South's commitment to the alliance and the U.S. troop presence.[65]

Gi-wook Shin and his co-authors make it clear that even within an ethnonational collective, "an in-group bias for desirable members" exists in tandem with "an in-group derogation for undesirable members . . . [where] downgrading unlikable ingroupers may be a cognitive strategy aimed at preserving the group's sense of positivity as a whole."[66] In Shin's work, he uses Social Identity Theory to identify North Koreans as the out-group that helps constitute the in-group of desirable Koreans—in the south. This "black sheep effect"[67] reveals the double-edged sword of nationalism. Not only is nationalism about "us" (nationals) versus "them"

(American, Japan, or the rest of the world), but the ethnonational "we" is divided and divisible by Koreans themselves, a division that persists to this day.[68] Despite the fanfare and hopes thrown about regarding the future unification of the peninsula, euphoric nationalism generated by the June summit did not change the U.S.-Korea alliance.

THE CHANGING CONTEXT OF NATIONALISM

Globalization and regionalization have presented South Koreans with changing opportunities for new ideas of political participation, cultural consumption, and identity formation by challenging and transforming norms, laws, institutions, and social relations within Korean society. Even though resurgent nationalism is often deemed a reaction to the pressures of globalization, Koreans tactically have used globalization as a way to advance national and individual power together with outward-looking, cosmopolitan tendencies. As the drive toward globalization became a state priority under President Kim Young Sam in the mid-1990s, the Korean political scientist Chung-in Moon emphasized the need for Koreans to use globalization as a way to thwart nationalistic tendencies: "[I]nward-looking and xenophobic biases cannot cope with the challenges of spontaneous globalization. Peace education, education for human capital formation and cross-cultural education constitute critical components of managed globalization. . . . [C]ross-cultural education assists individuals in transforming themselves into citizens of the world."[69]

It is important to remember the rapid social, economic, and political changes that Korea has been undergoing since the 1990s. For example, nearly overnight in the 1990s, South Korea became a labor-receiving country, with hundreds of thousands of migrant workers, documented and undocumented, coming from poorer countries, particularly China and Southeast and South Asia. In addition to sharing their labor market with foreigners, Koreans are also sharing their beds. By 2005, 13.6 percent of marriages involved a foreign spouse (compared to 4.6 percent in 2001), with never-married rural men and divorced urban men constituting the major groups seeking foreign wives.[70] In 2009 Korean researchers forecast that by 2050 the foreign-born population would compose 10 percent of the total population,[71] comparable to some western European societies today.

In 1997, the central government had changed the citizenship law from a patrilineal to a bilineal basis (allowing both mothers and fathers to bestow Korean citizenship on their children) in response to the growing number of "mixed race" children born of Korean parents and (mostly male) foreign workers. By 2008 the number of half-Korean children growing up in Korea increased to 44,000, along with the increase in "international marriages."[72] In October 2008 the Ministry of Education reported that the "number of Korean elementary, middle or high school students with multicultural backgrounds more than doubled over the past two years to 20,180."[73] One scholar accounted for 107,689 multicultural children in 2009.[74] By 2020, an estimated "5 percent of all South Korean residents will be either foreign-born or 'mixed-blood,' a level comparable with the proportion of non-autochthonous populations in some European societies."[75] The Korean state, under both Roh Moo Hyun and Lee Myung Bak, quickly responded to the challenges of the growing foreign population and "multicultural families" (*tamunhwa kajok*) by officially acknowledging that Korea is becoming a "multicultural society" and by formulating policies to facilitate integration and assimilation.[76]

Although some Koreans certainly have exhibited xenophobic reactions to the foreigners, "the normative aspects of globalization—emphasis on human rights, democratization, pluralism and cross-culturalism—have helped fuel the MWMs [Migrant Workers' Movements]" in Korea.[77] This may help explain why Koreans, who are ranked high on nationalism by the Pew Global Attitudes survey indicators (see the introduction to this volume) and are known to be highly ethnonationalistic (due to relatively high homogeneity in terms of language, ethnicity, and cultural practices), rank among the lowest in opposition to immigration restrictions among the nations included in the same Pew survey. In 2003, only 7 percent "completely agree[d]" that more restrictions should be placed on entry into their country. This contrasts with 46 percent of Americans who "completely agree[d]" with the statement, even though Americans live in a self-identified nation of immigrants that is one of the world's most ethnically and culturally diverse societies.

South Korea's own legacy of fighting both human rights violations and labor repression also has driven the rapid development of an advocacy movement for foreign workers. Amid confrontation with state authorities attempting to crack down on migrant workers and their supporters in the mid-1990s, Korean activists framed their fight on behalf of the foreigners as a fight on behalf of Korean democracy and also "adopted some symbolic and coalitional patterns that characterized democracy movements of the past."[78] In recent years, foreign workers and foreign wives have begun to organize among themselves to represent and articulate their interests to the rest of Korean society.

Korean identity is undergoing transformation in a complex flow and network of peoples, languages, customs, and loyalties, both old and new. Yoonkyung Lee has studied the ways in which Korean intellectual circles, the media, and civic organizations have been challenging ethnonationalism: "[T]hey concur that this nationalistic identity, which once had a liberating capacity [especially against Japanese colonial rule], tends to be a totalizing state ideology in Korean society today, stifling diversity, individuality, and democratic inclusiveness."[79] She offers the example of MBC TV's popular program *Nŭkkimp'yo* (2001–7), which featured "Asia Asia," a segment that highlighted a pan-Asian culture to which Korea belongs and "advocated an egalitarian identity for Koreans and migrant workers as co-equal Asians."[80] In addition,

> major newspapers, too, have produced special reports on the changing demographic composition of Korean society and the barriers and challenges "foreigners" and inter-racial Koreans face in everyday life. Such reports have appeared in liberal dailies such as *Hankyoreh, Kyonghyang,* and *Ne-il,* as well as in conservative newspapers like *Chosun, JoongAng,* and *Donga*. With titles such as "Don't Ask Me If I Am a Korean," "The Era of One Million Migrants," "The Era of One Million Multiethnic Families," and "A Korea Report on Multiethnic Society," these reports survey the influx of migrant workers and foreign brides and acknowledge that recent changes in the Korean demography are an irreversible fact of life. They also carry stories on the maltreatment nonethnic Koreans have experienced at the hands of Koreans who are ill prepared for multiethnic cohabitation. By advocating universal human rights, democratic inclusiveness, and global citizenship, the mass media have played a role in raising critical voices against Koreans' ethnocentrism.[81]

YOUTH AND GENERATIONAL GAP

There are many in the United States and Korea who attributed the deterioration of U.S.-Korea relations to Korean youth. A common assertion is that young Koreans suffer from historical amnesia (about how dangerous a threat Communism really was and the American sacrifices made in the Korean War) and political naïveté (by romanticizing their North Korean kin). Critics like to point out that Korean youth, who have grown up in a prosperous society without direct experience of war and suffering, exhibit prideful nationalism and wishful thinking about reconciliation and reunification with North Korea and harbor negative attitudes toward the United States and the bilateral alliance. In 2002, Nicholas Eberstadt of the

American Enterprise Institute remarked, "Such is the temper of the times that South Korea's most popular 'bubblegum pop' girl band—a heretofore entirely apolitical group with a reputation for extreme wholesomeness—released a harshly anti-American MTV-style video."[82] To underscore the correlation between naïveté and youth, he highlighted a 2001 survey of fifth- and sixth-graders in south Kyŏngsang Province, one of the most conservative regions in South Korea, which reported that 42 percent "identified North Korea as 'the friendliest nation toward South Korea,'" with the U.S. playing second fiddle (39 percent).[83] Eberstadt blamed the Kim Dae Jung administration and its overly optimistic brand of engagement policy for swaying the Korean public toward foolhardiness. Eberstadt is not a lone voice; numerous public opinion surveys and polls in both Korea and the U.S. have churned out numbers attesting to the generational gap as it relates to the United States and the U.S. forces in Korea.

Indeed, age and support for the U.S. and the bilateral relationship do correlate. In the midst of heavy protests in the winter of 2002–3, a U.S. State Department survey found that the younger generations viewed the United States less favorably than older respondents (32 percent of those in their twenties versus 69 percent of those in their fifties and older). Moreover, only 22 percent of the twenty-something cohort versus 42 percent of those over fifty considered the U.S military presence in Korea to be "very important."[84] A 2003 survey by *JoongAng Ilbo*, the Center for Strategic and International Studies (CSIS), and RAND found that 36.9 percent of those in their twenties and 32.4 percent of thirty-somethings viewed the bilateral relationship as "very beneficial" to Korea, compared to 62.4 percent of those over fifty.[85] Worse, only 15.2 percent of Koreans in their twenties and 19.5 percent in their thirties believed that the military alliance contributed "a lot" to peace and stability on the peninsula, versus 58.6 percent of those fifty and above.[86] Additionally, the same survey revealed that about 45 percent of those in their twenties and thirties thought that inter-Korean cooperation should take precedence over cooperation with the United States, while the reverse was true among older Koreans: 38.8 percent of the fifty-plus cohort believed that cooperation with the United States should come first.[87] With respect to anti-American sentiment as a major cause of the deterioration of the alliance, there was a clear consensus (44.6 percent) among those in the over-fifty category that "anti-American sentiment in Korea" was responsible, whereas only 28.1 percent of those in their twenties agreed.[88]

Young Koreans, however, are not unique in their critical attitudes toward the United States. According to the 2002 Pew survey, 44 percent of Canadians under thirty had unfavorable views of the U.S., compared to 20 percent in the fifty to sixty-four age group.[89] Almost three decades earlier, "[t]he German rejection of and mistrust toward the United States" was "especially pronounced among the younger generation."[90]

To place the burden of anti-Americanism on youth, with its associated idealism, rebelliousness, lack of historical understanding, and naïveté, is analytically misleading. First, the Pew 2002 report states that age generally has varying effects on attitudes toward the United States.[91] Second, where an age gap exists, it cannot necessarily be isolated as an explanation since there has been a "persistent" age gap in Korean people's regard for the U.S. during both good bilateral times and bad:

> In 1993, when opinion of the U.S. was considerably more favorable among all age groups, there was still a 15-point difference between youngest and oldest, and 25 points between the 20s and 40s. In 2003, there was a 37-percentage point difference between the much more negative attitudes of the 20-somethings and the widely positive views of those age 50 and above (roughly corresponding to the Korean War generation).[92]

Back in 1985, during the heyday of the student and democracy movement that protested both Chun Doo Hwan and Ronald Reagan, 78 percent of youth (versus 56 percent of the general public) believed that "Korea was too closely identified with the United States."[93] Major Korean surveys conducted later between 1990 and 1992, after the democratic transition and improved relations with the United States, still revealed that a higher proportion of Koreans in their twenties held a negative opinion of the United States than people in their fifties and older.[94]

Moreover, how to assess the impact of age (versus other factors) on political attitudes needs to be debated. A useful categorization of age cohorts is offered by the U.S. Department of State survey report of 1,556 Koreans aged twenty and over who were interviewed in January and February 2003:

> Changing public attitudes may be due to three effects—i.e., *aging* or *maturation* (as people get older and more socialized into their occupations and communities, their views become more like those of their elders), *generational* or *cohort* (attitudes are set at an early, formative stage in people's lives and tend to persist over time), and the *impact of events* (which affect everyone).[95]

The State Department study clearly recognizes the age gap between the young and old in Korea but also states that specific events (e.g., Winter

Olympics, "Axis of Evil" speech, killing of the schoolgirls) affected all generations and *eclipsed both cohort and maturational effects.*[96]

In addition, higher levels of education and social class/status correlated with negative perceptions of the United States and Korea-U.S. relations in both the early 1990s and the early 2000s.[97] According to the April 2003 State Department survey, education follows age as an anti-American variable: "In 2003, younger Koreans with a college education (over half of those under 40, over 60 percent of those in their 20s) tended to be the most negative toward the United States. College students stood out –as they did in the 1980s—for their negative opinion of the United States (only 17 percent favorable vs. 81 percent unfavorable)."[98] Gallup Korea's surveys in 2002 found that higher educational, occupational, and income status correlates with a higher degree of unfavorable attitudes toward the United States.[99] Specifically, 33 percent of respondents with middle-school education or lower, versus 68 percent of those with college degrees or above, expressed unfavorable views of the U.S., as did 37 percent of farmers versus 70 percent of white-collar workers.

With respect to U.S. troops, although 35.5 percent of Koreans with university degrees and/or advanced degrees associated the military presence with security and peace on the peninsula in August 2000, as did 36.4 percent of those with junior high-school education or less, their similarity stopped there: 32.6 percent of Koreans from the highest education background (versus 15.1 percent of the less educated) associated the military presence with crimes by Americans in uniform, and 16.2 percent (versus 5.2 percent of the second group) likened the military presence to military occupation.[100] Moreover, the older and the less educated the respondents, the more likely they were to hold the view that the U.S. is stationed in Korea in order to keep the peace on the peninsula (45.6 percent of those fifty and older and 43 percent of those with junior high-school education or less) and that the U.S. troops should stay indefinitely (28.6 percent of those over fifty and 23.1 percent of those with junior high-school or less).[101]

Earlier in a 1990 survey, which defined three categories of anti-American views—economic ("pressure to increase import of agricultural crops + trade friction"), political ("political interference + Kwangju incident + American military presence"), and nationalist ("growth of nationalist consciousness + subservient [*sadaejŏk*] politicians")—27.5 percent of respondents with middle-school education or less and 42.3 percent with college degrees articulated nationalism and political concerns respectively as reasons behind their negative attitudes. This is similar to the twenties cohort: 22.9 percent nationalism, 43.8 percent political concerns. By comparison, those with just elementary-school education had lower percentages: 11.2 percent nationalism and 29 percent political concerns.[102] Furthermore, in 1990 high-income earners in Korea (30.4 percent) outpaced both those in their twenties (22.9 percent) and low income earners (13.8 percent) in nationalist motivations behind their anti-Americanism.[103]

It is interesting that the 2003 *JoongAng*-CSIS-RAND poll reveals a convergence of older age (fifty and over), low educational achievement (middle-school graduates), low occupational status (36.3 percent of those in agriculture/fisheries, forest services), as well as unemployment, in blaming youth and anti-American sentiments for the deterioration of the alliance.[104] The unemployed were consistently most supportive of the alliance. Among all the occupational categories specified in the 2003 survey, the unemployed more than any other group viewed the U.S.-Korea relationship as very beneficial to Korea (58 percent). The only larger demographic group with that view was the fifty-plus generation (62.4 percent). Again, concerning the degree to which people believed that the military alliance contributed to peace and stability on the peninsula, the unemployed ranked among the highest across the age, education, and occupation categories: 45.3 percent of unemployed respondents believed that the U.S. contributed "a lot" ("somewhat" was the other possible positive response), together with 55.6 percent of those in agriculture/fisheries/forestry and 58.6 percent aged fifty and older. In response to the question whether the alliance should be reduced, strengthened, or maintained at the then-current (2003) level, again, there was a convergence of age, low occupational status, and unemployment: 36 percent among the fifty-plus cohort, 37.5 percent of the agriculture/fisheries/forestry workers, and 36.2 percent of unemployed respondents chose to strengthen the alliance. By contrast, only 17.9 percent in their twenties and 8.8 percent in their thirties, as well as15.7 percent of white-collar workers, held this view. But on this question, the common denominator was to maintain the status quo (thirties: 55 percent; fifty-plus: 53.6 percent; middle-school graduates: 58.1 percent; college and above: 52 percent; agriculture, etc.: 50.9 percent; white collar: 52.6 percent; unemployed: 44.2 percent). In these categories, those in their forties and those in blue-collar work held the highest percentage favoring the status quo: 65.7 percent and 64.7 percent, respectively.[105]

Japan in the 1950s offers an interesting cross-country, cross-time comparison of the importance of education and access to information over age as factors influencing one's attitude toward the United States. A 1957 survey of foreign policy views of citizens in urban, heavily Socialist Osaka and rural, Liberal Democratic Party–dominant Izumo found that across party lines, respondents with middle-school education or less were more likely to favor cooperation with the "American bloc" (rather than the "Russian bloc" or "Indian bloc" or "other/don't know") than those with high-school education or more.[106] Thirty-seven percent of the less-educated conservative voters in Osaka were pro-American, compared to 29 percent of Osaka dwellers under thirty. Surprisingly, 31 percent of the less-educated Socialist respondents in Izumo agreed with their less-educated Osaka counterparts. Even among the not pro-American Socialists in Osaka, education played a big role in determining the pro/anti stance on cooperation with the U.S.: 6 percent of the less educated were opposed, while 39 percent of those with more education and 25 percent of those Socialists under thirty were against such cooperation.[107] Similarly, "low political information" (rather than "medium" or "high") in both parties in both locations was a factor that yielded higher rates of pro-Americanism than generational difference.

Higher education and social mobility, rather than ignorance and naïveté, seem to incline one toward negative attitudes toward the U.S. This is true for the youngest cohort as well as the oldest. One might assume that educated respondents should hold more authority in foreign policy assessments than the less educated. However, analysts and the media in the U.S. and Korea did not raise that as an issue but focused primarily on generational differences. The reality is that the critical views that educated respondents tended to express were not what policymakers and public opinion makers—particularly of the conservative persuasion—in Korea and the United States wanted to hear. The fact that younger Koreans tend to be better educated and therefore might not be as naïve and uninformed as the older generations and critics of South Korean youth have assumed never became a part of the public debate.

Moreover, analytical attention to the ways in which the younger and older generations do agree was rare or understated; indeed, they do see eye to eye on some issues. For example, the *JoongAng*-CSIS-RAND survey shows that 51.7 percent of those surveyed in their twenties and 52.1 percent of those fifty and above disagreed with the U.S. decision to relocate U.S. forces south of Han River. Their opposition to the move was larger than that of those in their thirties and forties (44.5 percent and 42 percent, respectively). Moreover, in selecting a major reason for the decline in the U.S.-Korea alliance, there was intergenerational agreement: "improvement in inter-Korean relations" (24 percent of twenty-somethings, 23.8 percent of those in their thirties, 22.3 percent of those in their forties, and 25 percent of those fifty and older).[108] On the hot issue of SOFA revision, which had attracted most of the anti-American fervor and activist attention in the late 1990s and early 2000s (prior to the mass demonstrations against the deaths of the two schoolgirls in 2002–3), *Hankyore Sinmun* found significant overlaps among the generations regarding the need for revision: 88.4 percent of those in their twenties, 87.4 percent of thirty-somethings, 86.4 percent of those in their forties, 81.7 percent of those in their fifties, and 76.2 percent of those sixty and over.[109] Such a showing of public consensus was a significant cause of the renegotiation of the terms of the SOFA in 2000. Even after the U.S. "discovery" of North Korea's uranium enrichment program in the fall of 2002, large majorities in each age cohort continued to believe that changing the SOFA—despite the revisions in 2000–2001—was necessary in order to establish more equal bilateral relations.

Furthermore, the tendency to lump "youth" together, from the twenties to the forties (including the "3-8-6" generation),[110] has misled both analysis and understanding of demographic changes and their impact on Korean politics. As Sook-Jong Lee puts it, "[t]he mental world of Korean youth is *inevitably* different from those of the older generation and the 3-8-6 cohort" (emphasis added) and that in contrast to the latter, the younger group is "more responsive to cultural signs and symbols than political slogans."[111] She is one of the few analysts of anti-Americanism and nationalism in Korea to specify "youth" as primarily age 19–30 and to designate them a "distinct" cohort, different from those in the 3-8-6 generation. She finds that when those in the 19–30 group are politically active, they are also selective, responding toward specific events and issues. Additionally, *they are more responsive to issues they perceive to be "related to universal values."*[112] (emphasis added)

There is also a curious omission of factors besides nationalism among those who have tried to ferret out the reasons behind the sagging Korean support for the United States. Yet nationalism, even loosely defined as "nationalist concerns" and "subservient" domestic leaders, trailed significantly behind economic and political reasons for Koreans' avowed anti-American sentiments in media reports and policy analysis. In both 1990 and 2002, economic issues ranked highest as reasons for anti-American views. Gi-Wook Shin's research put economic reasons at the top with 39.5 percent (versus 20.8 percent "nationalist" reasons), with 55 percent of the most pro-American age cohort (fifty-five and older) in agreement.[113] A

2002 State Department survey also found that in a representative sample of 1,514 South Korean adults, economic and trade issues ranked highest (26 percent) as the main cause of tensions in U.S.–South Korean relations. By comparison, USFK and security issues ranked second (22 percent), while (poor) U.S. treatment of Koreans ranked third (13 percent), and U.S. policy toward North Korea came in fourth (11 percent).[114] To the more general question of "why some Koreans dislike the U.S.," respondents ranked "economic and trade pressures" second (21 percent) among nine available explanations and first (47 percent) as a combined ranking of first and second choices. U.S. unilateralism came in first place as both the first choice (35 percent) and as a combination of top two choices (50 percent).[115] *U.S. troop presence weighed in at a mere 5 percent for first choice* and at 10 percent for a combination of first and second choices. Yet if one took at face value the barrage of media coverage and utterances by public opinion leaders and policymakers about the crisis around the U.S. troop presence, one would have to imagine a complete inverse of the figures, with USFK issues occupying first place among the nine explanations for anti-American views.

An honest and inclusive assessment of survey research on Korean youth, nationalism, and anti-Americanism would have to conclude that a definitive correlation is nonexistent. There are both contradictory data and a variety of possible interpretations. For example, a regression analysis of a nationwide survey of South Korean college students in 2004 by Jun Young Choi and Myongsob Kim of Yonsei University concluded that there is no "supporting evidence for the argument that the rise of national pride leads to a drop in the level of trust for the United States."[116] In a related paper based on a survey of the general population, Kim, Choi, and Parker found that "national self-esteem *increases* trust in the USA and may contribute to attenuating tensions in the Korea–USA alliance" (emphasis added).[117]

Kim and Choi also negate two other commonly held beliefs about the declining regard for the U.S. among youth: that China's growing popularity is at the expense of support for the United States and that Korean youth who are exposed to "anti-American education" in elementary, middle, or high school by ideologically oriented teachers become anti-American. They found no statistically significant support for either claim. Noting that anti-American education's impact on the negative sentiments might have been exaggerated, Choi and Kim observe that "[g]iven the nature of media, which displays a voracious appetite for conflict and for stories that are simple, negative, and sensational, it is likely that anti-American education was framed in a negative and sensational way, creating images that the education system can be very harmful to a healthy relationship between South Korea and the United States."[118]

Regarding the common assumption of youthful affinity for North Korea as a source for the devaluation of America, Haesook Chai and her co-authors, who also conducted regression analysis of survey data on 1,076 university students at twenty-two institutions in South Korea in 2004, found that young Koreans "consider North Korea to be a serious security threat and nurse highly negative feelings against the Kim Jong Il regime."[119] They found absolutely no linkage between Korean students' opinion of North Korea and the North Korean threat and their opinion of the United States. "Rather, . . . it is not the perception of North Korea that explains anti-Americanism, but perceptions of the United States."[120] In a prior publication examining the youth factor, Youngshik Bong and I concluded that

> the alarmist arguments for "young and reckless" anti-Americanism brewing in South Korea and its pro–North Korean inclination are exaggerated in tone and underspecified in their causal mechanisms. It would be a gross misunderstanding if young Koreans were collectively deemed pro–North Korean dissidents or antagonistic nationalists, and their activism portrayed as one of destructive hostility.[121]

FEARING YOUTH

Although the U.S. is one of the youngest national powers and is known for a culture that glorifies and flaunts youthfulness, it casts a suspicious eye toward the political passions of young people, both at home and abroad. American reactions to expressions of anti-American sentiments in Korea were similar to those regarding anti-U.S. demonstrations in Europe over twenty years ago:

> Postwar Europeans have matured under circumstances of affluence and political stability. They do not remember the postwar reconstruction or the first, most difficult days of the Cold War: they have at best only a vague memory of the building of the Berlin Wall. They came of age during a period of détente, and their views of Soviet society have been colored by Leonid I. Brezhnev and Mikhail S. Gorbachev rather than Stalin. For them, America does not connote the Marshall Plan, the Berlin airlift, or even John F. Kennedy, but rather the Vietnam War and the installation of Pershing and cruise missiles.[122]

The analogy to South Korea is that nations that should remain grateful and loyal to the United States for its wartime sacrifices and postwar largesse become wayward and jeopardize good military and security relations with the United States because their youth forget the lessons of history—the abominable threats of Nazism and Communism, destruction and poverty—and become "soft" from U.S.-enabled prosperity and well-being.

Certainly there is an older generation of Americans for whom Vietnam and the 1960s youth protests serve as examples of the volatility of mixing youth and politics; the period left mental and emotional scars on many, both old and young. For some, youth activism can be interpreted as potential or real radicalism and social upheaval; indeed, Korean youth did undergo a period of radicalization in the 1980s. Whether in the 1960s context for Americans or the 1980s for Korea, the protests, countercultural tendencies, and challenging of established political authority all were deemed destabilizing and dangerous to society by those holding power by age or office in both countries. According to Sidney Hyman, who studied youth politics and "the 1970 congressional election as a referendum on American youth,"[123] "[t]he revolutionary posture of young militants—their inflamed rhetorical advocacy of 'revolution,' and their predictions about the 'inevitability' of it" "had a frightening effect on some observers who confused their cries for rebellion with a planned revolution, assumed all who preached for revolution had the same violent revolution in mind, and feared that the revolution being called for was near at hand."[124] Gary Schwartz is more specific and graphic about many American adults' reactions to the youth uprising and culture back then: the shock at witnessing students "spitting on the flag and taunting the police."[125] Moreover, "[y]oung people were experimenting with altered states of consciousness and casual sex. They were joining communes, religious cults, and radical political movements, and in general, turning their backs on the values of achievement, productivity, and success."[126] From the perspective of such elders, America's future was in jeopardy.

More recently, since the popularization of Samuel Huntington's "clash of civilizations" argument and the palpable destruction the United States experienced on September 11, 2001, many Americans have come to perceive the mixing of youth and politics as a dangerous combination. In 1999, Francis Fukuyama provocatively wrote that since biology trumps socialization, a West that is aging and "feminized"—("in terms of female franchise and participation in political decision-making")—would not be up to the challenge of dealing with a poorer and more "masculinized" part of the world: Africa, the Middle East, and South Asia: "So, even if the democratic, feminized, postindustrialized world has evolved into a zone of peace where struggles are more economic than military, it will still have to deal with those parts of the world run by young, ambitious, unconstrained men."[127] The assumption was that the economically dispossessed and politically unstable parts of the world will be teeming with hot-blooded youth bent on a politics of aggression and irrationality. Fukuyama named the full adult versions of "unconstrained" males—Mobutu, Milosevic, and Saddam Hussein—as examples of threats in world politics.[128] (It is ironic that Fukuyama was critiquing the "weaknesses" of American democracy at a time when "democracy promotion" was an integral part of U.S. foreign policy strategy.)

In a 2003 Brookings Institution report on youth and political radicalism in the Middle East, Graham Fuller stated that "large cohorts of youth from 18–24 years of age" in the Middle East were "being socialized in a more radical regional environment overall, one characterized by the power of radical Islamic ideologies and heightened political violence and growing anti-Americanism."[129] The image that Fuller portrayed was one of a Middle East overrun by young, lawless, delinquent youths who would be easy recruits for Islamist organizations. There is no sense of a social context that would serve to counter such reckless tendencies. But Diane Singerman, a well-known scholar of Middle Eastern politics and societies, pointed out that Middle Eastern youth do have avenues for participation in public discourse and institutions, even if many are corporatist bodies such as youth student unions and youth auxiliaries of political parties that do not have much autonomy from the state.[130] Moreover, youth do not run around without boundaries and direction. Rather, Singerman emphasized the "family ethos" that dominates and contains the lives of Middle Eastern youth: "the moral and economic presence of the family is pervasive and, since the state has slashed its social welfare policies after neo-liberal reforms, if anything, young people are more than ever dependent on their families."[131] Her work reminds us that youth have multiple contexts that they inhabit and negotiate.

Gary Schwartz challenges the notion of youth as a monolithic entity and focuses instead on the relationship between youth and what he calls the "community culture," and "youth subcultures," which include local institutions, youth groups, and friendship networks.[132] In this light, it would be important to disaggregate Korean youth—urban versus rural, Seoul dwellers versus those in smaller cities, and by different levels of education. Most of the protests and candlelight vigils we witnessed in the first half of the 2000s were composed overwhelmingly of urban dwellers, especially in the Seoul area. For many Korean youth, schools are not necessarily venues of community-building but of severe competition and seemingly needless hierarchy and authority. It is commonplace that both parents and children find school education, whether public or private, inadequate in preparing for college so that extracurricular tutoring and studies at *hagwŏn* (private tutoring academies or "cram" schools) are integral to a student's education. There is little time or energy for local community life as a youth, especially in the high-school years. In the college years, the campus becomes the local community, even if students live at home with their families. And given the lack of proximity to a common residential life—because they are scattered—students form virtual electronic communities. Much of the outpouring onto the streets after the deaths of the two schoolgirls in 2002 and 2003 and, more recently, to protest the Korea-U.S. Free Trade Agreement and the importation of American beef in 2008–9 was triggered by cyber-messages, often across friendship networks, calling for a meeting in a particular venue at a publicized protest spot without knowing what the issue was or harboring any anti-U.S. sentiment.[133]

For many Koreans in the 1980s, the leftist ideology that became popular among radical student activists was at least worrisome if not outright dangerous in a society that had imbibed and dwelled on anti-Communism. Radical students expressed curiosity about Marxism and socialism and considered North Korea a more "authentic" polity because of its resistance to U.S. influence and domination. For example, "[s]upporters considered North Korea 'a beacon because of its long practice of independence and self-reliance' and felt that only the North could claim revolutionary legitimacy for the nation of Korea."[134] According to Gi-Wook Shin, North Korean *chuch'e* (self-reliance) ideology appealed to these activists because of its emphasis on the following critique: "American military power had supported (and continued to support) antinationalist authoritarian regimes" in the south.[135]

The possibility that South Korean youth could feel sympathy toward the sworn Communist enemy, North Korea, rather than the "savior" from Communism, the United States, seemed irrational and menacing to the conservative South Korean elite, especially the military authoritarian leadership of the 1980s. The Chun Du Hwan regime exacerbated the situation by labeling student radicals as pro-Communist North Korea sympathizers. In such a loaded ideological framework, an all–or-nothing attitude prevailed, a nationalized version of the "you're either with us or against us" mentality. For both dissident youth and government authorities, compromise was viewed at best as cowardice and relinquishment, at worst as betrayal and anti-nation.

Sheila Miyoshi Jager makes a provocative observation that "[u]nlike most modern nations where the contests between various groups have been drawn along ethnic, religious, or linguistic lines, in Korea these contests have been drawn, broadly speaking, between two generations."[136] She analyzed, applying *chuch'eron* historiography, the tensions between the older and younger generations around nation, patriotism, failure, and redemption even before the media, policymakers, and social scientists tended to raise the "problem" of the generation gap. If we accept Jager's point, the generational gap is written into the psyches and political identities of modern Koreans: "While dissidents relied on the narrative of benevolent fatherhood and ancestral lineage in their vision of reunified nation, progovernment groups relied on the cult of virile manhood and ancestral piety in their search for national recognition."[137]

Today, the rivalry between the older and younger generation is exacerbated by the fast-changing economy, technology, and pop culture and the power that they provide to those who can master and wield them. Sook-Jong Lee has written that

> "[o]ne consequence of democratization and institutional reforms has been the economic decline of the older generation and the rise of the younger generation. . . . The older generation is also being pushed to the political and social sidelines. This generation is perceived as supporting the status quo and resistant to reform. . . . In addition, [the younger generation's] easy access to information [technologies] and ability to create and mobilize political networks gives them the ability to be an effective political force.[138]

Moreover, the younger generations, and especially "progressives," chafed for decades under the near-monopolistic control of Korea until recently by a small coterie of Korean "super elites" from privileged backgrounds (educated in the United States as early as the 1950s and 1960s, with excellent command over English, finely mannered, well-heeled, and so on). The ascent of Kim Dae Jung and Roh Mu Hyun to the presidential office was a kind of revolution in terms of changing high-level personnel tasked with overseeing the bilateral relationship after decades of conservative, elitist management.

But generational tensions need not be pathologized. Rather, they can be interpreted as normal and natural and in need of domestic and external adaptation. Jager states that "in the traditional language of Confucian family renewal,"[139] the elders' failures can be redeemed by the sons (the next generation) in what she calls a narrative of ongoing "transgenerational revitalization."[140] Viewed from this perspective, a generational gap does not signal a crisis or collapse of the achievements of the past generations but a new generation finding its way to claim the nation anew as one would create a family anew to keep the line of descent going and improve upon the past. Here, Schwartz's observation seems more fitting than the hyperbolic "generational divide" that captured many Koreans' and Americans' imaginations as a major cause of the decline of the U.S.-Korea alliance: "Instead of thinking of youth as a force for conserving or changing societal institutions, [they are] people who are working their way through tensions that exist in the environing culture."[141]

YOUTHFUL COSMOPOLITANISM AND PRAGMATISM

Even if one insists that public opinion figures support the claim that the generational gap is responsible for a decline in support for the United States and its bases in Korea, the life and times of Korean youth are too complex and in flux for the one-way correlation to stick. Put simply, the generational gap is not an adequate explanation. Regarding young Koreans as politically naïve or economically complacent because they grew up in times of relative wealth and stability and, therefore, as threats to the maintenance of the bilateral alliance does not make sense unless one also emphasizes the fact that they grew up in a social and political environment of relative freedom in the 1990s. They do not long for the right to speak out against the government or to express independent opinions as their predecessors had in the 1960s, 1970s, and 1980s; they take it for granted. In addition, no form of authority—whether it is their own government, the U.S. government and its troops, or their own parents—is sacrosanct to them. They revel in a vibrant youth culture that was never available (nor imaginable) to their parents and grandparents; eschew old-fashioned, restrictive expectations about marriage and social achievement; and never leave home without connections to the Internet and their social networks. Sook-Jong Lee describes this generation as the "fast" generation, given that "97 percent of young Koreans aged 6–29 use the Internet daily, while only 11 percent of Koreans aged 60 and over do so. They constantly call and send text messages through their mobile phones, which have practically become part of their bodies."[142]

The younger generations in Korea (those in their teens, 20s, and 30s) are in some ways the most globalized and cosmopolitan in their self-identity and social and political outlook, and are the least conventionally nationalistic among the population. This is not unique to Korea. Based on World Value Surveys from 1981 to 2001, Jai Kwan Jung asserts that "there is a global pattern in public attitudes toward supranational identity: the younger, the more supranational" (although there is no evidence that the pattern holds during the life cycle).[143] Young Koreans are the ones studying abroad,[144] learning foreign languages, and traveling in the region and beyond. The Korea Tourism Office reported that August 2007 marked the highest monthly increase of Koreans traveling abroad in 2007, with twenty-somethings leading the way with a 16.4 percent increase (compared to a 12.8 percent increase nationally).[145] Given the dynamism of Korean youth and their environmental context, it is illogical to attribute historical amnesia and resurgent nationalism to them as if those are the only political and cultural influences that surround them.

In reality, it is the younger people, in their twenties and thirties and some in their forties, who have been developing Korea's new consciousness about peace, human rights, and multicultural orientation, both in their society and around the world. In recent years, young Koreans have been pushing political issues that had long been impossible to raise or taboo during the decades of anti-Communism and military authoritarian rule, such as peace activism and opposition to the near-sacrosanct institution of the military draft. They have been making individual rights-based arguments and using the judicial system to emphasize religious rights, human rights, and gender equality. Specifically, they have advocated for legally sanctioned conscientious objector status[146] and against the draft for promoting gender discrimination in the civilian society (due to the work points system that automatically benefits males in employment situations).[147]

Younger Koreans also have been developing new consciousness and identities as civic activists, pursuing universalistic themes like peace, reconciliation, and multiculturalism, as well as practical methods of political expression. Leaders of the Korean House for International Solidarity (KHIS), an NGO that developed in the mid- to late 1990s to focus specifically on transnational issues, and their people-to-people campaign toward Vietnam serve as just one example. KHIS investigated and publicized both the atrocities Korean soldiers committed toward Vietnamese civilians during the Vietnam War and the need for reconciliation between Korea and Vietnam. In 2000, they helped organize a "goodwill mission" to Vietnam, in which Korean dentists and other medical professionals volunteered their services to Vietnamese villagers and their descendants who had suffered violence by Korean troops. They also organized music and arts festivals as fundraising events to assist Vietnamese victims of war and, together with *Hankyore Sinmun,* raised money for a "peace park" to be built in Vietnam. They conducted such efforts while simultaneously participating in the social movement to revise the Status of Forces Agreement with the United States (discussed in chapter 3). In spring 2002, one of the leaders of KHIS told me that their fundraising efforts for the Vietnam project drew larger sums than for any *banmi,* or "anti-American," protest or program.[148]

The work of KHIS is noteworthy for three reasons related to U.S.-Korea relations. First, in contrast to American officials' oft-mentioned complaint that Koreans only seek to criticize U.S. policies and actions but overlook their own government's and nation's faults,[149] KHIS insisted that Koreans must take responsibility for past wartime atrocities and assist the Vietnamese who survived, and not only point fingers at Japan and the U.S. for abuses against Koreans. Second, contrary to popular view that nationalism is what drives anti-Americanism, KHIS addressed an issue that was and is "anti-nationalist" and highly unpopular among Koreans, especially political elites and veterans.[150] Third, KHIS was intent on using new democratic freedoms and the transnationalizaton of ideas and activist networks in the 1990s to address issues, interpretive frameworks, and peoples, including foreigners, long neglected or ignored by the general Korean society. Yet KHIS was a key player in the People's Action to Reform the SOFA (PAR-SOFA) movement, belying the neat and simple label of "nationalist" or "anti-American" that too often have been placed on individuals and organizations.

Furthermore, young Koreans at rallies and on blogs may frame their political sentiments in the passionate rhetoric of patriotism, national sovereignty, and reunification, but they are clearheaded about policy choices. For example, Koreans in their twenties and thirties may have "denounced the U.S. war against Iraq as unjust invasion, but support[ed] the[ir] government's decision to dispatch troops for U.S.-Korean cooperation over the North Korean issue."[151] With respect to the alliance, young Koreans regarded the U.S. military presence as vital to the security and stability of their nation even through the period of heavy protests against the U.S. military in the winter of 2002–3: 78.1 percent of Koreans in their twenties and 84.3 percent in their thirties. And they showed no significant difference with their older cohorts' views.[152] Borrowing from Chung-in Moon's schematization of a historical range of attitudes toward the United States, Youngshik Bong observes that young Koreans—like their older and more conservative counterparts—have espoused both pro- and anti-American sentiments on a broad spectrum of affinity with and need for the United States.[153] Along this spectrum, Koreans historically have leaned toward *yongmi*, a "Korea-first philosophy at the leadership level" coupled with "a risk-averse, calculated pursuit of personal safety and well-being at the individual level."[154]

Despite the charge that young Koreans are irrational and naïve, they do calculate their regard for the United States in terms of self-interest and practical considerations. Although many young Koreans participated in the candlelight vigils and other protests in the winter of 2002–3, they had clearheaded notions of the value of an American education. The number of Koreans taking the Test of English as a Foreign Language (TOEFL) increased to 86,188 during the high-pitch period of anti-American protests—July 2002 to June 2003—from 73,093 in the same period of the preceding year.[155] Furthermore, among 227 geographic regions and native countries worldwide where the examination is offered, South Koreans make up the largest group by far in absolute numbers taking the test, followed by Japan (81,749) and China (24,075). Given Korea's much smaller population, Koreans are peerless in their aspirations to study in the United States and employ English in their career development.[156] Additionally, Bong cites a *Chosun Ilbo* poll of college students in which 44.8 percent chose U.S. citizenship, versus 55.5 percent who chose Korean citizenship, if given a choice between the two.[157] Moreover, according to a *Chosun Ilbo* survey in early 2003, 43.4 percent of Koreans in their twenties and thirties revealed that if a war broke out on the peninsula while they were abroad, they would not return to their homeland.[158]

Even with regard to the time-tested nationalism—anti-Japanese nationalism—Koreans, especially the young, have become avid consumers and leading producers of Japanese and other Asian forms of pop culture.[159] The lifting of legal prohibitions against Japanese cultural imports in 1998 and the elimination of bans on Japanese music, films, computer games, and comics in early 2004[160] under President Kim Dae Jung made possible the fact that "Asian youth are overcoming [their] conventional nationalism through the regionalization of pop culture, making connections across national and historical boundaries and stepping away from old enmities that governments and older generations seem unable or unwilling to give up."[161] *Daum*, one of Korea's most popular Internet portals, hosted 10,000 blogs and cafés dedicated to introducing Japanese culture to South Korea, as compared to just 50 blogs and cafés that promote anti-Japanese views.[162]

In *Chasing the Sun*, Morton Abramowitz and Steve Bosworth emphasize that these patterns are part of the "trend toward a greater East Asian consciousness, self-awareness, and confidence" that are "hard to stop, even if someone wanted to."[163] The two veteran U.S. diplomats and East Asia policy experts economically illustrate the depth and breadth of contemporary changes in the region with a clear warning that current U.S. policymakers need to open their eyes and wipe away the sand to get a realistic view of Asia's future and its relationship with the United States. They describe the "[f]everish activity [that] is going on in many [East Asian] countries below the radar screen of outside governments."[164] In addition to the boom in the variety and volume of intra-Asian trade and foreign direct investment, the cross-fertilization of social experiences—consumption, travel, education, employment, language, entertainment, arts, information, and identity—is occurring at a dizzying pace within Asia. Bosworth and Abramowitz clearly recognize that today, "the newly urbanized, more affluent Asians still consider themselves Chinese, Japanese, Korean, and so forth, but they also have begun to think of themselves as Asian in ways that their parents and grandparents never did," and "their aspirations are increasingly international in thought and action."[165] To focus only on the nationalist impulses of Koreans—and interpret them as anti-American—while ignoring or downplaying the fast-growing trends that thwart such impulses paints a false picture of South Korean society and turns nationalism into a tautology in Korean politics and policies.

NOTES

1. "20 Hurt in Protests at U.S. Base Near Seoul," *New York Times*, June 18, 2000, www.nytimes.com (accessed May 14, 2001).

2. "Anti-American" or "anti-Americanism" in this book refers to a multiplicity of grievances, complaints, and demands by Korean civilians with regard to U.S. bases. Ideologically anti-American activists form a small minority within the coalition that I discuss in the book. Also see the introduction.

3. *Ohmynews*, www.ohmynews.com/article_view.asp?menu=c10100&no=87744 (accessed November 24, 2002).

4. Alexander Cooley, *Base Politics: Democratic Change and the U.S. Military Overseas* (Ithaca, NY: Cornell University Press, 2008), 10.

5. *Hankyore Sinmun*, September 24, 2000, www.hani.co.kr/section-00300/00300401120000924225100 2.htm, (accessed February 26, 2002).

6. *The Korea Times*, April 30, 2002, www.koreatimes.co.kr/www/index.asp (accessed May 7, 2002).

7. Ibid.

8. Chaibong Hahm, "Anti-Americanism, Korean-Style," in *Korean Attitudes toward the United States: Changing Dynamics,* ed. David I. Steinberg (Armonk, NY: M.E. Sharpe, 2005), 224.

9. See Gi-Wook Shin and Kyung Moon Hwang, eds., *Contentious Kwangju: The May 18 Uprising in Korea's Past and Present* (Lanham, MD: Rowman & Littlefield, 2003); Linda Sue Lewis, *Laying Claim to the Memory of May: A Look Back at the 1980 Kwangju Uprising* (Honolulu: University of Hawai'i Press, 2002); John A. Wickam, *Korea on the Brink: A Memoir of Political Intrigue and Military Crisis,* (Dulles, VA: Brassey's Inc., 2000); William H. Gleysteen Jr., *Massive Entanglement, Marginal Influence: Carter and Korea in Crisis,* chapters 9, 10, epilogue (Washington, DC: Brookings Institution, 1999).

10. Wonmo Dong, "University Students in South Korean Politics: Patterns of Radicalization in the 1980s," *Journal of International Affairs* 40, no. 2 (1987), 238.

11. Gi-Wook Shin, "Marxism, Anti-Americanism, and Democracy in South Korea: An Examination of Nationalist Intellectual Discourse," *positions* 3, no. 2 (1995), 508–534.

12. John Kie-chiang Oh, "Anti-Americanism and Anti-Authoritarian Politics in Korea," in *Two Koreas in Transition: Implications for U.S. Policy,* ed. Ilpyong J. Kim (Rockville, MD: In Depth Books, 1998), 255–256.

13. Tim Shorrock, "The Struggle for Democracy in South Korea in the 1980s and the Rise of Anti-Americanism," *Third World Quarterly* 8, no. 4 (1986), 1212.

14. Ibid., 1211.

15. Sheila Miyoshi Jager, *Narratives of Nation Building in Korea: A Genealogy of Patriotism* (Armonk, NY: M.E. Sharpe, 2003), 100.

16. *Minjung* ideology "held that the division [of Korea] itself had led to Korea's political, economic, military, and cultural dependence on the United States. The second tenet was that the successive United States-backed regimes, which had ruled Korea since the founding of the republic, always opposed the people [*minjung*], the nation [*minjok*], and democracy [*minju*]." See Oh, "Anti-Americanism and Anti-Authoritarian Politics in Korea," 256; Dong, "University Students in South Korean Politics"; and Shin, "Marxism, Anti-Americanism, and Democracy." For a comprehensive study of *minjung* in Korean history and society, see Kenneth M. Wells, *South Korea's Minjung Movement: The Culture and Politics of Dissidence* (Honolulu: University of Hawai'i Press, 1995).

17. Jager, *Narratives of Nation Building,* 101.

18. Dong, "University Students in South Korean Politics," 246.

19. Jinwung Kim, "Recent Anti-Americanism in South Korea," *Asian Survey* 29, no. 8 (1989), 749–763 and Gi-Wook Shin, "South Korean Anti-Americanism: A Comparative Perspective," *Asian Survey* 36, no. 8 (1996), 787–803.

20. Shin, "South Korean Anti-Americanism," 798–800.

21. Ibid., 802.

22. Ibid., 796.

23. Ibid., 799.

24. Gi-Wook Shin, *Ethnic Nationalism in Korea: Genealogy, Politics, and Legacy* (Stanford, CA: Stanford University Press, 2006), 176.

25. *Washington Post,* June 21, 1988, www.washingtonpost.com (accessed January 5, 2000).

26. Amnesty International, *South Korea: Prisoners Held for National Security Reasons,* (New York, N.Y.: Amnesty International U.S.A., 1991), 6; See also Namhee Lee, "Anti-Communism, North Korea, and Human Rights in South Korea: 'Orientalist' Discourse and Construction of South Korean Identity," in Mark Bradley and Patrice Petro, eds., *Truth Claims: Representation and Human Rights* (New Directions in International Studies, Rutgers University Press, 2002), 43–72.

27. "South Koreans Redefine Ties to US, Resentment of Military Presence Spurs Talks on Security Alliance," *Christian Science Monitor,* January 3, 1989.

28. Youngshik Bong, "Flashpoints at Sea?: Legitimization Strategy and East Asian Island Disputes" (Ph. D. diss., University of Pennsylvania, 2002), chapter 3.

29. Ibid., 106.

30. Jin Song, "Financial Crisis in Korea: Implications for US-Korea Relations" (occasional paper, Honolulu: Asia-Pacific Center for Security Studies, May 1998), www.apcss.org/Publications/Ocasional%20Papers/OPKorea.html (accessed May 16, 2001).

31. "Many Proud South Koreans Resent Bailout from Abroad," *New York Times,* December 11, 1997 (accessed May 14, 2001).

32. Donald Kirk, *Korean Crisis: Unraveling of the Miracle in the IMF Era* (New York: St. Martin's Press, 1999), 43.

33. "Koreans Not Rushing to Shake the Hand Holding the Bailout Check," *New York Times,* December 5, 1997 (accessed May 14, 2001).

34. Kirk, *Korean Crisis,* p. 36.

35. "Asians Worry That U.S. Aid Is a New Colonialism," *New York Times,* February 17, 1998 (accessed May 14, 2001).

36. Ibid.

37. "Drop in Asian Wealth Can Affect the US," *New Straits Times,* February 7, 1998, www.nst.com.my (accessed May 15, 2001).

38. "Asians Worry That U.S. Aid Is a New Colonialism."

39. Song, "Financial Crisis in Korea," 4.

40. "Many Proud South Koreans Resent Bailout From Abroad."

41. Ibid.

42. Hyungna Oh, "Thoughts from the Korean Perspective," ezdragon, ezdragon.cortland.edu/archives/dp/dp06/06_08.htm (accessed May 14, 2001).

43. "Frugal Koreans Rush to Rescue Their Rapidly Sinking Economy," *New York Times,* December 18, 1997 (accessed March 21, 2007).

44. *The Gazette* (Montreal), December 14, 1997, www.montrealgazette.com (accessed March 21, 2007); "Frugal Koreans Rush to Rescue Their Rapidly Sinking Economy"; "TV Restrictions Broadcast a Message; Latest Measures Hint at Increasingly Frugal, Nationalistic S. Korea," *Washington Post*, December 13, 1997 (accessed March 21, 2007).

45. "EC, US Complain Over Korean 'Frugality' Campaign," *SUNS—South-North Development Monitor*, March 11, 1997, www.sunsonline.org/trade/process/followup/1997/03110097.htm (accessed March 12, 2007).

46. "TV Restrictions Broadcast a Message."

47. Laura Nelson, *Measured Excess: Status, Gender, and Consumer Nationalism in South Korea* (New York: Columbia University Press, 2000), 107.

48. Ibid., 110.

49. Ibid., 114. Nelson cites Chunghee Park, *Major Speeches by Korea's Park Chung Hee*, compiled by Shin Bum Shik. (Seoul: Hollym Publishers, 1970), 134–135.

50. Ibid., 130.

51. Kirk, *Korean Crisis*, 45.

52. Ibid., 44.

53. Ibid., 52.

54. Ibid., 56.

55. "New (Friendly) Craze in South Korea: The North," *New York Times*, June 20, 2000.

56. Roland Bleiker, *Divided Korea: Toward a Culture of Reconciliation* (Minneapolis, MN: University of Minnesota Press, 2005), 23.

57. Andrew O'Neil, "The 2000 Inter-Korean Summit: The Road to Reconciliation?" *Australian Journal of International Affairs* 55, no. 1 (2001), 55, 60.

58. "New (Friendly) Craze in South Korea."

59. Bleiker, *Divided Korea*, 23.

60. "New (Friendly) Craze in South Korea."

61. Victor D. Cha, "The U.S. Role in Inter-Korean Relations," in *Korean Attitudes toward the United States*, 26.

62. Mi-Young Ahn, "Korea: Anti-US Gripes Fuel North-South Warmth," *Asia Times Online*, December 12, 2002, www.atimes.com/atimes/Korea/DL12Dg02.html (accessed January 10, 2003).

63. Bleiker, *Divided Korea*, 23.

64. Ibid.

65. O'Neil, "The 2000 Inter-Korean Summit," 57.

66. Gi-Wook Shin, James Freda, and Gihong Yi, "The Politics of Ethnic Nationalism in Divided Korea," *Nations and Nationalism* 5, no. 4 (1999), pp. 473–4.

67. Ibid., p. 474.

68. I thank Erin Choi for some of these insights.

69. Chung-in Moon, "Globalization: Challenges and Strategies," *Korea Focus* 3, no.3 (1995), 66.

70. Yean-Ju Lee, Dong-Hoon Seol, and Sung-Nam Cho, "International Marriages in South Korea: The Significance of Nationality and Ethnicity," *Journal of Population Research* 23, no. 2 (2006).

71. "Korea in 2050: One in 10 Will Be Foreign," *Korea Herald,* September 4, 2009, www.koreaherald.co.kr (accessed September 4, 2009).

72. Seungsook Moon, "A Reflection on 'Multiculturalism' and Migrant Workers in South Korea," *AALA Newsletter* 7, Friends of Asia, (December 2008), 12.

73. "Biracial Students to Get Increased Support in Studies," *Korea Herald,* October 10, 2008 (accessed October 16, 2008).

74. Yi-seon Kim, "Measures to Support Children of Multicultural Families," *Gender Review* (autumn, 2009), available at www.koreafocus.or.kr/design2/layout/content_print.asp?group_id=102827).

75. Vladimir Tikhonov (Pak Noja), "South Korea—An Inverted Pyramid?" *AALA Newsletter* 7, 7.

76. Jiyoung LeeAn, "Resistance to 'Integration' by Marriage Migrants," *AALA Newsletter* 7, 15. The public policy framework has focused mainly on "maternity, protection of children, family relationship, and domestic violence."

77. Katharine H. S. Moon, "Migrant Workers' Movements in Japan and South Korea," in *Egalitarian Politics in the Age of Globalization,* ed. Craig N. Murphy (London: Palgrave, 2002), 195.

78. Katharine H. S. Moon, "Strangers in the Midst of Globalization: Migrant Workers and Korean Nationalism," in *Korea's Globalization,* ed. Samuel S. Kim (New York: Cambridge University Press, 2000), 154–155.

79. Yoonkyung Lee, "Migration, Migrants, and Contested Ethno-Nationalism in Korea," *Critical Asian Studies* 41, no. 3 (2009), 376.

80. Ibid.

81. Ibid.

82. Nicholas Eberstadt, "Our Other Korea Problem," *National Interest* (fall 2002).

83. Ibid., 113.

84. U.S. Department of State, Office of Research, "Trends in South Korean Opinion of the U.S.," opinion analysis M-42-03, April 9, 2003. Face-to-face interviews with 1,556 adults were conducted in Korea during January 24–February 4, 2003.

85. Derek J. Mitchell, ed. *Strategy and Sentiment: South Korean Views of the United States and the U.S.-ROK Alliance* (Washington, DC: Center for Strategic and International Studies, 2004), 148.

86. Ibid., 149.

87. Ibid., 142.

88. Ibid., 151.

89. The Pew Research Center for the People and the Press, *What the World Thinks in 2002. How Global Publics View: Their Lives, Their Countries, The World, America* (Washington, DC: Pew, 2002). www.people-press.org/2002/12/04/what-the-world-thinks-in-2002/.

90. Paul Hollander, *Anti-Americanism: Irrational and Rational* (New Brunswick, NJ: Transaction, 1995), 382.

91. Pew, *What the World Thinks in 2002.*

92. U.S. Department of State, "Trends in South Korean Opinion," 4.

93. W. Scott Thompson, "Anti-Americanism and the U.S. Government," in *Anti-Americanism: Origins and Context,* ed. Thomas Perry Thornton, special edition of *The Annals of the American Academy of Political and Social Science* (Washington, DC: SAIS, Johns Hopkins University, 1988), 25.

94. Gi-Wook Shin, "South Korean Anti-Americanism: A Comparative Perspective," *Asian Survey* 36 (August 1996), 795–796.

95. U.S. Department of State, "Trends in South Korean Opinion," 4.

96. Ibid.

97. Shin, "South Korean Anti-Americanism," 796–799.

98. U.S. Department of State, "Trends in South Korean Opinion," 4.

99. Gi-Wook Shin, *Ethnic Nationalism in Korea,* 177.

100. *Maeil Sinmun* and Hangil Risŏch'i yŏron chosa, August 2000 (included in a packet of reports about anti-Americanism provided to me by analysts at the Institute of Foreign Affairs and National Security, Seoul, Korea, spring 2001).

101. Ibid.

102. Shin, "South Korean Anti-Americanism," 798.

103. Ibid., 798–799.

104. Mitchell, *Strategy and Sentiment,* 15, 152.

105. Ibid., 148, 149, 150.

106. Douglas H. Mendel, Jr., "Japanese Views of the American Alliance," *Public Opinion Quarterly* 23, no. 3 (autumn 1959), 330. Mendel surveyed 196 Conservatives and 152 Socialists in Osaka and 304 Conservatives and 95 Socialists in Izumo in 1957. All of the statistics in this paragraph come from his study, tabulated on p. 330.

107. Ibid.

108. Mitchell, *Strategy and Sentiment,* 151, 157.

109. *Hankyore Sinmun,* www.hani.co.kr/section-00300/003004011200009242248004.htm. (accessed February 26, 2002).

110. The term "3-8-6" became a popular label in the 1990s, referring to the generation of student activists of the 1980s, who were in their 30s, came of political age in the 1980s, and were born in the 1960s.

111. Sook-Jong Lee, "The Assertive Nationalism of South Korean Youth: Cultural Dynamism and Political Activism," *SAIS Review* 26, no. 2 (2006), 126.

112. Ibid.

113. Shin, "South Korean Anti-Americanism,"798.

114. U.S. Department of State, Trends in South Korean Opinion," 10.

115. Ibid., 2.

116. Myongsob Kim and Jun Young Choi, "Can We Trust America?: An Empirical Analysis of Anti-Americanism in South Korea," (paper presented

at the Northeastern Political Science Association meeting, Boston, MA, November 11–13, 2004), 23.

117. "Holding other variables constant, a one-unit increase in the index of self-esteem results in a 1.031 increase in trust in the USA, on average." See Myongsob Kim, Suzanne L. Parker, and Jun Young Choi, "Increasing Distrust of the USA in South Korea," *International Political Science Review* 27, no. 4 (2006), 437.

118. Kim and Choi, "Can We Trust America?" 23–24.

119. Haesook Chae, Tiffany Carwile and Scott Damberger, "Understanding anti-Americanism among South Korean College Students," (paper presented at the annual meeting of the American Political Science Assocation, Chicago, September 2–5, 2004), 13–14.

120. Ibid.

121. Youngshik Bong and Katharine H.S. Moon, "Rethinking Young Anti-Americanism in South Korea," in *The Anti-American Century*, ed. Allan McPherson and Ivan Krastev (Budapest and New York: Central European University Press, 2007), 90.

122. *New York Times*, June 11, 1986. The author, Joseph Godson, was a former U.S. Foreign Service officer and the then Europe coordinator of the Center for Strategic and International Studies at Georgetown University. (Lexis-Nexis; accessed November 9, 2000).

123. Sidney Hyman, *Youth in Politics: Expectations and Realities* (New York: Basic Books, 1972), 5.

124. Ibid., 406.

125. Gary Schwartz, *Beyond Conformity or Rebellion: Youth and Conformity in America* (Chicago: University of Chicago Press, 1987), 1.

126. Ibid., 2.

127. Francis Fukuyama, "Women and the Evolution of World Politics," *Foreign Affairs* 77, no. 5 (September/October 1998), pp. 36–39.

128. Ibid., p. 36.

129. Graham E. Fuller, "The Youth Factor: The New Demographics of the Middle East and the Implications for U.S. Policy," analysis paper no. 3 (Washington, DC: Saban Center for Middle East Policy, Brookings Institution, June 2003), 18.

130. Diane Singerman, "The Economic Imperatives of Marriage: Emerging Practices and Identities among Youth in the Middle East," Middle East Youth Initiative working paper no. 6 (Wolfensohn Center for Development, Brookings Institution, September 2007), 37.

131. Ibid.

132. Schwartz, *Beyond Conformity or Rebellion*, 13–19.

133. Yi Chunghyŏng, Kang Kihyŏn, and Chang Chuyŏng, "Punsan kaech'ae ch'otbul chiphoe' ch'abunhaejyŏtta," news.naver.com/main/read.nhn?mode=LS2D&mid=sec&sid1=102&sid2=257 (accessed April 17, 2009).

134. Gi-Wook Shin, "Marxism, Anti-Americanism, and Democracy," 524.

135. Ibid., 523.

136. Jager, *Narratives of Nation Building,* xiv.

137. Ibid., xv.

138. Sook-Jong Lee, "The Rise of Korean Youth as a Political Force: Implications for the U.S.-Korea Alliance" (paper presentation, Center for Northeast Asia Policy Studies, Brookings Institution, Washington, DC, June 16, 2004), www.brookings.edu/fp/cnaps/events/20040616.htm (accessed July 5, 2004).

139. Jager, *Narratives of Nation Building,* 103.

140. Ibid., 105.

141. Schwartz, *Beyond Conformity or Rebellion,* 3.

142. Sook-Jong Lee, "Assertive Nationalism," 126. Lee cites a 2006 Ministry of Information and Communication finding that 98.5 percent of six- to nineteen-year-olds, 98.9 percent of those in their twenties, and 94.6 percent of those in their thirties regularly used the Internet. See mic.korea.kr/mic/jsp/mic1_branch.jsp?_action=news_view&_property....(accessed November 6, 2007).

143. Jai Kwan Jung, "Growing Supranational Identities in a Globalizing World? A Multilevel Analysis of the World Values Survey" (unpublished paper, Department of Government, Cornell University), 27.

144. The number of Korean youth studying abroad climbed steeply in the 2000s, with 10,000 in 2002 (versus 4,397 in 1998). By 2007, nearly 30,000 students were abroad, with about half enrolled in American schools. See "Fewer Go Abroad to Study," *Korea Herald,* October 17, 2008 (accessed October 17, 2008). From January to May 2004, Koreans spent U.S.$891 million on overseas education. See "More Than One Trillion Won Left the Country for Korean Students Abroad," *Dong-A Ilbo,* June 30, 2004, english.donga.com (accessed July 1, 2004).

145. *Herŏldŭ Kyŏngje,* October 12, 2007, www.heraldbiz.com/SITE/data/html_dir/2007/10/12/200710120171.asp (accessed November 6, 2007).

146. Seok-woo Lee and Sung-ha Yoo, "An Issue of Conscience: Conscientious Objection to Military Service in Korea from a Religious and International Viewpoint" (unpublished manuscript, 2005), 1–16; "Constitutional Court Upholds Security Law, Also Rejects Conscientious Objectors' Petition," *Korea Times,* August 26, 2004; "I Am Ashamed of Myself in Front of Jehovah's Witnesses," *Hankyore 21,* June 3, 2004, 87–89.

147. Seungsook Moon, *Militarized Modernity and Gendered Citizenship in South Korea* (Durham and London: Duke University Press, 2005), 123–146.

148. Korean House for International Solidarity, *Saram i saram ege* (People to people) (April–May 2000), 16–20.

149. For instance, as discussed in the introduction, some high-ranking U.S. officials and politicians expressed concerns about some Korean civic activist groups' vilification of General Douglas MacArthur as having been responsible for massive casualties of Koreans. See "Mi 'MacArthur Tongsang Chŏlgŏharyŏmyŏn Ch'arari Nŏmgyŏdalla'" (U.S. demands the handover of General MacArthur's statue, if it is to be demolished), *Dong-A Ilbo,* Septem-

ber 16, 2005; "Mi chidojung, ijen panHan nŏmŏ ch'orong kkaji" (U.S. leaders, from anti-Korean to mocking Korea), *Dong-A Ilbo,* October 28, 2005.

150. Hyun Sook Kim, "Korea's 'Vietnam Question': War Atrocities, National Identity, and Reconciliation in Asia," *positions* 9, no. 3 (2001), 621–635; Charles Armstrong, "America's Korea and Korea's Vietnam," *Critical Asian Studies* 33, no. 4 (2001), 527–540.

151. Youngshik Bong, "Yongmi: Pragmatic Anti-Americanism in South Korea," *Brown Journal of World Affairs* 10, no. 2 (winter/spring 2004), 161.

152. *Dong-A Ilbo,* donga.com/fbin/news?f=print&n=200304010323, April 1, 2003 (accessed April 14, 2003).

153. Bong, "Yongmi," 158–159.

154. Ibid., 161.

155. Educational Testing Service (ETS), TOEFL® Test and Score Data Summary: 2002–2003 Edition, TOEFL CBT Total and Section Score Means Table 10, 2003, Rep. no. TOEFL-SUM-0203, 8–9, available at www.ets.org (accessed September 4, 2009).

156. Bong, "Yongmi," 161.

157. Ibid., 165n34.

158. Ibid., 165n33.

159. "Close Harmony Memories of Japanese Occupation Still Pain Older Koreans and Reconciliation Has Often Seemed Reluctant . . . ," *Financial Times* (London), August 7, 2004, www.ft.com/home/us (accessed October 13, 2004). Also see *Time* magazine's Asia edition, in which Donald McIntyre describes the Asian fever for Korean pop music, or "K-pop," in recent years: "The $300 mil domestic market is the second largest in Asia, topped only by Japan's massive $2.9 billion in album sales last year [2003]. K-pop has broken across borders: teenagers from Tokyo to Taipei swoon over performers such as singer Park Ji Yoon and boy band Shinhwa, buying their CDs and posters and even learning Korean so they can sing along at karaoke. BoA [an iconic Korean female singer] this year became the first solo artist in more than two decades to have a debut single and a debut album reach No. 1 in Japan . . . . 'Korea is like the next epicenter of pop culture in Asia,' says Jessica Kam, a vice president for MTV Networks Asia." Donald Macintyre, "Flying Too High? The Korean Pop Music Biz is Asia's Hottest . . . ," www.time.com/time/asia/covers/1101020729/story.html (accessed September 30, 2004).

160. MacIntyre, "Flying Too High?"

161. Katharine H. S. Moon, "South Korea-U.S. Relations," *Asian Perspective* 28, no. 4 (2004), 55.

162. "Close Harmony Memories."

163. Morton Abramowitz and Stephen Bosworth, *Chasing the Sun: Rethinking East Asian Policy* (New York: The Century Foundation Press, 2006), 34.

164. Ibid., 30.

165. Ibid., 34.

2. Power and Democracy

If globalizing, cosmopolitan tendencies coexist with and undercut nationalistic tendencies in South Korea, what about the local? This chapter shows that the development and deepening of democracy in Korea have fostered new local political consciousness that challenges the notion of monolithic nationalism and the central government's control over the "national interest." The decentralization of government in the 1990s transformed the domestic structure and dynamic of power such that the central government no longer has a monopoly over foreign policy and national security. Power struggles between the center and the periphery have become an inevitable part of alliance politics.

The politics of military basing in a democratic South Korea is a highly complex process fraught with disparate and competing interests within and among government bureaucracies, and between the center and periphery, the state and society. Since the decentralization of government began in the 1990s, the local-national relationship in South Korean politics has generated new parameters of agenda-setting and policy implementation. Although the central government holds hierarchical, organizational, and fiscal levers over local governments, alliance policy is no longer a matter of top-down management, with Seoul's and Washington's interests leading the way. Moreover, the rise of local power has transformed the notion of national security and collective interest so that hitherto excluded conceptualizations, voices, and agendas regularly intervene in alliance politics, making the bilateral relationship much more complicated and difficult to manage.

Decentralization in the first half of the 1990s, an integral part of the country's efforts to deepen democratization, involved new laws to enhance local autonomy and citizen participation in many issue areas. A 1991 law enabled the establishment of local councils, and the 1995 Local Autonomy Law enfranchised Koreans to elect local and provincial officials for the first time in over thirty years. With votes at stake, candidates for local office became eager to promise economic development, improved social services, and stronger communities for local constituencies. The Korean sociologist Ho-Keun Song describes what I would term a new "hyperactivity" in local affairs after decades of top-down local governance:

> The heads of local governments know they should do something constantly in order to implement their campaign goals. It comes from either competition or commitment to their voters. Typically, they . . . take several development strategies into shape. . . . The government buildings [in Ch'unch'ŏn, for example] were covered by a torrent of pamphlets and booklets on campaign pledges and their implementation. Several conferences and public hearings were held. Special committees were organized.[1]

Specific policy interests tended to focus on residents' issues and social policy,[2] which, in the mid- to late 1990s, converged with the new democratic rhetoric and policy orientation of the Kim Young Sam administration. Jung-Hoon Lee characterizes the policy context as focused on "universally accepted values such as democracy, human rights, environmental protection, and social welfare."[3] In particular, "[i]mproving the quality of life, overshadowed over the years as a result of the country's growth-first strategy, was now to be an important part of the government's mission."[4] With respect to foreign policy and national security, "[m]ultiple dimensions . . . from economic and ecological security . . . to communal and societal security . . . were also emphasized."[5] Such a policy orientation at the center and the periphery generated a hospitable environment in which *kiji ch'on-* (military camp town) related concerns (quality of life, safety, environment, and so on) could garner public attention.

Institutional networks formed in quick response to the new laws and political process. The first association of local councils, the National Association of Local Authorities, was established in 1991, and the National Mayors Conference of Korea was established in 1996. Kyoung-Ryung Seong, a Korean expert on decentralization and democracy, deemed the new mayors' alliance as having "epochal importance" in representing the interests of lower-level units of government to central and provincial authorities.[6] Indeed since the obliteration of local autonomy in 1949, a new epoch in deepening and spreading democracy had begun.

Additionally, new laws that boost citizens' access to information, government transparency, and self-governance also emboldened local populations to voice opinions about their priorities and demand official accountability. For example, the implementation of the 1996 Laws Relating to the Disclosure of Information by Public Organizations took effect in 1998. In 1999, citizens were granted the right to enact, alter, or abolish municipal regulations as well as demand public audits and inspection.[7] The fact that much of these legal changes grew out of citizen initiatives speaks loudly to the new assertiveness of local interests and the central government's responsiveness to them.

Residents' movements rose in tandem with the growth of local autonomy laws. In many of the camp towns, citizens' committees, "citizens' classrooms," and neighborhood associations were created in the 1990s to raise awareness of issues concerning people's everyday lives. In the early years of decentralization, citizens' groups in the *kiji* (military base) areas tended to be led by self-declared progressives who targeted U.S. bases as objects of scrutiny, investigation, criticism, and local activism. In Tongduch'ŏn, which has housed the U.S. Second Infantry Division (2ID) for about half a century, resident-activists took pride in creating their own *siminhoe* ("democratic local citizens' committee") in 1990, purportedly the first nonstudent, local progressive citizens' organization. Other *kiji* areas also formed various citizens groups and resident associations.

Larry Diamond lauds such efforts toward decentralization and deems them indispensable to strengthening democracy and democratic participation. He cites a variety of venerable theorists of democracy, from John Stuart Mill, Benjamin Barber, Robert Putnam, to Robert Dahl to emphasize that

> [i]t is the arena of local and community life that offers the greatest scope for independent organizations to form and influence policy. At the local level, the social and organizational barriers to collective action are lower and the problems that demand attention—from social services to transportation and the environment—impact more directly on people's quality of life. Direct citizen involvement in the administration of public services at the local level generates an important opportunity to strengthen the skills of individual citizens and the accumulation of social capital, while making public service delivery more accountable.[8]

In advocating for decentralization in South Korea, Kyoung-Ryung Seong highlights the positive influence it may have in countering the fractious tendencies toward regional politics (for example, the south versus the southwest versus; south versus the Seoul metropolitan area) and the obsessive competition by regional leaders to "capture" national power that have plagued South Korean politics for decades: "If the powers of the central government are widely devolved to the local government, then the power struggles themselves will be localized, and democracy will be preserved from the dangerous virus of regionalism."[9]

But even in a hospitable political climate, decentralization necessarily involves power struggles between the central government and lower-level units because the central government must give up its grip and willingly set up new institutions with legal rights and permit new structures and processes of identity-building and organizing,[10] which then challenge and compete with national power and agendas. Ilp'yŏng Kim and Eun Sung Chung describe the center-periphery tensions as a "dialectic relationship."[11] As Diamond states, "[p]ower may be devolved from the center to the locality, but it may also be taken back in a myriad of ways, from major recentralizing initiatives to a gradual slicing away of local autonomy initiatives."[12] He adds that "[s]tates transitioning from authoritarian rule are especially vulnerable to recentralization, because the rules of the game are still in flux and can easily be changed."[13] We shall see the kind of push-pull dynamic exhibited by the center and the periphery regarding the U.S. bases, especially around local control and planning, environment, transportation, and more later in the chapter. Furthermore, we shall find that as much as local actors can cooperate with one another and put up united fronts, they can fight for leadership, influence, resources, and goals.

It is not only the Korean central authorities that present a challenge to local actors as the latter exercise their new democratic muscles. In the new democratic climate, the U.S. bases have come to represent the stark limits of and obstacles to local democracy, for Korean laws are not applicable on U.S. military compounds. Rather, it is the Status of Forces Agreement (SOFA) that governs the mutual rights, obligations, and protections between the Korean government and the U.S. bases. It is telling that 75.3 percent of local government officials surveyed in one recent study viewed the U.S. forces and bases as "completely outside of [their] jurisdictional authority" (with another 20.1 percent noting "very limited jurisdictional authority").[14] Limited access to and oversight of U.S. base activities was the norm during the three decades of authoritarian rule, but under democracy, such limits have caused frustration and the inevitable question of "who governs Korean territory and local life?" The *kiji undong* (bases movement) wanted answers to this question. In turn, activists' protests and demands since the 1990s did not fall on deaf ears. The Korean government at all levels has been sensitive to the volatile nature of the politics of U.S. basing in recent years and has employed various means to communicate with and respond to locals' interests' and concerns, to varying effect.

LOCAL POLITICS UNDER AUTHORITARIANISM

For much of its history as a modern republic, South Korea was a garrison state. Military-authoritarian governments tightly held the reins of power such that local autonomy was tantamount to political dissidence. Under Park Chung Hee (1961–79), Chun Du Hwan (1980–88), and Roh Tae Woo (1988–93), provincial and local officials were designated by Seoul to do its bidding.[15] Centralized authority was particularly useful in maintaining order in the *kiji ch'on* areas and in suppressing students and other activists who might politicize the presence of tens of thousands of foreign troops. The value of these locales lay in their ability to accommodate the foreign troop presence and, especially those near the demilitarized zone (DMZ), as frontline battlefields in case of military engagement with North Korea.

Given these concerns, the Korean government by and large applied policies of neglect and control to the areas housing U.S. bases. Economic and social neglect (e.g., educational, infrastructural, community development) was the order of the day, while periodic and selective control—through police surveillance, psychological operations, and the regulation of prostitution and bars/nightclubs—was exercised by both the ROK and U.S. authorities. For the Korean government, the key objective was to maintain a local population that would accommodate U.S. military personnel and facilities as civilian labor on the military compounds (e.g., translators, clerks, cleaners) or as service providers in the local economy (e.g., food vendors, shoeshine boys, marriage license brokers, bar owners, sex workers). Seoul needed the local populations' continued tolerance, if not eager support, of the foreign troops. To this effect, for decades the power of the dollar served as the carrot while police surveillance over local residents' dealings with "outsiders"—such as social welfare workers, political activists, student dissidents, and national and international media—served as the stick.

Government control, however, did not mean that the communities were completely compliant or quiescent. Local grievances were aplenty, even in the 1960s and 1970s when strong pro-American sentiment dominated Korean society, and to this day they are strikingly consistent: American arrogance and condescension toward Koreans, ignorance of

Korean customs and traditions, lack of information exchange and consultation with local residents, sexual crimes and abuse of women, and negative social impact and economic neglect by the central government. There are countless tales of taxi drivers being stiffed by GIs, peddlers and merchants catching GIs stealing their wares, bar hostesses being beaten up, and other variations on the theme of mistreatment, humiliation, and betrayal.[16] Some accounts have been depoliticized and incorporated as family stories of survival in hard times, but others have hardened through the generations as evidence of victimization and wrongdoing by Korean authorities and American troops. In many *kiji* areas, such as Maehyangni, locals have knitted together stories of past suffering with new grievances, along with accumulated frustration that neither their government (local and central) nor the U.S. authorities would listen and take them seriously.[17]

But once student activists raised their fists to rebel against military authoritarian rule in the 1980s, the U.S. bases fast became a source of political consciousness-raising and a symbol of trampled sovereignty under dictators-cum-"American lackeys." In the 1980s, patriotic nationalism, anti-government/pro-democracy activism, and anti-Americanism in the student movement increasingly became inseparable. By the mid-1980s, "virtually all efforts of the student movement would concentrate on the struggle against the United States,"[18] its troop presence, trade pressures, and relationship with the authoritarian regimes.

In the second half of the 1980s, camp towns became venues of political activism for some university students and dissidents. Democracy activists had developed "membership training" (MT) and field study/labor teams around the nation as a way to bridge the gap between intellectuals and workers/farmers, or the *minjung* (masses), to mobilize them against the authoritarian regime.[19] Thousands of young people went to work in factories and on farms, often under cover, as political organizers. Durebang (My Sister's Place), which was established in Tongduch'ŏn in 1988 and was the first shelter and advocacy group established to assist women who worked as barmaids and prostitutes, sponsored students from the start. These students and activists were some of the first Koreans to help challenge the pariah status of the *kiji ch'on* as places teeming with gangsters, crime, drugs, disease, immorality, and "bastard" Amerasian children. Since 1945, when U.S. troops stepped foot on Korean soil, and especially since the dislocation and chaos of the Korean War, the image of U.S. camp towns as pariah towns had become fixed in the imagination of the Korean people and instantiated in the policies of various governments.

While the rest of the nation modernized and prospered, these areas largely remained shantytowns, undesirable as recipients of economic and political investment.

While the general population marginalized and shunned the camp towns, it also accepted them as necessary evils in maintaining U.S. troops and deterring North Korean aggression. Yet they were sensitive to the negative images that Americans would collect as part of their Korean experience. A 1971 news article urging Koreans to pay attention to the "extreme goings-on in U.S. military camp-follower towns" is a good example: "various evils occur around 'CampTowns' almost daily both openly and secretly including trafficking in drugs, prostitution, begging, stealing, drunkenness, and rabble rousing."[20] The report warned that "nearly all of them [GIs] have left here with a poor image of our country," which has "led to a negative image of Korea on the part of U.S. public opinion."[21] And indeed, the racial rioting among U.S. troops that spilled over into conflicts with local Koreans in the summer of 1971 piqued the ire of several key members of the U.S. Congress, provoking them to question the rationale for keeping U.S. troops in an unwelcome environment and in some cases calling for a pullout altogether.[22]

The Camp Town Clean-Up Campaign (*chŏnghwa undong*, or "purification campaign") of the 1970s, waged by the Joint SOFA Committee, was the first concerted program to tighten law and order and regulate illicit activities in the camp town areas for the purpose of facilitating the maintenance of U.S. troops.[23] The campaign demonstrated the intimate link between local civil-military relations and the larger concerns of foreign policy and national security. Specifically, the troop withdrawal and restructuring that followed the Nixon Doctrine, which aimed to disentangle the U.S. from land wars in East Asia, created demographic dislocation and social chaos as U.S. forces moved out of some areas and into new ones, primarily from the DMZ regions to the Osan-P'yŏngt'aek area. Local civil-military relations were in such shambles that the U.S. and Korean authorities initiated the Clean-Up Campaign as a way to establish order, improve the physical and social environment of the camp towns, and facilitate cooperative relations among local Koreans and the GIs. This included stricter regulation of local Korean women who worked as sex workers and entertainers in the camp town bars.

Despite some improvements in local civil-military relations,

> the social cost of these camptown improvements was increased authoritarian control and militarization of people's lives. The number of police personnel, checkpoints, vehicles, and raids increased in most

> camptowns, and U.S. military patrol teams increased in number and kind to monitor the behavior of both U.S. personnel and Korean residents. Although increased policing was needed to control the excesses of camptown life, the Purification Movement reduced the amount of village space, especially that of camptown women, not subject to the surveillance of governmental and military authorities.[24]

During the authoritarian period, regard for these localities had little to do with the protection of individual rights and community development of Koreans, but largely with accommodating the alliance relationship.[25] But decentralization created new political opportunities, requiring local authorities to pay attention to residents' well-being and to pursue economic and social development.[26]

LOCAL AMBITIONS AND ACTIVISM

In contrast to the authoritarian period, when local officials suppressed residents' criticism of and protests against U.S. troops, decentralization often fostered cooperation between officials and residents and activists from other areas to assert local power *vis-à-vis* the U.S. forces and the central government. For example, in May 2000 the Inch'ŏn City Council joined with NGOs to form the Citizens' Congress for the Return of Land Used by the USFK in Pup'yŏng to reclaim land that the U.S. was using as a junkyard. The movement mobilized citizens from Pup'yŏng and the greater Inch'ŏn area to demonstrate in front of U.S. Camp Market for its relocation out of downtown Pup'yŏng. Participants claimed that the military facility was "obstructing city plans to build a new boulevard and that the camp's garbage dump and incinerator [were] harmful to the environment."[27] In my interviews with several officials of the Ministry of Foreign Affairs, there was serious recognition that the "development of cities has been limited" because of the bases.[28]

Pup'yŏng received national and international news coverage in the late 1990s and early 2000s for the "human chain" protests around Camp Market and various sit-ins (including one that started on May 27, 2000, with the goal of continuing until the U.S. base is returned to the locals) and hunger strikes in front of the U.S. installation and the local city hall.[29] On some of these occasions, National Assembly members from both the liberal Democratic Party and the conservative Grand National Party, as well as Inch'ŏn city officials, joined the protest gatherings.[30]

Local politics in Pup'yŏng was typical of the camp towns that are urban centers, in that urbanization since the 1980s and 1990s helped transform them from politically and economically marginal to more densely populated, influential areas. Pup'yŏng, whose population exceeds one-fifth of the total Inch'ŏn area, lies at the center of major commercial, residential, and transportation thoroughfares. And the Inch'ŏn area has in the 2000s increasingly become a spillover extension of Seoul; hence the sensitivity to the fact that U.S. Camp Market occupies a swath of coveted land to house a variety of support services for the U.S. military (e.g., Kimpo Postal Detachment, Defense Reutilization and Marketing Office, Printing and Publications Command—Korea, and the Air Force Exchange Services Bakery and Distribution Center)[31] and lies at the center of pedestrian and automobile traffic. Residents living in the high-rises that tower over the Market complain about the empty unused spaces within the compound, including a large playing field. Members of the Coalition for Changing U.S. Military Camps into Parks, which staged sit-ins and other demonstrations, complained that the camp was of no strategic use and housed only ten active-duty U.S. soldiers and about three hundred Korean employees.[32] For decades, the local government and citizens sought to expand the road system near the U.S. installation but had been thwarted repeatedly by the U.S. base authorities.[33] Additionally, Pup'yŏng residents and activists have complained about environmental damage, especially oil leakage and seepage (into soil and water), caused by U.S. military activities.[34]

Ch'unch'ŏn, which lies about 90 kilometers northeast of Seoul, is the capital and administrative center of Kangwŏn Province and is the longtime home of U.S. Camp Page. Like their counterparts in Pup'yŏng, Ch'unch'ŏn residents have complained that the U.S. base creates various problems and hazards for the locals. The fact that Camp Page, home of the Apache unit of the 2ID, is immediately visible upon arrival at Ch'unch'ŏn Station, that it blocks the main road in the downtown area so that "a direct distance of less than 600 m requires more than 6 km of circular travel" (thereby creating constant traffic jams), and that noise and fuel pollution from the helicopter training activities disrupts the education and damages the health of children in the nearby elementary school were some of the specific grievances. Activists reported that most new teachers at the school leave even before their second year is over because of the difficult teaching and learning conditions.[35] In this regard, such complaints parallel those of Ginowan residents on Okinawa, who have sought the closing and removal of the Futenma Air Base. And former Governor Masahide Ota of Okinawa, who aggressively had pursued local autonomy, also lamented the distorted development of towns near U.S. bases in Okinawa as "erratic sprawls."[36]

Moreover, since the mid-1990s, Ch'unch'ŏn (and Kangwŏn Province in general) has aspired to become a high-tech research and development area, in addition to continuing as a main tourist attraction for its natural beauty and as the host of international gatherings (e.g., international mime and *animē* festivals). Since 1995, in the new era of local autonomy, Ch'unch'ŏn City developed plans and infrastructure to become a major international center for animation technology and business. In 1998, the new provincial governor and the mayor of Ch'unch'ŏn proposed a development strategy that focused on "knowledge and information society."[37] Such activist local officials have transformed what used to be a "dormant periphery" of Seoul into a city with "a vision of [a] multimedia valley as a base for bio-venture support center and advanced visual industry."[38] In this context, the U.S. base represented, for many officials and activists, an old obstacle—dating back to 1951—that prevents or interferes with the hopes for a more dynamic and prosperous economic, global, and high-tech future.[39] (In 2005, Camp Page was closed and transferred to the South Korean government as part of the Land Partnership Program.)

The transformation of P'aju, just miles away from the DMZ, from a militarized buffer town to a "high-tech hub," provides a role model for *kiji ch'on* residents and officials who seek an alternative, more lucrative future. The P'aju area, which housed Camps Edwards, Gary Owen, Greaves, Giant, Howze, and Stanton until 2004 and had been part of the invasion route for North Koreans during the war, became a hotspot in the 2000s for real estate investors, developers, and businesses, like LG Philips LCD. As a consequence of the new demand, land prices rose "tenfold, faster than in Seoul."[40] Sohn Hak Kyu, the former governor of Kyŏnggi Province, which has housed many of the significant U.S. installations, emphasized that the northern part of the province, which is relatively uncharted in land-scarce and densely populated South Korea, has been experiencing a boom. Before democratization, decentralization, and the thawing of North-South relations under Kim Dae Jung and Roh Mu Hyun, P'aju had been a major pariah town for the vast majority of South Koreans.

Common Grievances and Demands

Complaints about land use, noise, environmental damage, accidents, and criminality ensuing from the U.S. military presence are not unique to

Korea.[41] Variations on the themes abound from Okinawa and Misawa, Japan; to Kaiserslautern, Germany; to Kyrgyzstan, which houses the Manas Air Base;[42] as well as Aviano, Italy. The infamous gondola accident of 1998, in which Marine captain Richard Ashby's aircraft sliced cables that caused a gondola to drop 300 feet to the ground, killing twenty people, occurred near Aviano. "The U.S. military charged the pilot with twenty counts of involuntary manslaughter" but acquitted him, while the "U.S. Congress paid $20 million to rebuild the cables" and Italians demanded the closing of the Aviano Air Base.[43]

Mark Gillem, who has studied land/space use and the politics of architectural development on and around overseas U.S. bases, lists a (long) sampling of U.S. tank, aircraft, and other accidents that have occurred in Japan and Korea. Some of the major accidents that took place in Korea in the late 1990s and early 2000s alone follow:

- August 1999: "Two F-16s collide above Kunsan Air Base and two live bombs drop into the sea at the end of the runway";
- June 2001: "An F-16 crashes into a rice paddy near Kunsan Air Base" (pilot is killed);
- August 2002: "An Apache helicopter crashes on a hillside near Camp Page" (two crewmembers are killed);
- January 2003: "A U- reconnaissance plane crashes near Osan Air Base" (four are injured, and a home and repair shop are destroyed);
- May 2003: "An F-16 crashes shortly after take-off at Osan Air Base; falling debris injures one person;"
- August 2003: "An Army C-12 crashes into a field seven miles from Camp Humphreys;"
- September 2003: "An F-16 crashes off of Korea's west coast."[44]

Of course, the most devastating and politically volatile accident in Korea in the early 2000s was the armored vehicle accident that killed Sin Hyosun and Sim Misŏn, who were walking along a road en route to a birthday party. Most of the media coverage highlighted public demands for the revision of the SOFA (so that the Korean government can have legal authority over such cases) and the massive "anti-American" candlelight vigils that swept through Korea. But local governments and residents near U.S. bases had more mundane, practical, and immediate quality-of-life demands. Their emphasis was on safety and control over daily activities. A major source of complaint was the military's use of land and roads frequented by local residents without due regard (caution and protection) for the residents' needs. Critics referred to the fact that the armored vehicle's width was greater than that of the road itself, leaving the girls (or any pedestrian) no room to move.[45] The death of the two girls brought out other accidents and civilian casualties associated with the U.S. military—grievances that had accumulated over time—including a tank accident that destroyed farming equipment in a different camp town in March 2002 and yet another in 2001 that led to nine Koreans' being injured.[46]

The Korean government and the U.S. military took seriously local residents' demands for more information on troop movements and provisions for their own safety. The ROK Ministry of National Defense acknowledged the inconvenience to locals caused by the USFK troop training and committed to improving local living conditions.[47] In the immediate aftermath of the accident, the Korean central and local governments made plans to widen the roadway on which the accident occurred and to pave a sidewalk (which had not existed at the time of the incident), install other safety features, and to urge the USFK to publicize better its plans for troop training and movement so that residents could be better informed and prepared.[48] Altogether, about $94 million were set aside for road development in Kyŏnggi Province, particular the roads used by the 2ID. The central and provincial governments engaged in burden-sharing, and the province was prompted to pay for agricultural roads, a responsibility that usually falls to the city government.[49]

In tandem, the USFK announced "corrective measures" to avoid similar accidents, stating that "the Second Infantry Division is taking over 20 significant measures to improve safety during training," including:

- More detailed notification of local leaders concerning training activities
- Intercom systems upgrades to improve communication between the vehicle driver and vehicle commander
- Additional mirrors and other vehicle reconfigurations to improve the visibility of vehicle drivers
- Front and back guide vehicles for vehicles like the one involved in the accident
- All unit movements will be rehearsed and approved by senior leaders two levels above the unit commander
- Two-way convoys on two lane roads are prohibited.[50]

The statement ended with this announcement: "The Second Infantry Division is also taking all vehicles of the type involved in the accident off the roads. The vehicles will be moved on large transport trucks."

In the armored vehicle case, the tragic loss of two lives, access to and use of land and public space, as well as authorities' regard for locals' safety and convenience converged. In short, the public outcry, at least on a local level, was not a simplistic, emotional matter of nationalistic outrage but a complex amalgam of multiple concerns. In this regard, Gillem offers surprising and telling information about the primacy of material interests among the local populations that host U.S. forces: "Despite widespread media attention focusing on tragic stories of rapes, deadly accidents, and environmental damage, surveys of local residents near some of these outposts reveal not so much an all-consuming desire for their demise but disgust, above all, with the excessive use of land by American forces."[51] With respect to Korea, we learn that a survey of 1,200 locals living near U.S. bases (conducted by Kyŏnggi Research Institute in 2001) found that

> 30 percent of the 1,200 . . . said that either they or their family members have suffered due to the presence of American military bases near their homes. . . . When asked to describe what they considered pressing concerns regarding U.S. troops, 56 percent pointed to environmental pollution and 62 percent noted crimes and undisciplined activity. Most significantly, *68 percent cited the U.S. military's excessive use of Korean land as the burning issue*.[52] (emphasis added)

Particularly vexing to some Korean landowners is the fact that they were never compensated for the land the Korean state granted for USFK use. According to Chang-hee Nam, privately owned land "accounted for about 25 percent of the total land that the ROK granted to the USFK in the form of either exclusive-use land or restricted areas," yet the government "has been reluctant to pay rents for these lands because of the enormous expenditure it would entail to satisfy the landowners' demands."[53] Moreover, grievances of long ago—people who lost their land to government expropriation during the Korean War and the later establishment of military bases—abound. Some have gone to court to press their claims; others pushed their farming activities onto U.S. base areas. And landowners and activists alike resent the Korean government's reluctance to pay "rent" when they learn of the Japanese government's policy to do so: In 2000, "the Korean government spent only $1.1 million in rent . . . , whereas the amount paid by the Japanese government for the USFJ [U.S. Forces, Japan] facilities and grant lands was $801 million."[54]

Koreans are not alone in resenting the U.S. bases' consumption of land. Mark Gillem discusses at length the replication of Americana overseas, with large shopping malls and parking lots "surrounded by asphalt and grass,"[55] which offers a sense of familiarity and home to U.S. service personnel living abroad. But what creates comfort for Americans causes discomfort for local hosts: "Exporting suburban [architectural and landscape] morphology exacerbates the negative effects of spillover and contributes to the excessive use of land so detested by America Town's [camp towns'] neighbors."[56] Just one example he offers is the plan for a school and shopping center on Misawa Air Base in Japan, whose "footprints [are] five times larger than the largest building in Misawa City."[57] Gillem takes particular issue with the amount of leisure space that the U.S. military occupies around the world,[58] especially golf courses: "In 2002 the USAF [Air Force] owned sixty-eight golf courses" and had "more than double the number of golf courses per capita than the United States as a whole. This gluttony of golf comes with a spatial price since an eighteen-hole golf course consumes approximately 120 acres."[59]

The politicization of land use, especially for leisure play such as golf, is part and parcel of Korea's legacy of rapid economic growth and democratization. Upon assuming office, Kim Young Sam, the first civilian to be elected president in over thirty years, vowed to inject new morality and modesty into political life. He publicly declared that "he would not play golf during his tenure of office, and urged his senior officials and party members to follow his example. "[60] James Cotton and Kim Hyun-a van Leest describe this move as a "self-conscious gesture . . . to signal a break with the past,"[61] specifically the "golf republic" of the Roh Tae Woo era (1988–1993). Roh apparently facilitated the proliferation of golf courses owned by *chaebŏl* (business conglomerates) and other elites. The authors emphasize that golf and leisure activities generally represented "three fundamental conditions; [sic] money, power and connections."[62] Yet the Roh administration was riddled with contradictions, since it also initiated frugality campaigns in the early 1990s against conspicuous consumption as a way to fight the growing national deficit, the declining savings rate, and the public's chafing at elite privilege. In this context, golf courses and other leisure space on U.S. bases, which from the 1960s to the 1980s had symbolized rare and truly privileged space (for the very few Koreans who were permitted to enter), increasingly became a target of Korean resentment and envy as expectations of equal access among the new middle class in a new democracy encountered hegemonic power structures like the *chaebŏl* and the U.S. bases.

Even though much of the coverage of local Korean-American civil-military relations has assumed anti-American nationalism and the swaying of "simple" locals by seasoned nationalistic activists, the truth is that local populations have their own self-interest in mind. They have learned to take seriously the notion of local autonomy. Gi-yong Yang, who conducted a survey of local residents and officials in camp towns P'aju and Ŭijŏngbu, found that the large majority of respondents (70.7 percent) who approved of the stationing of U.S. forces in Korea did so for "national and regional security" reasons, but almost 50 percent did not want their locality to play host.[63] It is an obvious example of NIMBY-ism, "not in my backyard."

Towns that have not housed U.S. bases also have become politically active in order to preempt or prevent their becoming another *kiji ch'on*. For example, residents and local officials of Songp'a-ku (ward) took action when their town was mentioned in 2001–2 as a possible site for the relocation of the U.S. Yongsan Garrison, an issue that had been pending since 1991. In a public statement on January 21, 2002, the Songp'a-ku Office and residents stated, "'We are against moving the U.S. military compound into our region, or even raising the possibility for discussion.'"[64] Upset over the lack of consultation, the community "called on the South Korean and U.S. militaries to make public all information about the decision-making process over the selection of an alternative site for the main U.S. military base."[65] The ward flexed its local autonomy muscles, exhibiting a kind of cooperation between local residents and officials that marked a startling reverse course from the near-fifty years of government dereliction of duties toward local communities: "Nearby military facilities are great disadvantage, such as limits on the height of buildings, to the residents of Songp'a. . . . An opinion poll on the matter will be conducted soon for conveying the residents' view to the government."[66] The ward council committed itself to "struggle against the movement of the Yongsan base to Songp'a."

Emboldened by laws and citizen support, fifteen local governments of areas housing U.S. bases convened first-ever meetings in 2000 to address local grievances toward the central government. They also submitted to the National Assembly a proposal for a special act that would recognize the disproportionate burden suffered by the local communities that house U.S. troops. In particular, they demanded financial compensation as a form of redress, as well as central government attention to economic development planning and environmental impact assessments in the camp town areas. They claimed that "[t]he law . . . would also help raise the negotiating power and voice of local governments and their residents in future negotiations with the U.S. side."[67]

The new collective call for local development planning and assistance had roots in the "return-of-land," or *panhwan,* movement that began in the mid-1990s and spread to various camp towns (see chapter 3). Activists, residents, and local government officials joined together to demand the return of land used by U.S. forces to the locals. The movement participants usually argued that in many cases, the U.S. military was occupying land that was idle or marginally put to use (such as storage and dump sites), blocked urban planning and development, or endangered the safety and well-being of local residents (e.g., strafing fields and noise pollution). Camp Market in Pup'yŏng was one such target. Kunni strafing range in Maehyangni was another. Throughout the second half of the 1990s, just about every town adjoining U.S. bases developed a branch of the national Return of Land movement.

In addition to challenging the U.S. presence and activities through public demonstrations and local government processes, Koreans have been quick to file class-action lawsuits in Korean courts and demand compensation from the national government for personal injury and/or the loss of or damage to personal property. According to my interviews with Korean officials in the Ministry of Foreign Affairs and Trade, as of November 2004 there were over twenty class-action suits pending in courts, alleging damage due to environmental and noise pollution and threats to public safety.[68] In 2001, in a first-ever ruling of its kind, the Seoul District Court decided in favor of fourteen defendants from Maehyangni who alleged that U.S. activities on the Kunni bombing range had caused the destruction of property and the disruption of people's livelihood. The court ordered the central government to pay 132 million *wŏn* (U.S.$99,660) to the defendants who were party to the class-action suit.[69]

This decision came after decades of individual complaints about the same kinds of problems, which the government and the larger public had long ignored. Maehyangni villagers had claimed that since the arrival of the U.S. Air Force at the end of the Korean War, nine people had "died in accidents linked to the range."[70] In spring 2000 the dropping of six bombs by a U.S. fighter jet reinvigorated local frustrations and generated loud and at times violent public protests against the base. Locals charged that six people had been injured and property damaged by the bombing incident and demanded the closing of the bombing range. This in turn led to an official joint U.S.-Korean investigation of the claims.

LOCAL VERSUS NATIONAL INTERESTS

In November 2001, the South Korean Minister of Defense Kim Dong Shin and U.S. Secretary of Defense Donald Rumsfeld signed a Letter of Intent at the 33rd U.S.-ROK Security Consultative Meeting (SCM) to develop and implement a ten-year plan to restructure and consolidate U.S. installations and facilities in Korea. The Land Partnership Plan (LPP), which the USFK had suggested to the Korean government in March 2000 and was formalized by both governments in March 2002, was a joint U.S.-ROK government response aimed at politically reducing the "U.S. footprint" and increasing organizational efficiency. It called for the reduction of major installations and training areas by at least 15, from the then 41 to 26 "enduring installations," with no reduction in the 37,000 troops stationed in Korea. The plan intended for the return of approximately 33,000 acres (41 million *p'yŏng,* more than 50 percent of the land granted for use by the U.S. Forces) of highly coveted commercial land to the South Korean government. This would entail about a third of the U.S. forces moving from one venue to another around the formation of seven "hubs" consisting of a headquarters and command-and-control center in Seoul (Yongsan Garrison), two Air Force war-fighting hubs at Osan and Kunsan, an Army war-fighting and training hub around the 2ID at Tongduch'ŏn (Camp Casey and Camp Hovey) and Ŭijŏngbu (Cam Red Cloud and Camp Stanley), an expanded Eighth Army combat-support hub in P'yŏngt'aek (Camp Humphreys), an Eighth Army combat-service support hub in Taegu, and a port hub around Pusan.[71] The Korean government had agreed to purchase or acquire approximately 1,258 acres (1.54 million *p'yŏng;* one *p'yŏng* equaling about 3.3 square meters) of land adjacent to existing installations or as replacement installations as needed by the USFK to facilitate the move.

Both the Korean and U.S. governments acknowledged that the reduction and consolidation of areas were needed to address the growing civic and local concerns regarding urban development, environmental protection, and public safety of citizens living around the bases. For both sides, "the accord [was] largely aimed at addressing growing anti-U.S. sentiment" regarding the bases.[72] Additionally, for the USFK, the "timing of the Land Partnership plan [was] directly linked to funding by the US Department of Defense to improve the quality of its facilities. The US Army [planned to] fund new barracks and support facilities through 2008."[73] For the Korean government, the agreement was intended to "help settle 'many unsolved civic petitions' related to U.S. installations"[74] and to assure the central government's responsiveness toward citizens' concerns.[75] To that end, the North America II Division of the Ministry of Foreign Affairs and Trade (MoFAT), which deals with the SOFA and the USFK, delegated an official to serve as liaison to the local governments that would be involved in and affected by the LPP. The liaison would visit with local officials and explain the central government's plans and procedures as well as those of the USFK and solicit questions and concerns from the localities. A MoFAT official offered the example of a Suwŏn official who expressed his gratitude for the central government's attention and assistance to his area because he was unfamiliar with dealing or negotiating with the USFK. Such local visits also allowed the MoFAT to get a better idea of local grievances and interests, many of which they deemed were utterly reasonable from the perspective of local residents.[76]

Despite the two governments' efforts to respond to citizens' demands, critics argued that the LPP was mostly an empty gesture because the U.S. was mostly relinquishing land that it did not need or use and that the Korean government would have to pay a high financial cost to accommodate the U.S. side. They reserved their sharpest criticism for the omitted areas, that is, facilities and villages that were not listed for return. Maehyangni activists aggressively demanded that the Kunni range be included for closure and return. Planning a major protest in front of the U.S. Embassy in downtown Seoul, Chŏn Mangyu, a village leader and activist, stated that "[w]e are enraged by the United States' infringement upon our human rights and our very right to live"[77] and that not closing the range "constitutes infringement of South Korean national sovereignty."[78]

Seoul-based activists were particularly incensed by the absence of the Yongsan base on the list of planned closures.[79] Some even demanded a complete revision of the LPP to include the return of Yongsan land to Seoul. The fact that the USFK was planning to build a new apartment complex to accommodate about 1,600 personnel provoked opposition from both the Seoul Metropolitan government and CSOs. They insisted that the central government and the USFK should honor the 1991 Memorandum of Understanding (MOU) to transfer the base out of Seoul. Bases activists did what came most naturally—demonstrate in front of Yongsan Garrison and the National Ministry of Defense building nearby. But officials also took on activist coloring as the Association of Seoul City officials "threatened to tackle the [building] plan in coalition with civil officials nationwide and international labor groups."[80]

Civil society activists reserved the harshest criticism for their own government. They "blasted the military [Ministry of National Defense; MND] for conceding too much to the United States."[81] Kim Yonghan, a leader in the *panhwan* movement and the People's Action to Reform the SOFA, which I discuss in detail in chapter 3, criticized the deal: "Compared with a preliminary plan reached during last year's Security Consultative Meeting (SCM) [November 2001], there is almost no increase of land that will be returned to the country while the land to be granted to the US side increased from 750,000 *p'yŏng* to 1.54 million *p'yŏng*."[82]

Such critics, however, tended to ignore or downplay the issues on which the Korean government did manage to exert pressure on the U.S. side. *JoongAng Ilbo* observed that "compared to last November's LPP negotiation, the inclusion of *tosim* (urban) areas for return is the most noticeable result" (original in Korean).[83] The article listed Camp Hialeah in Pusan, Camp Page in Ch'unch'ŏn, Camp Market in Pup'yŏng, and Camp Walker in Taegu as installations for return the USFK had resisted, despite the locals' desire for their removal. But the MND had urged the U.S. that if the LPP were to proceed without exacerbating anti-American sentiment, the urban bases would have to be included.[84]

From the Korean government's perspective, *tosim* areas were politically active and volatile places, some of which had held legitimate grievances against the constraints and inconveniences that the U.S. facilities presented. For example, an MND document on the LPP acknowledges that places like Ch'unch'ŏn and Pup'yŏng had long suffered problems in urban development due to the geographic location and structure of the U.S. facilities, and that Pusan had sought since the 1990s to rid itself of Camp Hialeah so that it might pursue modern construction and development projects. In particular, Pusan had officially begun negotiations with the MND at the end of 1995 to remove the bases so that the city would be able to erect facilities to accommodate the 2002 Asian Games. The MND emphasized that with regard to these key areas, the Korean government exerted strong pressure to persuade U.S. negotiators to concede and sought practical means to meet local citizens' demands without compromising national security. The document also clearly states that the "current system of local autonomy" fostered people's view of the U.S. bases "as detestable facilities" to house in their environs, making urgent the need to return base lands.[85]

Even though interested civic groups and local camp town residents paid attention to the LPP process, the consolidation and return-of-land procedures were by and large a matter of management and bureaucratic negotiations under the SOFA Joint Committee and not a major item of foreign policy or public debate. By contrast, the Pentagon's plans to restructure U.S. troops as part of its Global Posture Review (GPR) aroused Koreans' fears of abandonment and suspicion of U.S. intentions on the Korean peninsula. Ever since former U.S. Secretary of Defense Donald Rumsfeld mentioned the Pentagon's intention to remove and redeploy U.S. troops in Korea in his testimony before the U.S. Senate Armed Services Committee on February 13, 2003, Korean speculations ran rampant. Koreans on the left conjectured that Washington wanted to move its forces south of the Han River so as to conduct military strikes against North Korea's nuclear program sites; Koreans on the right blamed the "anti-American" protests in the winter of 2002–3 for creating a rift with the U.S. They condemned the newly elected Roh Moo Hyun for his poor stewardship of the alliance and his role in abetting anti-Americanism among his left-leaning followers.

Washington's announcement in June 2005 to reduce 12,500 troops (a third of its forces) by the end of 2005 exacerbated the strains in the bilateral relationship. Even though some policy elites and the media had speculated since 2003 that a reduction was possible, most Koreans were shocked and angered by the abruptness and the condensed time frame of the announcement, and newspapers on the left and right echoed these concerns. For example, the conservative *Chosun Ilbo* remarked that the way in which the U.S. delivered its reduction plan was particularly problematic: "The U.S. side, in fact, 'notified' the Korean side of its reduction plan. The U.S. side did not appear to be interested in conducting 'negotiations' on its reduction plan."[86] The *Dong-A Ilbo* echoed, "More than anything else, the U.S. must not press the size and timing of the USFK reduction in a unilateral manner, if it respects the ROK-U.S. alliance and the concern of the Korean people."[87]

Korean political elites resented the unilateral nature of Washington's decision and the plan to move U.S. forces away from the DMZ. They interpreted this as a major turn away from the "tripwire" role that they believed the U.S. served in deterring North Korean aggression. A group of 133 National Assembly members, mostly from the conservative opposition Grand National Party, even led a signature campaign under the auspices of the Coalition against U.S. Troop Withdrawal to prevent the removal of the 2ID away from the border with North Korea.[88] And the *Korea Times* (April 11, 2003) noted that the "gap between the two sides on the timing of relocating the Second Infantry Division seems to be so wide that President Roh Moo-hyun once again expressed his wish to keep the division where it is near the inter-Korean border until the North Korean nuclear crisis is resolved." The Korean government did manage to negotiate a longer time schedule for the removal of U.S. forces, stretching it out until 2008 rather than the end of 2005.

The actual end date of relocation has continued to be an issue of contention. By late 2006, Koreans were seeking a 2013 date, with officials citing "protests by [P'yŏngt'aek] residents and anti-American activists" as the cause of delay, while some analysts cited the Korean government's wish to keep U.S. forces near the DMZ, especially while the transition to Korean wartime operational control of troops takes place in 2012.[89] As of April 2009, USFK officials insisted on a delayed target year of 2016 for the relocation of Yongsan Garrison and the 2ID, while Korean officials insisted on 2014 for the 2ID and 2015 for the garrison. Both sides have stated financial constraints as reasons for postponement.[90]

The reduction and repositioning of troops seemed like a repeat of what Koreans had experienced under the Nixon Doctrine back in the early 1970s. The impact on Korea at that time was dramatic, reducing 20,000 troops from the total force of 64,000 (the U.S. Seventh Infantry Division, one of two divisions that had been based in Korea since 1955, and three Air Force fighter squadrons were withdrawn). The abrupt announcements of the change in troop policy under both the Nixon Doctrine and the GPR were (1) based primarily on changes in U.S. strategic assessments, (2) unilaterally announced, (3) opposed by a wide spectrum of Korean political society, and (4) interpreted by many Koreans as destabilizing Korean security and economic prosperity.

Moreover, on both occasions, local populations got caught up in the maelstrom as people feared economic collapse in areas that were being vacated by U.S. troops and competed for local resources in those areas marked for the expansion of U.S. forces and facilities. For example, by June 1971, "6,000 Koreans (out of a total of 32,000) employed at various U.S. installations" were losing their jobs; real estate prices in most camp towns plummeted; and *kiji ch'on* businesses and workers, particularly those in bars and the sex industry, suffered economic losses and physical dislocation.[91] According to one set of records, the withdrawal of the Seventh Division led to the closing of thirty-nine bars in P'och'ŏn, sixty-two in P'aju, and twenty-seven in Pup'yŏng within a one-year span.[92]

In recent years, Tongduch'ŏn residents have faced similar fears of economic decline following the reduction and eventual withdrawal of 14,000 U.S. troops from the region, and local residents and merchants have held demonstrations since the announcement of the planned U.S. departure from the area. Like his predecessors over thirty years ago who were forced to close or move, Jimmy Chu, the owner of a bar in Ŭijŏngbu (home of 2ID Camp Red Cloud), emphasized that "moving major bases like Red Cloud to the South [of the Han River] would cause great economic hardship for little purpose."[93] In his estimate, 50,000 people would be forced to leave the area. But unlike his predecessors, who had blamed the U.S. for changing its commitments toward Korea, Chu, who was experiencing these shifts in the context of "anti-American" vigils and protests, cursed those Koreans who oppose the presence of U.S. troops.[94]

Having been synonymous with the 2ID for about half a century, the Tongduch'ŏn and Ŭijŏngbu areas will have to reconfigure their economic base and local identity. Fearing *sŭrŏmhwa* ("slumification") of the area, the central and provincial governments submitted legislation in late 2004 intended to bolster the local economy and welfare over the next five years, including special funds for economic development, the establishment of a research and development science complex, the extension of the highway system to attract Seoulites to the Tongduch'ŏn region, and the expedited adjoining of a subway line to connect Seoul and the northern regions.[95] During an interview in November 2004, Yu Insŏn, the head of the USFK Relocation Planning Office of Kyŏnggi Province, mentioned that the government had already committed 200 million *wŏn* for development purposes in the Tongduch'ŏn area. Stating that there was no luxury of a long timeline, he hoped that five years of hard work would ensure that the area could stand on its feet.[96]

Cities like Tongduch'ŏn, P'aju, and Ŭijŏngbu, which have been major hosts of U.S. forces, drafted their own development plans. Tongduch'ŏn's is most ambitious (because of the vast areas that will be vacated by the U.S. forces), including a university, industrial complex, and golf course. But financial costs and conflict with the central government over how much budget support the latter will provide to these former *kiji ch'on* has dogged economic and infrastructural development since the mid-2000s. In 2006, Mayor Kim Mun-wŏn of Ŭijŏngbu sharply stated: "It is only reasonable, that the central government must extensively back up these regions. . . . If our city does not receive as much support as the other local governments, our residents will not stand it." He also reminded Seoul that "[t]hese regions had to endure the military bases for the sake of national security."[97] *Dong-A Ilbo* pointed out that the return of land has raised tensions and competition between the central government and local governments as well as among the latter.[98]

Local governments have been keen to reap as many benefits as possible from the return of land and to avoid falling behind other localities in terms of development opportunities. The Kyŏnggi localities expect the central government to relax various regulations on construction and industrial development, especially to "expand information technology related manufacturing facilities of conglomerates," and to exempt them "from the total maximum factory load regulation defined in the Seoul Metropolitan Area Readjustment Planning Act."[99]

The return of land has prompted new assertiveness on the part of Tongduch'ŏn authorities, who produced a ten-minute video, "After the Clearing of the Rain," to promote public support for more development assistance and attention from the Seoul government. They targeted sympathies in relation to a proposal in the National Assembly in winter 2009 that would allow thirty percent of future land sale proceeds to go to the local government. The Ministry of Defense, however, wanted the funds to pay for the relocation of U.S. troops to P'yŏngt'aek. One local official called even the thirty percent "too menial for the severe sacrifices the city has endured" over the decades of hosting the foreign bases, which grew to cover about forty percent of the city.[100]

As the reduction and redeployment issue took hold, the Korean and U.S. sides had to haggle over the size and specificity of lands needed to accommodate the redeployment and consolidation of U.S. facilities, particularly the transfer of the Yongsan base from Seoul to Osan-P'yŏngt'aek. During the ninth round of the Future of the Alliance Initiative talks (FOTA), government representatives on both sides disagreed over how much land in Osan-P'yŏngtaek should be given in return for Yongsan, and the Korean media publicized these tensions. According to an editorial in the progressive *Hankyore Sinmun,*

> [t]he Korean delegation claimed the base size in Osan-P'yŏngt'aek should rationally decrease in accordance with the USFK reduction. The U.S. delegation, however, said that up till now, the reduction plan has been, for all intents and purposes, reflected in the negotiations. On the contrary, the U.S. is claiming it needs hundreds of thousands more p'yŏng of land for unit facilities and housing in order to merge the UN and Combined Forces commands with the bases in Osan-P'yŏngt'aek. We have said the USFK reduction of 12,500 men has not been sufficiently reflected and providing around 3 million p'yŏng of land . . . was going too far, and moreover, it was unreasonable for us to pay the entire cost of relocating the U.S. Yongsan Garrison, so we need to renegotiate this deal from square one.[101]

The conservative *Dong-A Ilbo* did not call for a renegotiation of the entire Yongsan plan but stated, "It makes little sense that the U.S. said it would cut U.S. military personnel in Korea by one-third while it demanded more land for its new base site."[102] The issue of how much and which parcels of land should be made accessible to the U.S. forces were politically sensitive for the Korean government. On the national level, it had to weigh the desire for a reduced U.S. footprint with the logistical and organizational effectiveness of the U.S. troops. It also had to project the image of being tough in negotiating with the United States and getting the best deal possible for the Korean people. *Hankyore* challenged the Roh government's competence in this way: "Suspicions will not disappear that this result [U.S. unwillingness to accept reductions in the base size or share moving costs] was brought on by the humiliating negotiating attitude of our delegation, which could not stand up for our rights."[103]

The central government has had to straddle demands and complaints from various camp town constituencies. For example, while areas facing a reduction or withdrawal of U.S. troops, like Tongduchŏn, fear economic devastation, those facing an expansion of U.S. personnel, like P'yŏngt'aek and P'aensŏng, experience splits between those who favor such expansion and those who oppose it. In addition, the authorities would have to come up with ways to compensate landowners who would have to give up their land to accommodate incoming U.S. troops, while arbitrating and prioritizing among numerous commercial and civic interests that would compete for access to the returned areas.

In order to manage such concerns, the central government established in 2003 the Special Commission on USFK Affairs in the Office of the Prime Minister. The Commission represents staff members from fifteen ministries (e.g., Ministry of National Defense, of Foreign Affairs and Trade, of Finance, of Environment) and relevant provinces (e.g., Kyŏnggi) who coordinate policy regarding domestic matters related to reduction and relocation, such as the purchase of new land needed for the move, the provision of budgets for relocation, the formulation of measures for relocating people's homes and livelihoods, and central government efforts to address the demands of local governments and residents.[104] In addition, the USFK Relocation Task Force was established in the Kyŏnggi provincial government in April 2004 to serve as a middleman between the central government and local areas. (Yu Insŏn, who headed the new task force, commented that prior to its establishment, local people lodged their complaints directly to the central government.[105]) In the history of USFK-ROK relations, this marked the first time that central and provincial bodies were dedicated to the purpose of mediating interests and disputes among residents and the various levels of government and between the USFK and the local Korean governments. But the commission and the task force were to serve as temporary vehicles of management and mediation, aimed solely at facilitating the U.S. reduction and relocation. This stands in contrast to the Okinawa Prefecture government and the Japan Defense Facilities Administration Agency, which have institutionalized mechanisms and procedures for dealing with the U.S. bases and between Tokyo and Okinawa.

Expansion plans for P'yŏngt'aek entailed a threefold increase in the land around Camp Humphreys by 2008,[106] with the small village of P'aensŏng becoming the new home of the 2ID. Residents and activists opposing the expansion staged demonstrations and protests, with numerous organizations coalescing to form the Committee against the Expansion of P'yŏngt'aek. In 2004 (at the time of my interview), its leaders claimed to represent a total of about 20,000 members and sought to raise public awareness of the potential negative impact of U.S. expansion (increased militarization of the area; environmental and noise pollution; the spread of underworld culture such as prostitution, drugs, and gangsterism; and the exacerbation of the area's image and reputation), residents' rights and political participation, and perceived dangers to the North-South reconciliation process. This group spanned local and national NGOs.[107]

On a smaller scale, the P'aensŏng Committee against U.S. Base Expansion represents mostly small landowners who are unwilling to give up their land to accommodate the expansion. They particularly resent what they perceive to be unilateral decision-making on the part of the central and provincial governments to offer up their land to the U.S. military. In an interview in November 2004, Kim Chi T'ae, Policy chief of the P'aensŏng Committee, listed residents' grievances toward the Korean government: no consultation with locals regarding local interests and needs; no discussion of alternative sites to P'aensŏng and P'yŏngt'aek; no environmental impact study; lack of transparency regarding the relocation process and costs.[108] He railed against the "unilateral decision" of the government and its penchant "to prioritize ROK-U.S. relations over Korean people who live off the land." He clarified that private interests should not necessarily come before the public interest but that "on a human level, this is wrong, inhumane to have families uprooted."[109]

The central government promised 1.4 trillion *wŏn* to P'yŏngt'aek City to cover costs of the troop expansion and to assist local development. Sheila Smith, an expert on the politics of U.S. bases in Japan, observed that "as in the Japanese case, the national government is offering the

P'yŏngt'aek government considerable subsidies for urban development, special legislative exemptions for community facilities, and tax exemptions."[110] Central and provincial officials have also emphasized that they will not abandon P'yŏngt'aek to become another militarized city; rather, they have promised to help develop it into an international "peace city," regional educational center, and free trade zone.[111]

Despite these efforts, anti-expansion activists continued their resistance. Many have viewed the government's promises as propaganda to influence local public opinion. For example, Lee Hosŏng of the Committee against the Expansion of P'yŏngt'aek, who was seconded to P'aengsŏng from the committee, criticized the local government for raising the hopes of P'yŏngt'aek citizens that Seoul will grant extra development aid as part of the base expansion for the USFK. He cited examples of "traditional areas where U.S. bases have been—Kunsan, P'och'ŏn, Tongduch'ŏn, Munsan—which experienced limited development and rather became "closed economies" catering to the U.S. troops. He feared that P'yŏngt'aek will face additional restrictions on building construction and infrastructural development to accommodate the U.S. military's priorities. Additionally, he feared a decline in tax revenues and a consequent economic burden on P'yŏngt'aek's citizens since no tax revenues would be collected from the expanded land space the U.S. military would occupy. He predicted the decline of the P'yŏngt'aek area as inevitable.[112] Anti-expansion activists also took great offense at the Kyŏnggi Provincial Council's passing of a resolution to support the expansion of the P'yŏngt'aek area back in March 2003. They opposed the "antidemocratic" procedures of the provincial council as well as the repositioning of U.S. troops from Yongsan into their area.[113]

But the central government, for its part, often found the opposition's tactics undemocratic and outright frustrating. For example, it had invited residents to public meetings in 2004 to articulate their priorities concerning the expansion. But they apparently were not constructive. During an interview with this author and other researchers in November 2004, Deputy Minister of the Special Commission on the USFK Yu Chŏngsang stated that "public hearings are done," meaning that they are of no use, because when the government tries to hold them, they get the same response: *panghae* (resistance/oppositional intervention) by anti-expansion activists. He offered an example: the public hearing that his office had scheduled for September 1, 2004, at P'yŏngt'aek University had been preempted by anti-expansion groups.[114]

Conversely, the opposition believed that the government was insincere in its outreach efforts because it had already made a *fait accompli* decision to use P'yŏngt'aek for USFK purposes, leaving residents no real choices. In addition, they believed that the government heeded the views of business lobbies that sought to benefit from the expansion. In Yi Hosŏng's view, the government then "interprets" such support as reflective of positive interest on the part of the locals. Yet government officials like Yu Chŏngsang and Yu Insŏn emphasized that local citizens' needs and interests were incorporated into the special legislation on P'yŏngt'aek.[115]

In addition, there are local interests who seek to gain from the increase in U.S. troops, including merchants who cater to U.S. military personnel, construction companies, landowners who seek to strike it rich by selling off their land, and farmers who wish to quit their traditional way of life. It is interesting to note that P'yŏngt'aek was one of the very few places in Korea that sponsored pro-U.S. rallies in early winter 2003 when the national trend was the opposite. During these demonstrations, veterans' organizations as well as self-proclaimed patriotic associations spoke out against sympathizing with North Korean Communists and for welcoming the expansion of U.S. forces into the region.[116] Both groups favoring expansion and those opposing it continued to use the streets, local government offices, and the media to publicize their views.

By 2005, the government's *Yonhap News Agency* reported that the central government "took legal control of about 3.49 million *p'yŏng* (one *p'yŏng* equals 3.3 square meters) [around Camp Humphreys] and has since been seeking to clear the area of people who remain there."[117] Although many farmers in Taech'uri and Toduri eventually yielded and accepted the government-determined lump sum in return for the expropriated land, the holdouts—about 200 farmers—put up fierce resistance. In addition to petitions, demonstrations, a protest tour around the country on tractors, and candlelight vigils that ran for 935 days,[118] some engaged in new planting of rice crops as a way to keep the government out. The government in turn escalated its tactics: "In a last-ditch effort to halt farming and ensure the occupants' eviction, the [defense] ministry sent thousands of troops [and riot police] to help build a barbed wire fence around the area near the U.S. camp"[119] and evicted the residents in spring 2006.[120] The Ministry of Defense also threatened violent protesters with punishment under military law for what a spokesman called a 'premeditated frontal challenge to authority.'"[121]

Analyzing the *kiji undong* and the politics between local and national actors demonstrates that organizational politics is actively at play; simply put, where you sit determines what you see. And often, local and central units cannot see eye to eye because of their different structural parameters and mandates. Interviews with MoFAT officials revealed that naturally, local governments have local issues on their minds, specifically residents' welfare, opposition to housing U.S. bases even if they support their presence in Korea, and environmental contamination. As one official stated, "Local governments don't think about national security or the national interest."[122] These MoFAT officials found that Seoul metropolitan government officials were almost solely focused on getting the Yongsan Garrison moved and on environmental pollution/contamination from the bases. Also, they adamantly insisted that the U.S. must be subject to "our domestic laws."[123] Another official stated that such views are understandable because local residents ask questions and demand accountability from their local governments, but when it comes to U.S. bases, "local officials can't even explain the problem or represent their constituents' interests because they have no legal access to the U.S. bases."[124] However, the MoFAT—and the MND to some extent—is by definition "outward" in orientation, is obligated to observe the legally binding Status of Forces Agreement, and, like other agencies of the central government, has "larger [national] concerns." Its constituency is not local residents but foreign governments and embassies (and the USFK), along with international organizations. [125]

DECENTRALIZATION IN EAST ASIA

South Korea had good company when it underwent decentralization in the 1990s: Both Japan and the Philippines, U.S. allies and hosts of U.S. military facilities and personnel, undertook a similar process during the same decade. Concerning Japan, the United States, which was motivated by a desire to liberalize the Japanese economy, pressured the highly centralized Japanese political establishment to democratize. Fueled by economic frustration and American nationalism,[126] "Japan-bashing" became commonplace in the United States. "Senator John Danforth publicly referred to Japanese as 'leeches' as U.S. politicians began to publicly blame the Japanese for the $59 billion bilateral trade deficit."[127]

Of course, internal demands for decentralization were also at play. Takashi Inoguchi wrote that the "United States government may not have been the only actor engineering the 1993 dismantling of the LDP's one-party dominance; nevertheless, it played an important part."[128] The year 1993 ushered in Morihiro Hosokawa as prime minister, whose particular cause was deregulation and decentralization. The U.S. government found a Japanese politician who was willing to push a political and economic liberalization agenda, but one of those agenda items, decentralization, had the effect of redistributing power to local governments and civil-society organizations (CSOs) in the localities that house U.S. bases, most prominently Okinawa. For the United States, Okinawa Governor Ota's challenge to central authority and the hegemony of the bases in Japan-U.S. relations, a popular referendum on the bases and the blocking of the construction of a U.S. air station at Henoko, and other policy initiatives by residents were just some of the costs—for the U.S.-Japan alliance—of local empowerment. Decentralization and local empowerment in Japan caused serious and enervating headaches for the managers of the U.S.-Japan alliance as they did for the managers of the U.S.-Korea alliance.

But decentralization and democracies do not necessarily generate the same strains on U.S. alliances and access to host territory everywhere. In the Philippines, the logic of decentralization yielded a very different outcome: eager support for U.S. troop presence through the Balikatan ("shoulder-to-shoulder") military training exercises in 2002. Initiated by the United States as a way to address Abu Sayyaf activities in the southern island of Mindanao, Balikatan turned the Philippines into the Asian front in the war against global terrorism. Although the arrival of 660 U.S. troops, with the purported goal of training 5,000–7,000 Philippine soldiers to hunt down Abu Sayyaf members, created a political crisis in Manila, the locals welcomed the Americans in uniform. For example, when in January 2002 the U.S. troops arrived in Zamboanga City, Mindanao—the site of their training camp—they were greeted with friendly placards: "Welcome back, GI Joe."[129] Later in March, Zamboanga residents "staged a large march . . . to thank the Americans for their presence."[130]

Although the Filipino public held a favorable view of the U.S. military presence in the southern islands, the people of Basilan, where the actual exercises were concentrated from winter through July 2002, were particularly eager to host the foreigners. According to the *Manila Standard* (July 30, 2002), "before the [U.S.] soldiers came, the Basilan folk lived in constant fear. It was, for them, a hellish existence as the Abu Sayyaf bandits sowed their seeds of terror on the island and neighboring areas. Some of the Basilan women were raped and killed; many of their men and children were forced into servility or slaughtered by the bandits during murderous orgies." So, official sighs of relief at the American presence seemed logical: "'I trust the Americans,' said Wahab Akbar, a former Muslim rebel who had become the island's governor. 'We're very thankful the U.S. government has not abandoned this corner of the world.'"[131]

Pro-Americanism stemming from the U.S. troop presence was the prevailing sentiment in the southern islands throughout 2002. By contrast, a small minority of left-oriented students, activists, and intellectuals staged public demonstrations against Balikatan and U.S. hegemonic policies, including daily protests in front of the U.S. Embassy in Manila during the winter of 2002. They carried "Yankee Go Home!" signs and by late February burned American flags at rallies (some of which counted up to 2,000 people). They campaigned aggressively against the re-entry of U.S forces into the Philippines on two grounds: nationalism and Philippine sovereignty, and constitutional authority. For many Filipinos, the return of American soldiers was not only a reminder of a bygone colonial era, but also a source of fear that the U.S. was seeking to reclaim former bases that had been returned in the 1990s. As one Manila resident put it, "I think that the American government would be happy to have us as a colony again." Such suspicions were spray-painted on Manila's street curbs: "U.S. troops out now."[132]

The relationship between the center and the localities significantly determines the nature and force of bases activism and their effect on policymaking. Although leftist students and intellectuals in the Philippines began targeting the U.S. bases and the local camp towns as incarnations of American neo-imperialism and militarism as early as the 1960s and 1970s, they were never able to mobilize the larger population around such issues. Their successors issued statements and protests against Balikatan, the U.S. war in Iraq, and their government's support of the George W. Bush administration, but they were ineffective. For one, they formed a very small minority, and second, the ideological and social gap between them—intellectuals and urban activists concentrated in Manila—and the poor villagers of the southern islands was very wide. For the residents of Basilan and Mindanao, the U.S. military presence was more about immediate daily survival, as long as the Abu Sayyaf and other "bandits" could be eliminated. They, especially the Muslim populations, were not enamored of the U.S. presence, but poverty and underdevelopment bound the various communities together to support the temporary presence of U.S. forces.

In Japan, despite the politicization of the bases and the political activities in Okinawa that targeted the U.S. bases and the Japan-U.S. SOFA—for example, the referendum on the U.S. bases, legal battles with Tokyo over base-related policies, and widespread media coverage of citizen movements—mainland Japanese activists never adopted the cause as their own. (See chapter 4 for a more detailed discussion of Okinawan activism.) The fact that the overwhelming majority of U.S. forces resides on an island whose cultural and historical identity is already marginal to the mainland's meant that overlapping interests, CSO personnel, and coalitions were weak. However, South Korea's much smaller and intact land mass makes communication and travel between Seoul and the localities much more accessible. Plus, there is no historical separation per se between Seoul and the countryside, especially since the late 1970s and the 1980s when the democracy movement made the bridging of the urban-rural gap an integral part of activism.

Additionally, democracy activists and radical students began targeting U.S. military camp towns in the mid- to late 1980s as symbols of subjugation by the U.S. government and its authoritarian "lackeys," former presidents Chun Du Hwan and Roh Tae Woo. And after the murder of Yun Kŭmi, a former prostitute, by Private Kenneth Markle in 1992, military camp towns increasingly became incorporated into CSO activism on foreign policy, national security, and reunification issues (see chapters 3 and 5). The growth of such activism was part and parcel of the dynamic spread of civil society participation in politics.

In tandem with decentralization in the three countries has been the exponential growth of and public interest in civil society organizations (CSOs, including nongovernmental organizations [NGOs], nonprofits [NPOs], and transnational networks), local residents' associations, and volunteerism, such that Tadashi Yamamoto argues that "the development of civil society itself has become the issue of governance."[133] In the 1990s, East Asian CSOs broadened and diversified their issue areas, ranging from consumer rights, social welfare, political reform, environment, and human rights to peace, defense spending, national security, and troop deployment to Iraq. In the Philippines, NGO communities regarded the Local Government Code and the potential for new "people power" as "arguably the most significant legislation passed under the Aquino administration."[134] The code empowers local governments by substantially increasing their access to financial resources,[135] enhancing their regulatory powers, and broadening their authority over planning, development, and social service provision. In order to facilitate capacity-building and delivery of services, the central government transferred tens of thousands of workers from central bureaucracies to localities: "The Department of Health alone devolved forty-five thousand staff—two thirds of its total personnel—to provincial and municipal government from 1992 and 1994."[136]

It is also important to recognize that the identity and interests of

NGOs in the Philippines have become moderate and society-oriented rather than state-oriented since democratizaton. That is, they believe that societal changes must occur first before the state can act constructively, whereas before democratization, most civic organizations were either pro or anti-state (Marcos). NGOs also tend to be development-oriented, reflecting economic rather than national security priorities in the Philippines. It is also not a coincidence that heavy funding by foreign/international sources, particularly the U.S. Agency for International Development (USAID), tends toward moderation in issue orientation and political activities. In general, NGOs in the Philippines have paid less sustained attention to security issues than socioeconomic ones. This is in stark contrast to Korea, where economic development is no longer a driving policy concern, but national security, regional balance of power, and reconciliation/reunification with North Korea are hot issues.

In Korea, the major resistance to U.S. base expansion has passed, since the Korean government's authority—and use of force—was exercised, but the government's power to seize private land came with political costs. Various human rights groups within and outside Korea have criticized the treatment of villagers and called for petitions and other forms of protest against the Korean government. For example, Amnesty International circulated a statement which included the following depiction and called on the government to release the activists who were arrested at the sites of protest:

> The residents of Taech'uri village, mostly farmers in their 60s and 70s, suffered bloodied noses and were pushed over while resisting the latest eviction attempt on 15 March and during an earlier attempt to evict them on 6 March. They say the compensation offered will not be enough to buy equivalent land elsewhere and their livelihoods are at stake.[137]

Anti-expansion activists have continued to network in cyberspace and international conferences to publicize their cause. American antiwar groups, such as ANSWER and Code Pink, which protested against the U.S. war in Iraq, sponsored activists from Korea at events such as P'yŏngt'aek International Solidarity Night in Los Angeles in July 2006. The Korean activists also traveled to Washington, DC, San Francisco, and New York. In September 2006 (American) Veterans For Peace (VFP) sent a delegation to Korea to participate in a march and rally for P'yŏngt'aek farmers. VFP urged Americans to support "the just struggle of the P'yŏngt'aek farmers against the unnecessary, dangerous expansion of the U.S. military base in P'yŏngt'aek *by writing a letter to our members in the Congress, especially to members of both Armed Services Committee* (emphasis in the original).[138] The Italian NGO Centro Internazionale Crocevia (CIC) also covered the P'yŏngt'aek issue and urged Italians and others to write letters of protest to President Roh Mu Hyun and other high-ranking officials of the Korean government.[139] As the next two chapters will show, local politics can easily become more than local and occupy the attention of not only domestic governments but also that of domestic and international CSOs.

NOTES

1. Ho-Keun Song, "Local Government and Social Development: Leadership, Development, and Participation" (paper presented at the conference "New Developments in Local Democracy in Asia: Appraising a Decade of Experience, Problems, and Prospects," Seoul National University, Seoul, April 8–9, 2002), IV-3-3.
2. Ibid.
3. Jung-Hoon Lee, "Globalization, Nationalism, and Security Options for South Korea," in *Democratization and Globalization in Korea: Assessments and Prospects,* ed. Chung-in Moon and Jongryn Mo (Seoul: Yonsei University Press, 1999), 240.
4. Ibid.
5. Ibid.
6. Kyoung-Ryung Seong, "Delayed Decentralization and Incomplete Democratic Consolidation," in *Institutional Reform and Democratic Consolidation in Korea,* ed. Larry Diamond and Doh Chull Shin (Stanford, CA: Hoover Institution Press, 2000), 77.
7. Bong-Scuk Sohn and Chung-Si Ahn, "Citizen Participation in Local Governance in South Korea" (paper presented at the conference "New Developments in Local Democracy in Asia: Appraising a Decade of Experience, Problems, and Prospects" (Seoul National University, Seoul, April 8–9, 2002).
8. Larry Diamond, *Developing Democracy: Toward Consolidation* (Baltimore: Johns Hopkins Press, 1999), 124.
9. Kyoung-Ryung Seong, "Civil Society and Democratic Consolidation in South Korea: Great Achievements and Remaining Problems," in *Consolidating Democracy in South Korea,* ed. Larry Diamond and Byung-Kook Kim (Boulder, CO: Lynne Rienner, 2000), 105.
10. For general discussions of the institutional and political tensions surrounding decentralization, see Diamond, *Developing Democracy,* 132–139; Desmond King and Gerry Stoker, eds., *Rethinking Local Democracy* (London:

Macmillan, 1996), chapters 1 and 2; and Dilys M. Hill, *Democratic Theory and Local Government* (London: Allen & Unwin, 1974), chapter 8.

11. Ilpyong J. Kim and Eun Sung Chung, "Establishing Democratic Rule in South Korea: Local Autonomy and Democracy," *In Depth* 3, no. 1 (1993), 212.

12. Diamond, *Developing Democracy*, 149.

13. Ibid.

14. Gi-Yong Yang, "Attitudes, Issues and Agenda for New Relationship between Local Communities and the USFK" (working paper, Pukyong National University, November 5, 2004).

15. On the dismantlement of the 1949 Local Autonomy Law and the centralized selection of local officials, see UNESCAP, Human Settlements section, "Country Paper: Republic of Korea," in *Local Government in Asia and the Pacific: A Comparative Analysis of Fifteen Countries* (n.d.), www.unescap.org/huset/lgstudy/country/korea/korea.html (accessed March 24, 2009).

16. People's Solidarity for Participatory Democracy, *Ch'amyeo sahoe* (Participatory society) (April 2002), 28–29.

17. For a longer discussion of local grievances against U.S. troops, see Katharine H. S. Moon, "Citizen Power in Korean-American Relations," in *Korean Attitudes toward the United States: Changing Dynamics*, ed. David Steinberg (Armonk, NY: M. E. Sharpe, 2005), 233–240.

18. Jae-kyoung Lee, "Anti-Americanism in South Korea: The Media and the Politics of Signification" (Ph.D. diss., University of Iowa, 1993), 131.

19. Membership Training (MT) refers to consciousness/awareness-raising field trips and "internships" that were popular in the 1980s student movement (and continue today among university students). The aim was to break the division between the intellectual/educated elite and the masses in Korean society and to encourage students to witness, participate in, and assist in the life and labor of factory workers and farmers, in particular. The MT movement later diversified to include various field settings and social issues, including the *kiji ch'on* and related prostitution.

20. Eighth U.S. Army, (IR) Civil-Military Office, Album of Incidents and Civil-Military Affairs press clippings, English translation from Korean, "Good Image of This Land," most likely a *Dong-A Ilbo* report of June 18, 1971.

21. Ibid.

22. Katharine H. S. Moon, *Sex among Allies: Military Prostitution in U.S.-Korea Relations* (New York: Columbia University Press, 1997), 108.

23. Ibid., chapters 3 and 4.

24. Ibid., 83.

25. See ibid.

26. Jong Soo Lee, "The Politics of Decentralization in Korea," *Local Government Studies* 22, no. 3 (1996), 68.

27. "Inchon Groups Call for Moving of U.S. Base, Citing Environmental Harm and Obstruction of City Plans for New Boulevard," *Korea Herald*, January 17, 2001, www.koreaherald.co.kr (accessed July 12, 2001).

28. Interviews with a team of officials at the ROK Ministry of Foreign Affairs, Seoul, April 24, 2002.

29. Pyŏnggil Yi, "Pup'yŏng Migun Kiji Twich'atgi wa chiyŏk undong" (Pup'yŏng return of land and regional movement), in Chu Han Migun munje haegyŏll undongsa (The Korean people's movement for solution of U.S. Forces Korea Issues), *Nogŭlli esŏ Maehyangni kkaji* (From Nogunri to Maehyangni) (Seoul: Dosŏ Publishing, 2000), 131.

30. *Yonhap News,* September 10, 2000, english.yonhapnews.co.kr (accessed May 2, 2002).

31. For a brief history of Camp Market, see GlobalSecurity.org, www.globalsecurity.org/military/facility/camp-market.htm (accessed April 1, 2009).

32. "Inchon Groups Call for Moving of U.S. Base."

33. Pyŏnggil Yi, 128.

34. Ibid.

35. Ubyŏng Chŏn, "Pom i onŭn maŭl e saebom ch'atgi" (Finding a new spring in the village of spring), In *Nogŭlli esŏ Maehyangni kkaji,* 131.

36. Masahide Ota, "Governor Ota at the Supreme Court of Japan," in *Okinawa: Cold War Island,* ed. Chalmers Johnson (Cardiff, CA/Albuquerque, NM: Japan Policy Research Institute, 1999), 208.

37. Ho-Keun Song, "Local Government and Social Development," IV-3-3.

38. Ibid., IV-3-4.

39. See ibid. for a comprehensive discussion on the financial and other difficulties of meeting the development goals, as well as the gap in priorities and aspirations between urban area dwellers (including officials) and rural dwellers.

40. "Koreans Find Prime Property Near the DMZ," *New York Times,* January 15, 2006.

41. For a survey on local residents' and officials' concerns over these matters, see Gi-Yong Yang, "Attitudes, Issues and Agenda."

42. In December 2006, a U.S. serviceman shot and killed a fuel-truck driver servicing the base, alleging that he was an armed terrorist. The driver carried no weapons. This incident generated severe criticism of the U.S. presence and emboldened the Kyrgyz government to renegotiate the terms of the basing agreement.

43. Mark L. Gillem, *America Town: Building the Outposts of Empire* (Minneapolis, MN: University of Minnesota Press, 2007), 173.

44. Ibid., 44–45.

45. National Campaign for the Eradication of Crime by U.S. Troops in Korea, "Migun changabch'a e ŭihae sumjin tu yŏjungsaeng e chugŭm ŭl aedohamyŏ" (Statement of condolence over the death of the two schoolgirls killed by the U.S. armored vehicle), June 14, 2002, www.usacrime.or.kr (accessed September 24, 2002).

46. Ibid.

47. ROK Ministry of National Defense, "Mi 2 sadan kwedoch'aryangsago

kwallyŏn," (U.S. 2 ID track vehicle accident), news release, August 7, 2002, 3-3.

48. Ibid., 3-2 to 3-3. Also, interviews with officials at the North America Division, ROK Ministry of Foreign Affairs and Trade (MoFAT), echoed the urgency of improving local conditions for residents (Seoul, November 1, 2004).

In December, 2002, a Special Joint Task Force with the USFK to improve the implementation of the revised SOFA was established and in six months undertook "intense work to resolve the biggest issues" (e.g., USFK operational/training procedures, increased safety standards and traffic control, and environmental protection surveys). I obtained these documents from the MoFAT.

49. "S. Korea Widening Project to Help Prevent Repeat of 2002 Accident," *Stars and Stripes*, February 8, 2004, www.stripes.com (accessed June 24, 2009).

50. U.S. Forces Korea, "USFK Retains Jurisdiction, Takes Corrective Measures in 13 June 02 Accident," news release no. 020802, August 7, 2002.

51. Gillem, *America Town*, xv.

52. Ibid., 68–69.

53. Chang-hee Nam, "Relocating the U.S. Forces in South Korea: Strained Alliance, Emerging Partnership in the Changing Defense Posture," *Asian Survey* 46, no. 4 (2006), 617.

54. Ibid., 618. Nam cites U.S. Department of Defense, *Report on Allied Contributions to Common Defense* (Washington, D.C.: DOD, 2002), D-8.

55. Gillem, *America Town*, 79.

56. Ibid.

57. Ibid., 78.

58. Ibid., 94–103.

59. Ibid., 95.

60. James Cotton and Kim Hyun-a van Leest, "The New Rich and the New Middle Class in South Korea: the Rise and Fall of the 'Golf Republic,'" in *The New Rich in Asia: Mobile Phones, McDonald's and Middle-Class Revolution*, ed. Richard Robison and David S. G. Goodman (New York: Routledge, 1996), 198.

61. Ibid.

62. Ibid., 190.

63. Yang, "Attitudes, Issues, and Agenda," 6.

64. "Local Residents Protest Proposed Relocation of U.S. Military Base," *Korea Herald*, January 22, 2002.

65. Ibid. See also *Yonhap News Agency* in English, January 21, 2002 (Foreign Broadcast Information Service translation), in *Special Press Summary: Land Partnership Plan and Yongsan Relocation*, U.S. CINCPAC Virtual Information Center (January 31, 2002), 21.

66. Ibid.

67. "Local Gov'ts Push for Legislation on U.S. Military Facilities," *Korea Herald*, June 20, 2001 (accessed February 1, 2002).

68. Author interview with ROK Ministry of Foreign Affairs and Trade, North American Division, Seoul, November 1, 2004.

69. "NGOs to Launch Body for Legal Action on U.S. Troop-Related Incidents," *Korea Herald*, April 17, 2001 (accessed April 18, 2001).

70. Associated Press, "Activists Demand U.S. Troop Withdrawal from South Korea" July 19, 2001 (accessed March 29, 2003).

71. *Stars and Stripes*, Pacific edition, November 25, 2001 (accessed April 28, 2003).

72. "South Korea, U.S. Sign Land Swap Deal," NewsMax, March 29, 2002, www.newsmax.com/archives/articles/2002/3/29/61543.shtml (accessed July 7, 2003).

73. U.S. Forces-Korea, "Land Partnership Plan Questions and Proposed Answers," March 29, 2002. I obtained the documents from the USFK.

74. "South Korea, U.S. Sign Land Swap Deal," 2002.

75. See ROK Ministry of Foreign Affairs and Trade, North America Division, "Sŏlmyŏng charyo-LPP Hyŏbjŏng Palhyo" (Materials for explaining the LPP agreement), October 31, 2002, www.mofat.go.kr/main/index.jsp (accessed November 24, 2002).

76. Interviews with a team of officials at the ROK Ministry of Foreign Affairs and Trade, Seoul, May 8, 2002.

77. "Activists Demand U.S. Troop Withdrawal from South Korea."

78. *Stars and Stripes*, Pacific edition, July 28, 2001 (accessed April 28, 2003).

79. Green Korea United, "Report on Land Readjustment Plan," www.greenkorea.org/english (accessed March 5, 2002).

80. *Korea Times*, January 12, 2001, in *Special Press Summary: Land Partnership Plan and Yongsan Relocation* (provided by officials at MoFAT).

81. BBC, March 29, 2002, www.bbc.co.uk (accessed March 29, 2003).

82. Ibid.

83. *JoongAng Ilbo*, March 29, 2002, in usacrime.or.kr (accessed April 15, 2002).

84. Ibid.

85. ROK Ministry of National Defense, "LPP kwallyŏn kisa ch'amgo charyo," in LLP-related information materials, March 29, 2002 (provided by officials at MoFAT).

86. *Chosun Ilbo*, June 9, 2004, in "Reduction of U.S. Forces in South Korea Labeled 'Shocking,'" U.S. Department of State, International Information Programs, June 16, 2004, www.globalsecurity.org/military/library/news/2004/06/wwwh40616.htm (accessed November 16, 2004).

87. *Dong-A Ilbo*, June 8, 2004, in "Reduction of U.S. Forces in South Korea Labeled 'Shocking,'" in ibid. See also similar *Hankook Ilbo* article that follows the *Dong-A Ilbo* article.

88. "Lawmakers to Collect Signatures," *Korea Herald*, April 10, 2003 (accessed April 10, 2003).

89. "Korea, U.S. Differ on Base Relocation," *Korea Herald*, December 15, 2006 (accessed June 24, 2009).

90. "South Korea, USA Discuss Setting Timeline for Base Relocation," BBC International Reports (Asia), April 29, 2009 (accessed June 22, 2009).

91. *Korea Herald*, March 19, 1971; *Pacific Stars and Stripes*, July 15, 1971; "Feature: Slump Hits 'GI Town' throughout Nation amid Rumors of U.S. Troop Cut," CA News Service, July 10, 1970, found in files on community relations in the Office of International Relations, EUSA, Seoul.

92. Interview with an official of the Korea Special Tourist Association, Seoul, May 26, 1992.

93. "Along Korean DMZ, G.I.'s Ponder Order to Pull Back" *New York Times*, June 8, 2003 (accessed June 10, 2003).

94. Ibid.

95. Shifting Terrains Project (STP) interview, Yu Insŏn, Director of the USFK Relocation Task Force, Kyŏnggi Provincial Government, November 2, 2004.

96. Ibid.

97. "Base Closures Leave Locals Wondering," *Dong-A Ilbo*, September 8, 2006, english.donga.com (accessed June 22, 2009).

98. Ibid.

99. Ibid.

100. "Tongduch'ŏn Hopes Film Brings Support as Troops Leave," *Stars and Stripes*, January 23, 2009 (accessed June 20, 2009).

101. *Hankyore Sinmun*, June 9, 2004, in "Reduction of U.S. Forces in South Korea Labeled 'Shocking,'" U.S. Department of State, International Information Programs, June 16, 2004, www.globalsecurity.org/military/library/news/2004/06/wwwh40616.htm (accessed November 16, 2004).

102. *Dong-A Ilbo*, June 9, 2004, as cited in ibid.

103. *Hankyore Sinmun*, June 9, 2004, as cited in ibid..

104. STP interview, Yu Chŏng-Sang, ROK Deputy Minister, Special Commission on USFK Affairs, Office of the Prime Minister, Seoul, November 3, 2004.

105. STP interview, Yu Insun, USFK Relocation Task Force Office, Kyŏnggi Provincial Government, November 2, 2004.

106. "Evictions to Pave Way for U.S. Base Relocation," *Yonhap News Agency*, May 4, 2006 (accessed May 5, 2006).

107. STP interview, Yi Hosŏng, P'aengsŏng, November 2, 2004.

108. Interview, Paengsŏng, November 2, 2004.

109. STP interview, Kim Chi T'ae, Paengsŏng, November 2, 2004.

110. Sheila Smith, *Shifting Terrain: The Domestic Politics of the U.S. Military Presence in Asia*, (Honolulu: East-West Center, 2006), 35.

111. STP interview, Yu Insŏn, November 2, 2004.

112. STP interview, Yi Hosŏng, P'aengsŏng, November 2, 2004.

113. Katharine H.S. Moon, "Citizen Power in Korean-American Relations," 239.

114. STP interview, Yu Chŏng-Sang, ROK Deputy Minister, Special Commission on USFK Affairs, Office of the Prime Minister, Seoul, November 3, 2004.

115. STP interview, Yu Insŏn, November 2, 2004, Kyŏnggi Provincial Government, and interview with Yu Chŏngsang, Seoul, November 3, 2004.

116. *P'yŏngtaek Sinmun,* January 15, 2003, www.pttimes.com (accessed March 27, 2003).

117. "Evictions to Pave Way for U.S. Base Relocation."

118. Sang-Won Kang, "The Korean Anti-Base Peace Movement, Focused on P'yŏngt'aek," Global Network against Weapons and Nuclear Power in Space, April 17, 2009, www.space4peace.org/actions/gnconf_09/focus%20 on%20pyeongtaek.htm (accessed June 20, 2009).

119. *Yonhap News Agency,* May 4, 2006.

120. For an account by activists, see Land Research Action Network, "South Korea: US Military Expansion Plan Threatens the Right to Food of 200 Rice Farmers, Taech'uri, P'yŏngt'aek, Kyŏnggi-do Province," June 29, 2006, www.landaction.org/display.php?article=435 (accessed June 20, 2009). See also the documentary film *War in Taech'uri,* by Il-gun Chŏng (Purn Productions, 2006; available through Third World Newsreel, New York).

121. "U.S. Base Protestors Face Sentence under Military Law," *Chosun Ilbo,* May 8, 2006, english.chosun.com (accessed June 20, 2009).

122. Interviews with a team of officials at the ROK Ministry of Foreign Affairs and Trade, Seoul, May 8, 2002.

123. Ibid.

124. Ibid.

125. Ibid.

126. Japan bought Rockfeller Center, and so on.

127. Keith A. Nitta, "Paradigms," in Steven K. Vogel, ed., *U.S.-Japan Relations in a Changing World* (Washington, D.C.: Brookings Institution, 2002), 81.

128. Takashi Inoguchi, "Three Frameworks in Search of a Policy: U.S. Democracy Promotion in Asia-Pacific" in *American Democracy Promotion: Impulses, Strategies, and Impacts,* ed. Michael Cox, G. John Ikenberry, and Takashi Inoguchi (New York: Oxford University Press, 2000), 280.

129. www.worldpress.org/article_model.cfm?article_id=501&dont=yes (accessed November 19, 2003).

130. www.globalsecurity.org/military/library/news/2002/03/mil-0203 01-ss02.htm (accessed November 19, 2003).

131. *Washington Post* Foreign Service, January 28, 2002.

132. *Stars and Stripes* (Pacific edition), March 1, 2002, www.global security.org/military/library/news/2002/03/mil-020301-ss02.htm (accessed November 19, 2003).

133. Tadashi Yamamoto, *Deciding the Public Good: Governance and Civil Society in Japan* (Tokyo: Japan Center for International Exchange 1999), 104.

134. Terrence George, "Local Governance: People Power in the Prov-

inces?" in *Organizing for Democracy: NGOs, Civil Society, and the Philippine State,* ed. G. Sidney Silliman and Lela Garner Noble (Honolulu: University of Hawai'i Press, 1998), 228.

135. For details, see ibid., 225.

136. Ibid., 227.

137. Amnesty International, "South Korea: Elderly Farmers Forcibly Evicted for US Army Base" (press release, March 17, 2006), www.amnesty.org/en/library/asset/ASA25/001/2006/en/a0b7676cd44c-11dd-8743-d305bea2b2c7/asa250012006en.html (accessed July 28, 2009).

138. Veterans For Peace, "Report of the VFP Delegation to South Korea," October 5, 2006, www.veteransforpeace.org/File/pdf/Korea%20Delegation%20Report.pdf (accessed July 18, 2009).

139. Centro Internazionale Crocevia, "Rilasciate i contadini coreani subito! Scrivete la vostra indignazione alle autorità coreane" (Release the Korean villagers now! Express your indignation to the Korean authorities), semionline.croceviaterra.it/news/rilasciate-i-contadini-coreani-subito-scrivete-la-vostra-indignazione-alle-autorita-coreane (accessed July 18, 2009).

3. Protesting America

Cooperation and Conflict in Civil Society Activism

In the beginning months of 2003, by popular determination, South Korea seemed inhospitable, at best, and outright hostile, at worst, to maintaining close military cooperation with the United States. The massive "anti-American" protests during the winter of 2002–3 and the political activism behind them took many by surprise, but they did not emerge in a vacuum. For many years, Koreans' fundamental complaint against the United States and its relationship with Korea was the perceived inequality between the two countries and the disregard by both governments for the personal and social costs of hosting U.S. troops. In the early 1990s, activists and local residents of the *kiji ch'on* (camp towns near U.S. military installations) had attempted to focus public attention on and galvanize public support for these two basic grievances. They considered the revision of the Status of Forces Agreement (SOFA)—to grant Korea more power and authority as a sovereign (advanced industrialized) nation—and the removal of U.S. forces from Yongsan to be necessary solutions. The seeds of what later erupted in the early 2000s as nationwide and mainstream protests that rocked the alliance were sown by small numbers of disparate and sometimes random individuals and organizations throughout the 1990s.

In 1997, Father Mun Chŏnghyŏn, a Catholic priest who had been a political activist since his youth, began a campaign against the U.S. military in Kunsan—where the U.S. Kunsan Air Base is located—over a fee increase for runway usage by Korean civilian aircraft. Based on an earlier agreement, which was due to expire in early December, the runway served as a civilian airport for Korean air traffic. Local residents learned of the U.S. command's plans to negotiate a memorandum of understanding (MOU) with the Korean government for a three- to fourfold increase in usage fees and a doubling of the maintenance and renovation fees (from 25 to 50 percent), to which the Korean side would be obligated for a five-year period. Local newspapers assiduously covered the story, inciting Father Mun and other Kunsan leaders like Ch'oe Yŏngwŏn, a managing official of the Kunsan YMCA, to organize against the fee hikes. It was Ch'oe who first publicly raised the "injustice" of the USFK's plans and mobilized various residents. In September 1997, the Kunsan YMCA, a local association of Catholic priests, and the Kunsan branches of Korean Citizens for Economic Justice (Kyŏngsilnyŏn) and the National Alliance for Democracy and the Reunification of Korea (Chŏn'guk Yŏnhap), in addition to eighteen other groups, established the "Citizens' Committee to Stop the Fee Increase." Father Mun became one of the three co-representatives of the organization.[1] This group staged weekly demonstrations in the camp town and in front of the air base, demanding "local sovereignty" (respect for and protection of local residents' rights) and the revision of the SOFA to enable the exercise of Korean sovereignty.

Later on, the Citizens' Committee claimed relative success in getting the two governments to extend the negotiations for another three months and to agree to a gradual fee increase over a five-year period rather than a lump sum increase at the outset.[2] The Citizens' Committee also changed its name and focus to "Citizens' Committee to Reclaim U.S. Bases Land" and became famous for its "Friday protests" (which later got changed to Wednesdays) and their "five-point" demands: (1) SOFA revision; (2) U.S. payment of "rent" for land use; (3) elimination of and accountability for U.S. crimes against Korean civilians; (4) the release of unused public lands; and (5) resolution of environmental problems. Many of these issues became part and parcel of the larger *kiji undong* (bases movement)[3] in the late 1990s and early 2000s.

Contrary to popular belief, *kiji* activism was not about emotional and irrational eruptions of nationalist sentiment. Rather, it involved the kind of careful, rational issue selection, prioritizing, balancing of internal capabilities with external resources, mobilizational appeal, and issue framing that all social movements must consider if they are to have any impact on the larger society and those in positions of authority. Second, any pre-existing anti-American and/or nationalist sentiment was not the driver behind the motivations and actions of the movement; only a very small minority of the coalition participants, represented predominantly by Chŏn'guk Yŏnhap and Hanchŏngnyŏn (National Association of University Student Councils), held a purely ideological anti-U.S. and anti-bases agenda. A third and related point is that contrary to common perceptions by Korean and U.S. policy elites and many in the media, the movement had no monolithic intention or organizational capacity to act against the alliance or the United States.[4] To the contrary, as a coalition movement, it was riddled with infighting over leadership, goals, methods of activism, gender conflicts, issue framing, and other forms of discord. At the same time, disparate groups, large and small, urban and rural, veteran activists and newcomers to collective action, learned to compromise, agree to disagree, build social capital, and make new connections over issues and among the participants. At the outset of the collectively authored book *Nogunri esŏ Maehyangni kkaji* (From Nogunri to Maehyangni), which documents the history and purpose of the *kiji*/bases movement, the publication committee introduces the book by stating that it is the work of numerous individuals who held very different opinions on the issues raised in the book and that there was no great effort made to unify the perspectives.[5]

KIJI UNDONG (BASES MOVEMENT): THE START

"We need to do some *pan-Mi* (anti-American) activism, don't we?" Father Mun propositioned some younger activists whom he had called down to the countryside from Seoul in 1999. "By doing activism, we can try to change the SOFA," he continued. Ch'a Migyŏng, a leader of a new nongovernmental organization (NGO), the Korean House for International Solidarity (KHIS), replied, "If we want to get the SOFA revised, we should not just bring together a bunch of (former) *pan-Mi* activists." Later in 2001, while preparing Father Mun for his first trip to Washington, DC, as a representative of People's Action for the Reform of the SOFA (PAR-SOFA), Ch'a urged him not to unleash his anti-American rhetoric: "Please, I beg you, don't go around yelling Yankee Go Home! If you do that, Americans will not want to join in solidarity with us."[6] During many hours of formal interviews and informal conversations with me in 2002, Ch'a elaborated on her reasoning: (1) individuals willing to do activism, despite the fact that they probably had participated in anti-American demonstrations as college students in the 1980s, were not available (they have become housewives and "salarymen"); (2) the NGO scene in Korea was so crowded and diverse that a narrow focus by a few on the SOFA or the U.S. military would be ineffective; and (3) globalization requires and enables transnational cooperation and dialogue, and not a simplistic anti-U.S. stance.

Ch'a was in her thirties at the time and Mun in his sixties. Ch'a came of political age in the 1980s, as part of the 3-8-6 generation. She was influenced by the left-leaning activism of the student democracy movement of the 1980s, but by the mid-1990s had set up one of the first NGOs in Korea with the express purpose of doing transnational and international advocacy on a wide range of political and social issues (KHIS). Father Mun was a veteran of anti-government activism for much of his adult life, had been jailed under the authoritarian regimes, and was a militant in his approach to politics and style of political expression. Mun came from the older generation of *t'ujaeng* (struggle) fighters in the *minjung undong* (people's movement) of civil society activists.[7] Members in this camp were influenced by leftist, anti-imperialist, and ethnonationalistic views and had exercised their political muscle in the anti-authoritarian movements of the 1970s and 1980s. They were used to expecting confrontation with the establishment and toeing a thin line between political expression and self-sacrifice in the face of repression. Ch'a, on the other hand, represented the younger generation of more professionalized NGO workers, with a clear identity as a legitimate political actor in Korea's civil society—not a dissident—and as a citizen of the world. Although she was influenced by the *minjung* culture in which she came of political age, Ch'a was interested in issue-oriented advocacy and in building bridges with likeminded people in the *simin undong* (citizens' movement) camp of civil society.

In addition to her work for PAR-SOFA and activism around the 2000 Maehyangni bombing incident (discussed below), Ch'a led some of the first advocacy projects for female foreign workers (and continues to do so), and while involved in *kiji* issues, she led a grassroots campaign to offer apologies and assistance to Vietnamese civilians who had experienced violence at the hands of Korean soldiers during the Vietnam War. "People-to-people reconciliation" was her aim, and personal responsibility and accountability as a citizen in a globalized world was her claim to politics. The contemporary bases movement reflects the political experiences and expectations of both the old guard and the new guard of activists.

Before PAR-SOFA was launched, the National Campaign for the Eradication of Crimes against Civilians by U.S. Troops (Undong Ponbu) had been in operation since 1993 with the purpose of raising public attention to various incidents of violence, crime, and unrest allegedly and actually perpetrated by U.S. service personnel in the various camp town areas. Chŏng Yujin was one of the co-founders and leaders. For many years before then, Chŏng had worked as a staff member at Durebang (My Sister's Place) in Tongduchŏn, the first counseling center established to serve

Korean women who worked as "entertainers" in the hundreds of Korean bars and nightclubs that catered to U.S. servicemen. She had started her work at Durebang as a form of political activism and *pan-Mi* expression (Chŏng also came of political age in the 1980s and participated in the student democracy movement). But over the years as she assisted the women who were considered social outcasts and moral pariahs in Korean society, her feminist consciousness and her understanding of the personal toll exacted on the *kiji ch'on* sexual laborers grew. After the brutal murder in Tongduch'ŏn of twenty-three-year-old Yun Kŭmi, a prostituted woman working in a camp town bar, by Private Kenneth Markle in October 1992, Chŏng joined hands with new partners to establish the National Campaign in order to investigate crimes against Korean civilians, disseminate information about the living and working conditions of camp town residents, and pressure both U.S. and Korean authorities to protect and respect the lives and rights of Korean camp town residents. She codirected the National Campaign throughout most of the 1990s and then gained a post in the new national Human Rights Commission in the early 2000s. The National Campaign became a key member of the PAR-SOFA coalition.

Kim Yonghan, a resident of P'yŏngt'aek who in 1990 had begun his own campaign to oppose the relocation of U.S. military headquarters from Seoul (Yongsan) to P'yŏngt'aek, became the first chairperson of the National Campaign's Subcommittee on U.S. Crimes/Investigation of the Situation around U.S. Installations (Migun pŏmjoe mit kiji silt'ae chosa wiwŏnhoe). He also agreed to become the resident-expert on the subcommittee for the revision of the SOFA and to work with Prof. Yi Changhŭi of Hanguk University as the scholar-expert. Kim, unlike most of his fellow activists in the National Campaign, had no experience in activism and had not paid much attention to such politics before the events of the early 1990s. In an interview with me, he stated that he had "gotten wind of the proposed move of the Yongsan base to his home area through the newspapers and then looked around to see who else might have concerns about the proposed *ijŏn*" (move of U.S. bases to P'yŏngt'aek). Together with two friends, he held meetings to see if people wanted to work against the relocation of the base to their town, going door to door with flyers and pamphlets and holding meetings to discuss the issues. When he learned of Yun Kŭmi's murder in the fall of 1992, Kim called up the Tongduch'ŏn Minju Siminhoe (Democratic Citizens' Committee) and asked what he might do. He then went to Tongduch'ŏn to learn about "doing *undong*" (activism/movement) regarding the U.S. bases from people who were more familiar with the issues and experienced in activism. He called this his "self-education."[8] Kim became a leading figure in the PAR-SOFA movement.

With the active participation of Kim Yonghan in U.S.-base-related activism, the *sigol* (countryside) was no longer left behind on the margins of national activism and politics. The bases movement could not become solely a nationalist cause or a leftist cause; nor could it remain in the hands of experienced and committed activist elites in Seoul. The movement became as much about the rights of local governments and citizens as about challenging U.S. hegemony. It was also about improving citizens' access to information and policymaking on national security issues in tandem with redressing heretofore suppressed grievances. In the process of diversification, new political entrepreneurs came and went and new lines of solidarity were tied and severed. In addition, the organizational agendas of various movement actors were forced to compete for influence and dominance, and clashes over goals, methods, and leadership occurred together with coalition-building, cooperation, and the generation of social capital among the participants.

CREATING A COALITION AND DEEPENING DEMOCRACY

Coalition activism explains how and why disparate activist groups, local officials, and residents successfully mobilized public sentiment around the issue of U.S. bases and troop conduct. The civil society organizations (CSOs) participating in the bases movement have represented a wide range of groups, ideological perspectives, issues, activist experiences, intensity of personal commitment, and political and policy agendas. Constituent groups have included the National Campaign for the Eradication of Crimes against Korean Civilians by U.S. Troops (Undong Ponbu); women's groups; religious activists; law professionals, including Lawyers for Democratic Society (*Minbyŏn*); human rights organizations; environmental organizations such as Green Korea United (GKU) and the Korea Federation of Environmental Movements (KFEM) academics; radical students; peace activists; both progressive and conservative labor organizations; and local residents and government officials. Small, localized groups have been able to voice their grievances and call for redress through larger, more well-known, and more powerful national civil society organizations, such as the Citizens' Coalition for Economic Justice (CCEJ or Kyŏngsillyŏn) and the People's Solidarity for Participatory Democracy (PSPD or Ch'amyŏ yŏndae). Large and more established organizations are considered instrumental to building successful coalitions because they can provide valuable resources like internal leadership, "organizational infrastructure,"[9] and public name recognition. In turn, these larger organizations with broader scope and expertise have become more familiar with grassroots matters related to life in the political and geographical periphery, the U.S. military camp areas (*kiji chiyŏk*). The bases issue has allowed groups and individuals at the center and the periphery of Korea's new civil society to eschew old habits of division and to create a new web of connections related to the U.S. military presence.

What is particularly interesting about the bases movement is that it has brought together groups and individuals that previously tended to identify themselves in opposition to one another. For example, Sunhyuk Kim has characterized the CCEJ as representative of "citizens' movements" (*simin undong*) in civil society, organizations that consciously sought to toe a moderate line in the 1990s, in contrast with the more radical "people's movements" (*minjung undong*) dominant in the 1980s. According to Kim, in the first half of the 1990s

> [t]he citizens' movement groups, such as the Citizens' Coalition for Economic Justice, the Korea Federation for Environmental Movement, and others, generated publicity and popularity for their campaigns for economic justice, environmentalism, fair elections, consumer rights, and gender equality. . . . [T]hey became dominant, exponentially proliferating and impressively outperforming the radical people's movement groups. Emphasizing that they would lead a new generation of social movements, the citizens' groups rejected the class-based and confrontational strategies of the past in favor of a nonviolent, peaceful, and lawful movement style and specific policy alternatives.[10]

In reaction, the more radical groups became "disconcerted and underwent a serious identity crisis."[11] Kim comments that civil society in the first half of the 1990s seemed "fragmented and even chaotic," torn between "'petty' interest groups and those committed to the 'great democratic revolution."[12] In the second half of the 1990s, both *simin* and *minjung* groups came together occasionally for nationwide campaigns, and organizations like People's Solidarity for Participatory Democracy (PSPD) emphasized bridging the divide between the two types of movements.[13] But as Kim points out, the two camps coexisted mostly in competition throughout the 1990s and maintained their differences in strategy and style.[14]

But the *kiji* movement of the late 1990s and early 2000s brought the two poles closer and gave them a common "national" purpose and occasions for cooperation and resource mobilization.[15] This occurred in the larger context of CSO efforts to unify, consolidate, and deepen their involvement in democratic politics. For example, in February 2001, two major coalition members of the PAR-SOFA, the CCEJ and GKU, forged a nationwide network of NGOs called the Solidarity Congress of Civic and Social Groups. Their initial agenda items—enhancing local autonomy, the abolition of the National Security Law, and the enactment of the Human Rights Commission Law—were issues that coincided with the interests of the bases movement.[16] In particular, the *kiji* coalition's work to expose and protest the dumping of formaldehyde into the Han River (February 2000) and the consequent official apology by the U.S. Forces-Korea (USFK)—the "first ever," as Korean newspapers and civic groups were quick to note—seems to have encouraged and emboldened civic groups to forge the broader Solidarity Congress.[17]

Fred Rose, the author of *Coalitions across the Class Divide: Lessons from the Labor, Peace, and Environmental Movements*, emphasizes that coalitions help decrease the parochialism and homogeneity among single-issue movements, like labor and environment, and enable formerly unconnected and opposing actors to "go beyond isolated interests or abstract values" that reproduce divisions.[18] He bases this observation on his study of the process by which disparate and opposing interest groups—labor, peace, and environmental movements—came together to push for military-to-civilian conversion of local economies in the United States in the late 1980s–early 1990s. According to Rose,

> [m]ovements [as distinct from coalitions] attract self-selected segments of society who share beliefs, experiences, and assumptions and exclude people with divergent perspectives. In general participants are drawn from fairly narrow class, race, or geographic backgrounds. Community organizations and single-issue movements can reinforce the exclusion of outsiders or the protection of local privileges.[19]

Such a tendency is stronger in mass organizations that rely on dues-paying members. Robert Putnam points out that although such associations are important, they play less of a role in building social capital because "[f]or the vast majority of their members, the only act of membership consists in writing a check for dues or perhaps occasionally reading a newsletter. . . . Their ties, in short, are to common symbols, common leaders, and perhaps common ideals, but not to one another."[20]

The CCEJ and the main green groups are examples of mass dues-requiring movements, and both are distinctly (urban) middle class in membership and leadership.[21] But Putnam misses the possibility that such organizations, through coalition work, can be "cross-fertilized" to diversify their interests and operations, at least in the short term. Having become major coalition partners in the PAR-SOFA, the larger, Seoul-based organizations had to broaden their agendas to include issues external to their organizational foci. Their members went out to the "field," to the countryside or regions (*chibang*), where most of the large installations and camp towns are located, in order to investigate alleged environmental damage and economic deprivation; to demonstrate in solidarity with the locals; and to debate, compromise and cooperate. These developments reflect what Larry Diamond has emphasized as crucial to the development of civil society and the strengthening of democracy: the extension of "multiple organizational ties that cut across and complicate existing cleavages and generate moderating cross-pressures on individual preferences, attitudes within civil society.[22]

Contesting and debating differences of opinion are also necessary for the development of civil society. Indeed, internal dissonance in the *kiji* movement abounded. It is clear from my interviews with some of the key activists that the biggest contention within the bases movement centered on defining the problem of the U.S. bases, as well as the necessary and practicable prescription to deal with them. Even if critical views of U.S. policy and the conduct of troops was generally shared by the *kiji* activists, the clash between the more ideologically nationalist and anti-U.S. leaders (e.g., Chŏn'guk Yŏnhap and Seoul Yŏnhap, Hanch'ŏngnyŏn) and those who were more moderate and issue-oriented (e.g., from the National Campaign and local autonomy/rights groups) was intense. Kim Yonghan went so far as to call these conflicts a "war of words" (*nonjaeng*), as the more ideologically anti-U.S. groups insisted that kicking out the U.S. bases (withdrawal or *ch'ŏlsu*) was the bottom line issue and solution, while the moderates insisted on confronting specific and known problems that individual civilians or locales face and then articulating specific demands for remedy.

PEOPLE'S ACTION FOR THE REFORM OF THE SOFA (PAR-SOFA)

At the outset, it was not clear that a political movement centered on local grievances regarding U.S. bases and the desire to revise the legalese in a treaty-like instrument (SOFA) would actually take off. Initiators like Father Mun and Ch'a Migyŏng could not foresee the progression of events that would put the PAR-SOFA in the public limelight as the umbrella organization for over 100 disparate groups. Regardless of their success as a social movement and the possible effects their activism might have on policy, Ch'a was clear from the start that, given the dynamic playing field of political activism in the country, cooperation with various established organizations and interests was necessary. In her initial response to Father Mun's query about doing *pan-Mi* activism, Ch'a insisted that they must reach out to issue-oriented groups, such as environmentalists, human rights activists, labor, and more, and that their work must be something that all these groups can do together.

PAR-SOFA was composed of a hodgepodge of disparate groups—from the predictable partners like the National Campaign and Lawyers for Democratic Society (Minbyŏn) to those that require a long stretch of the imagination, like groups seeking to protect Korean (film) screen quotas.[23] When I asked Father Mun to consider the pros and cons of working with such varied groups in his PAR-SOFA coalition, he laughed, acknowledging that some groups just "hang their nameplate" (*irŭm man kŏrŏ*) without contributing or participating in a substantive and consistent way, whereas he and his fellow committed activists were clear about what "action" in movement is: demonstrations, protests, petitions, and so on. Yet he was quick to add that when there are important occasions, like press conferences, the great many show up. He acknowledged, "This can be a real show of force at times. . . . We need the collective cooperation of these groups to give the SOFA *undong* size, widespread support, perhaps legitimacy."[24]

Indeed, Father Mun's perception is not unique among social movement actors, for scholars point out that "agreeing to lend a group's name to a common effort" is a regular occurrence among coalition movements.[25] Public legitimacy can serve as an important resource for activists who are intent on getting a movement off the ground, recruiting supporters and media attention, and gaining traction among political decision makers.

Activists in social movements play the same political game as any other keen political actor. They seek out individuals and organizations that can generate funds, workers and supporters, social connections, name recognition, office space and supplies, and other such needed resources. Resource mobilization theorists emphasize the rational cost-benefit decision making that organizations and individuals engage in when determining whether to join a movement or to invite new members into the movement. This approach emphasizes the organizational, tactical, and interactive dynamics among social movement organizations, rather than specific grievances that give cause to a movement or the identities that might sustain it.[26] By definition, resource mobilization brings disparate groups together with varying goals, commitments, and organizational cultures, and of course, resources. And the "strength of ties and their permanence can be related to the level of contribution of resources, including financial and human, along with the stability of those contributions, and to common efforts."[27]

In the *kiji*/bases movement, environmental groups turned out to be a significant resource and source of much-needed organizational support, technical expertise, and public legitimacy. According to Kim Yonghan, as he dove more deeply into *kiji* activism and the *panhwan* (return-of-land) movement, it became apparent that environmental issues were a big concern for camp town people but that he did not have the knowledge of the issues or a method of dealing with environmental problems. So, he approached Hwan'gyŏng Yŏnhap (Korea Federation of Environmental Movements, or KFEM) and met with its leading officials in order to explain the environmental problems around the U.S. bases and to ask them to join his cause. KFEM promptly rejected his proposition. To Kim's understanding, KFEM did not want to get involved in such controversial issues: "They said it was not the way they wanted to orient their group." So, Kim went next to Green Korea United (GKU), a brand new and smaller environmental group, and met with a few young, low-level officials. Apparently, they exhibited a "can-do" attitude and agreed to work with him. GKU set up a new position and named a person (Yi Hyŏnch'ŏl) to handle U.S. base-related matters (*Migun kiji silmu ch'aeg'imja*).[28]

KFEM was certainly the established organization, with national organizational and mobilizational reach. They were also international players—having partnered with Greenpeace International in 1999 to oppose the transfer of weapons-grade plutonium from France and Britain. Calling the scheduled shipment "Floating Chernobyl," the organizations had threatened protests and a naval blockade. Ch'oe Yul, then the secretary general of KFEM, had argued that "South Korea needs 'decisive action'" because the "narrow straits between Korea and Japan are about to become a plutonium freeway."[29] In 1997 they had played the leading role, with GKU and Greenpeace as coalition partners, in protesting and stopping plans by Taiwan to sell nuclear waste to North Korea.[30] But large and well-known CSOs face a more complex task of negotiating competing internal priorities and investment of resources, support from its membership or support base, and public perceptions of "image" and "approval." According to a PAR-SOFA leader, KFEM had been known and respected by the larger society for its investigational role and was viewed as a rational, issue-oriented, "pure" organization and not a radical rabble-rouser.[31]

GKU, on the other hand, was a relative newcomer to the environmental scene, much less encumbered by organizational structure and commitments, and in need of raising its name value among other CSOs, the media, and the general public. Kim Yonghan himself believed that GKU readily signed up because "they were a small, less known group." When I asked him why he hadn't approached them first, he replied: "They were too small." Kim admitted that he had wanted a big fish to join his cause.[32]

For the GKU, *kiji* activism not only provided opportunity for broader CSO involvement and public exposure but also an apt organizational and political "fit." GKU at its roots had an explicit orientation toward "healing and beautifying the divided land."[33] The component groups, including Paedal Nation, emphasized a nation-focused notion of the Korean land or soil as a common or unifying resource for Koreans on both sides of the Thirty-Eighth Parallel; reclaiming the national territory was as an environmental imperative. (One PAR-SOFA activist commented to me that the name of this group "smelled of nationalism."). So, for GKU, partnering environmental recovery as a cause with the reclaiming of USFK-used land made conceptual and practical sense.

Although KFEM considered itself and was recognized by society as a successful interest-oriented CSO that is representative of the *simin* movements, its origins lie in the dissident movements of the authoritarian period. According to Su-Hoon Lee, "[e]nvironmental movements in Korea in the 1980s were equal to democratization movements,"[34] and "South Korean democracy movements often disguised themselves as environmental movements in order to avoid political suppression"[35] because anti-pollution "was one of the few arenas in which the Korean military regime allowed public demonstrations."[36] Comparing environmental movements in East Asia, Yok-shiu Lee and Alvin So observe that many environmental organizations share a history of resistance to external domination (imperialism), authoritarian rule, and opposition to economic development measures that favored the elites and the rich at the expense of workers, farmers, and the environment.[37]

Many of Korea's contemporary environmental leaders cut their political teeth in the student/democracy movement of the 1970s and 1980s. For example, Ch'oe Yul, the founder and former secretary-general of KFEM, was imprisoned for six years by the Park Chung Hee regime for dissident activities as a student. After his release, Ch'oe embarked upon a new and fledgling environmental crusade in the 1980s. He co-founded the Korean Research Institute of Environmental Problems (KRIEP) with progressive Christian church leaders in 1982, which later merged with other environmental groups to form the Korean Anti-Pollution Movement Association (KAPMA) in 1988. Four of the eight members of the executive committee of KAPMA also had been democracy activists.[38]

Here it is important to point out that personal, political, and ideological orientations do not necessarily translate into organizational agendas and goals. Given the personal political histories of KFEM leaders and the ideological heritage of the environmental movement, KFEM should have jumped immediately on the bandwagon criticizing the U.S. bases, but it did not. According to a key *kiji* activist, it was not because individual leaders of KFEM were pro-American or lacking sympathy for the bases movement. Rather, KFEM's self-identified organizational purpose was to pursue work that was oriented toward research, investigation, public education, international collaboration, and policy influence through institutionally established channels (in addition to public demonstrations). Therefore, KFEM steered clear of activities that would be readily identified by the public and policymakers as *chaeya* (dissident) or *pan-Mi*.[39] As one veteran activist commented during a conversation in the spring of 2002, "most CSOs, as they grow larger and more influential, increasingly worry about what the public thinks." Put another way, individual CSO leaders can espouse nationalist sentiments or lean leftward in political views, but their organizational logic and mandate are separate priorities.

Conflating environmentalism and political dissent is a typical tactical approach taken by social movements that face high opportunity costs for political mobilization. From a comparative perspective, Jane Dawson's work on "eco-nationalism" in Russia, Lithuania, and Ukraine illustrates the instrumental role of environmentalism (specifically anti-nuclear activism) in social and political mobilization. Dawson states:

> In mobilizing against Moscow's nuclear power decisions, movement participants had the opportunity to explore not only their attitudes toward the environment but also their own roles as members of a political community. . . . While contesting and exploring precisely how far the shift in power from state to citizenry should go, members agreed that the state's monopoly over decision making should be eliminated. In all of the cases observed, resentment of Moscow's complete dominance over local decision making played a key and explicit role in mobilizing opposition to nuclear power.[40]

Similarly, in 1988, local protests over toxic nuclear and chemical plants in then Soviet Armenia turned into calls for the independence of Nagorno-Karabakh from Azerbaijan and its unification with Armenia.[41]

In Germany and Japan, too, the rise of environmental movements occurred in tandem with citizens' push toward the further democratization of state power.[42] Miranda Schreurs emphasizes that the 1960s German "student movement's concern with democratic decision making and the direction of national and foreign policies were later incorporated as central elements of the environmental movement."[43] Thus, environmental movements often ride on the broader challenges to dominant power. At the same time, environmental movements get used and coopted for non-environment-specific purposes by disparate interests. Focusing on Asia, Lee and So state that "[e]nvironmental perspectives and related arguments are always motivated by particular interests, which may not be based on genuine concerns for environmental and ecological integrity."[44] In other words, "environment" can serve as a form of "frame alignment" that gives outward coherence, political focus, and media coverage to an internally dissonant social movement.

FROM MOVEMENT POLITICS TO SOFA POLICY POSITIONS

The 1967 Status of Forces Agreement (SOFA)[45] is a legal document that outlines the mutual rights and obligations of both the United States and the Republic of Korea regarding permanently stationed forces and facilities. Its oversight ranges from the mundane (the use of specific facilities) to such grave matters as the murder of Korean civilians (and legal jurisdiction over the cases). Although it is primarily a regulatory instrument, Korean activists and the media have tended to regard it as a political symbol of U.S. power *over* South Korea. Put another way, the SOFA has become a mirror on Korean sovereignty, which *kiji* activists have viewed as compromised by U.S. power. They have singled out specific provisions or lack thereof regarding jurisdiction, custody (of the accused), environmental responsibility, and more to criticize the document as yet another "unfair treaty" in Korea's history of relations with big powers. When a sensitive issue arises, such as the 2002 deaths of the two girls who were run over by a U.S. armored vehicle, and the court martial and subsequent acquittal of the U.S. military drivers, civic groups are quick to claim the "violation of Korean sovereignty" and related powerlessness in a mantra-like manner. Korea is not exceptional in this regard.

For the most part, SOFAs are highly technical and colorless documents written in mind-numbing legalese. But they easily can serve as symbols of compromised sovereignty since they outline the rights, privileges, and restrictions regarding the presence and conduct of a foreign military and the host government's obligations and prerogatives. Each host government that formulates or revises its SOFA interests seeks to get more of its own demands met than to give in to those of the negotiating partner. And each host government tries to learn from the mistakes of other host governments and cut the best deal possible. For example, by comparison with other SOFAs that the United States has negotiated, the one with Iraq (which the Iraqi parliament ratified at the end of November 2008) goes out of its way to favor Iraqi sovereignty.

The US-Iraq SOFA is unique in several ways. First, it contains numerous and explicit references to the sovereignty of Iraq—in territory, airspace, cultural assets, laws, and political process—that simply do not exist in the SOFAs with Korea, Japan, or NATO. Phrases like "with full respect for the sovereignty of Iraq" or "with full respect for the relevant rules and laws of Iraq" abound. Second, even in the midst of warfare and daily threats to peace and stability, the SOFA with Iraq has a clear withdrawal deadline (at the time of ratification, December 31, 2011). By contrast, Korea and Okinawa (Japan) have no clear end in sight, and critics lament what they view as their government's weakness in pushing for finite terms of the foreign military presence. In their eyes, Iraq would appear to have achieved a miracle in its negotiations with the mighty United States, especially given the fact that the U.S. had initially wanted an open-ended agreement.

Third, whereas it took Koreans five decades to get the U.S. just to plan for its departure from urban areas, including Seoul, their capital, Iraqis built in the date of June 30, 2009. Fourth, astoundingly, U.S. military missions will require the consent of and coordination with the Iraqi government. In Korea, the U.S., as head of the United Nations Command, held operational control over not only its own forces but the majority of units in the Korean military until the Combined Forces Command was established in 1978. That was about twenty-five years after the permanent stationing of U.S. troops through the Mutual Defense Treaty. Fifth, the SOFA with Iraq gives full legal jurisdiction over civilian contractors in Iraq, whereas the agreement with Korea severely restricts Korean jurisdiction. Even with respect to the mundane matter of license plates on official vehicles used by the U.S. military, the proposed SOFA with Iraq mandates Iraqi plates, whereas as the 1960 SOFA with Japan set up a special category of plates for U.S. vehicles.

Finally, there are bonus features that simply don't exist in the other major SOFAs, such as a U.S. promise to help Iraq "obtain forgiveness of international debt" inherited from the former regime, "to achieve a comprehensive and final resolution of outstanding reparations claims inherited from the previous regime," and "to protect from United States judicial process the Development Fund for Iraq and certain other property in which Iraq has an interest." These and other U.S. commitments written into the document amount to policy and have nothing to do with the technical and procedural requirements and protocols related to the functioning of U.S. troops and facilities that constitute the pages of other major SOFAs. Iraq's SOFA with the U.S. is a gold-plated one in many respects. Yet these favorable terms for Iraq still are not be enough to stop political resistance to the U.S. presence.

The bottom line is that there is no perfect SOFA, and even if there were, committed opponents would find reason to oppose it. Korea is a good example. Since the 1990s, Korean political activists have turned the military SOFA into a household word by campaigning aggressively for its revision. The politicization of the SOFA has accompanied democratization and civil society development. During the authoritarian decades, local residents lamented over the weakness and or indifference of their own government to protect and promote the rights and welfare of citizens, but the anger did not center on the SOFA. For one, human rights were not observed by the Korean government, and the rule of law existed in name more than substance. During the 1970s and much of the 1980s, Koreans were busy fighting for the creation and recognition of rights by their own government; they did not project the focus on rights vis-à-vis a foreign government until the late 1980s when democratization and the first revision process took effect.

But with the dynamic growth of civil society and local power, the SOFA became a near-mantra during the revision process of 1995–2001. This period, which witnessed the massive proliferation of NGOs, especially around human rights, women's rights, children's rights, and the environment, marked the diversification of political actors and issues in the bilateral relationship between Korea and the United States. The central government lost its monopoly over foreign policy and national security discourse and decision making, as organized civic groups, "netizen" (Internet-citizen) networks, a multiplicity of media outlets, the National Assembly, local governments, and transnational activists inserted their voices and agendas into alliance politics.

The main point of contention has been over the issue of which country has legal jurisdiction over specific criminal cases involving SOFA personnel and custodial rights over the accused. Until the third SOFA revision of 2001, the Korean government could not obtain custody of the accused until he/she was convicted and until the appeals process had been exhausted. Moreover, for decades, the Korean government was restricted to a fifteen-day period within which to request criminal jurisdiction of a case, after which an "automatic waiver" provision would allow for U.S. jurisdiction. Korean citizens bitterly complained that such conditions reflected disregard for Korean law and that consequently, U.S. personnel accused of crimes against Koreans or Korean property were exempt or shielded from legal and moral accountability.

Accordingly, in the negotiations that led to the 1991 and 2001 revisions, the issues of jurisdiction and custody, respectively, became the centerpiece of the process. Since 1991, the USFK's access to the "automatic waiver" of Korean jurisdiction over a criminal case has been curtailed, such that the U.S. side must request jurisdiction in writing to the ROK Ministry of Justice, which then has twenty-eight days (with a possible fourteen-day extension) to provide a written answer. Absent the response, the U.S. assumes jurisdiction. As for custody of U.S. personnel, the 2001 SOFA granted more power to the Korean government, such that Korean custody upon indictment (and upon request) in twelve categories of serious crime (including murder, rape, kidnapping, arson, drug trafficking or manufacturing, robbery with a dangerous weapon, and drunk driving or fleeing the scene of an accident resulting in death) would be possible. In murder and rape cases, if the Korean police were to arrest a SOFA personnel in the act, in hot pursuit, or before he/she returns to U.S. military control, Korean custody would prevail, provided that due process rights specified by the SOFA be observed while the accused is in Korean pretrial custody or confinement.[46]

Members of PAR-SOFA, the coalition of over a hundred organizations, had campaigned aggressively for a revision of the SOFA since the late 1990s. Their cause was boosted by a series of accidents involving the USFK and Korean civilians. In February 2000, Private Christopher McCarthy of the U.S. Second Infantry Division admitted to strangling the barwoman/prostitute Kim Sŏnghui, although he stated that he did not intend to kill her. While under U.S. military custody (in accordance with the Status of Forces Agreement in force at the time), McCarthy escaped on the day of his trial before a South Korean court. He was recaptured about eight hours later. Outraged citizens exerted more pressure to revise the SOFA in favor of strengthening Korean legal authority and custody over alleged American perpetrators. The Korean court eventually tried, convicted, and sentenced McCarthy to eight years in prison. His appeal led to a two-year reduction.

Public sensitivity to the USFK rose even higher after a May 8, 2000, bombing accident by a U.S. fighter plane in Maehyangni, which angered and incited local residents to demand compensation for the alleged damages they had suffered. Civic groups and local residents held demonstrations near the Kunni strafing range in Maehyangni, calling for the cessation of drills, the closing of the base, and a formal U.S. apology for the alleged injuries and damage created by the practices. Some of the gatherings turned violent, as thousands of residents and activists "clashed with baton-wielding riot police."[47] About 6,000 riot police were deployed around Kunni in the volatile aftermath of the initial accident and protests.

Activists also employed a strategy of comparing the terms and application of various SOFA documents that the United States had with other countries, primarily Japan and NATO-Germany. Their fundamental claim was that upon comparing Korea's SOFA with those of Japan and Germany, "it becomes obvious that specific imbalances and differences exist. As a matter of fact, when creating a scale it evidently appears that the Korean agreement is the most disadvantaged and the German one the most favorable."[48] Specifically, Koreans took issue with the more limited legal jurisdiction over military "dependents," no stipulation of a time limit or "contract period" for the use of land or facilities, and higher environmental and labor standards, particularly in Germany.

Political elites were quick to pick up on citizen discontent and eager to echo their sentiments in universities; the National Assembly; the Ministries of Foreign Affairs and Trade, Labor, Environment; and the media. The *Korea Herald* reported that "[i]n a rare suprapartisan move, the entire political circle called yesterday for the revision of unfair and outdated clauses in the Status of (U.S.) Forces Agreement (SOFA)."[49] Ruling party (MDP) representative Ahn Dong-sun, a key member of the National Assembly's National Defense Committee, elaborated, "Some aspects of the SOFA are too one-sided and seem to define Korea as a third-rate country," and "[r]evising it is the task of our times."[50] Opposition party (GNP) representative Kim Won-ung published his own "white paper" on the unfairness of the SOFA: "SOFA is a document demonstrating the arrogance of a super power and comprises inequality, prejudice and discrimination, when compared with the similar agreements the United States inked with Japan and Germany."[51] He also took issue with the "free" use of land, allegedly almost 9 billion *won* ($7.8 million) worth of real estate, and complained that the USFK also "received discounts of 3.08 trillion *won* ($268 million) worth of electricity for the last 20 years."[52] Former MOFAT Minister Hong Soon-young was noted as the first Korean foreign minister or cabinet member in the Kim Dae Jung administration to speak out assertively about the need to revise the SOFA and reflect the public's sense of urgency to renegotiate the terms. In a speech to the Korean-American Association in Seoul, Hong stated: "A mature, responsible friendship between democratic and open countries finds lasting enrichment in equality and mutual respect"; "[t]he vitality of the friendship will be better sustained in the continued process of review and renewal."[53]

Although the SOFA had remained off-limits as a subject of public discourse and political debate during the authoritarian decades, political and societal elites came to develop a vested interest in addressing the issue of revision in the 1990s and early 2000s. For one, many were genuinely worried that "anti-American" sentiments would grow and radicalize, especially among the student population, if popular complaints were not addressed. Second, a new spirit of democratic nationalism inspired lawmakers in particular to press for more equal, "symmetric" relations with the U.S. And third, to do nothing would have made establishment elites look inept and impotent, a charge that many activists have made regarding Korean officials' allegedly deferential or yielding orientation toward the United States ever since the period of occupation and war. Even if nationalist sentiment inspired the politicians, both self-interest and maintaining "face" in the public eye pushed them to "talk tough" to the United States.

Local authorities chimed in with their own demands pertaining to the granting and use of land and facilities by the USFK, for example, calling for the removal of the "unilateral power and obligation of the [ROK] government to grant the areas and facilities requested by the U.S. Armed Forces, but to allow consultation with the local government under whose jurisdiction the land and/or landowner exist[s]."[54] Another often repeated demand has been to change the "free" use of granted lands to "contracted rental as found in Japan and the Philippines." More specifically,

> [a]greement on the use of bases and facilities should be concluded by the two States on the basis of the views of land-owner, be in individuals or local governments, without going through the Joint Committee. Such an agreement must contain stipulations on the period the contract remains valid, the rate of rent levy, and the conditions or procedures for renewal of the contract.[55]

Two more related demands were enumerated, the first being provisions requiring the USFK to "notify the relevant Korean authorities in case of deployment of dangerous weapons, conduct of dangerous military exercises, and occurrence of major accidents which may cause serious danger and damage to the safety of neighbouring population and community."[56] The other was to require the U.S. side "to seek prior consent for construction of buildings and facilities which are not directly for military purposes."[57] An example of the former came to life in the armored vehicle maneuvers that led to the deaths of the two girls. Objection to the construction of apartment buildings and a new hotel on Yongsan base is an example of the latter.

Specifically, local governments demanded that U.S. commands take the appropriate measures to request permits for construction and observe local zoning laws. The U.S. military leader found this to be particularly irksome and in violation of their understanding of the SOFA. During his report to the Senate Armed Services Committee regarding the 2001 revisions, General Thomas Schwartz stated:

> We also agreed to notify and consult with the ROK Government concerning planned modification or removal of indigenous buildings and concerning new construction or alterations that might affect the ability of local communities to provide relevant utilities and services, or may affect the public health and safety. This does not mean a veto, but consultation. Subsequent discussions regarding the implementation of this provision indicate that the ROK Ministry of National Defense still insists that USFK should submit building plans to and obtain building permits from local governments; however, that is inconsistent with our agreement to consult at the central government level. We cannot be forced into the position of having to deal with each and every local government. It is the responsibility of the central government to elevate any concerns they may have to the government-to-government level.[58]

As the SOFA revision process took shape, activists, local residents, and government officials also pushed environmental concerns into the public debate about the responsibilities of the USFK toward Korean citizens. Although the environment had never been a substantive topic for SOFA discussions from the early 1960s to the early 1990s, it became "crucial" in the mid-1990s.[59] In the earlier attempts to renegotiate the SOFA (1995–96) and at the outset of the 2000 round, the Korean government pressed a broad range of issues to be discussed, particularly environment and labor rights (of Korean nationals working on the U.S. bases), whereas the U.S. government was willing to discuss primarily the issue of criminal custody.

It was the intense activism of environmental groups, which actively networked between the regions and the capital, and their various public awareness efforts, media reports, and government lobbying, particularly to the new Ministry of Environment, that led to its official adoption as an indispensable agenda item. They especially wanted to oblige the U.S. government to pay for the cleanup and restoration of environmentally damaged areas, even after vacating or departing from such locations. But the U.S. was emphatically against such stipulations for the fear of setting a costly precedent in other parts of the world where its military installations were located and because such an obligation would be inconsistent with Article IV of the SOFA.[60] Therefore, the U.S. side agreed to the remediation of new incidents or spills but not to the environmental restoration of existing facilities and areas upon their return to the ROK government. Although environmental activists themselves were disappointed that environmental concerns and obligations did not make their way into the main body of the revised SOFA, their interests and power were reflected in the separate "Memorandum of Special Understandings on Environmental Protection," which outlines cooperation between the two governments on environmental governing standards (EGS) and the sharing of information and consultation regarding access to facilities and areas and related environmental risks. None of the PAR-SOFA organizations were satisfied with the revisions, and they had collectively stated their opposition to the ratification of the revised SOFA by the National Assembly. However, in some ways, the environment emerged the "winner" more than any other issue area and quickly became a salient framing device that helped bridge the gaps among the various activist types and their agendas.

In general, the coalition leaders were of four minds: (1) *ch'ŏlsu* (withdrawal), (2) *ijŏn* (transfer of bases to less urban and populated areas), (3) *panhwan* (reclaiming/recovering land used by U.S. troops), and (4) *chaejŏng* (revision of the SOFA). Clashes in terms of ideology and movement goals were severe, especially because Chŏn'guk Yŏnhap leaders tended to have a maximalist or zero-sum approach to politics and Korea's relations with the United States.[61] Formed in 1991 as an umbrella organization of several interest groups, including labor, university students, farmers, and unification activists, it boasts a self-identified history of opposing military authoritarian rule and advocating a Korean nationalism based on fighting for the masses (*minjung*). Well-known dissidents of the 1970s and 1980s such as Kim Dae Jung and Mun Ikhwan were inspiring forces in the *chaeya* movement from which the Chŏn'guk Yŏnhap descends. The organization continues to proclaim itself the representative of the *chaeya* legacy and its ideals.[62] In "preamble" and "platform" on its website, Chŏn'guk Yŏnhap explicitly states its purpose and goal to be the democratic fight for liberation and sovereignty from U.S. domination (*pan-Mi chajuhwa*) and the pursuit and achievement of a unified Korea. According to their documents, the rejection of all unfair and unequal treaties, including the SOFA, and the stationing of U.S. troops in Korea are integral to its *raison d'être*.[63]

When Kim Yonghan of P'yŏngt'aek first met with leaders of the Seoul branch of Chŏn'guk Yŏnhap (Seoul Yŏnhap) to discuss their potential cooperation in the *kiji undong*, he realized that it would likely be impossible to work with them because they were too ideological and committed only to the removal of U.S. troops from Korea. He argued with them that *ch'ŏlsu* (withdrawal) might be what the Seoulites want, but it is *not* what the *chibang* (regional/local) people want. He carried on this battle for several months in 1993, taking a train up to Seoul from P'yŏngt'aek each week to have hours of debates with the Seoul Yŏnhap people. Over time, advocates of withdrawal had to cede ground in the face of opposition by other organizations, and they reluctantly had to accept the fact that the public would not support a radical restructuring of Korea's alliance with the United States.[64]

The radicals then came to the decision that the transfer of the Yongsan base out of Seoul to the *chibang*, specifically P'yŏngt'aek, would be the next-best goal, given the impossibility of withdrawal. However, Kim Yonghan and other individuals with regional affiliations adamantly fought back, charging that what the radical Seoul activists sought was tantamount to "criminal activity" (*pŏmjoe haengwi*): pursuing NIMBY-ism[65] (*nimbi chuŭi*) at the expense of the poorer and less powerful regions, such as his hometown. Protesting against the "tendency to locate society's undesirables, such as trash disposal sites, crematoriums, cemeteries, and military bases in the countryside," he argued that the Seoul radicals were playing the same kind of "strong dumping on the weak" game that was so familiar to Korea's modern history of authoritarian politics. In a clever rhetorical twist, he raised his voice and threw Chŏn'guk Yŏnhap's ultranationalist rhetoric right back at them: "If Seoul people say that having the U.S. base in the capital is anti-nation, then why is it okay to have the base in the *chibang* (regions)? Are the *chibang* not part of the nation?"[66]

Other issue-oriented leaders, like Lee Sohŭi of the National Campaign, also argued that withdrawal was not possible within the current political and social context of the nation and that mobilizing people around it would be difficult (if not impossible). Rather, she insisted that the *kiji undong* should stay focused on specific problems or grievances regarding specific misdeeds by U.S. troops and the specific harm or damage that civilians endure, and aim to change the legal and administrative framework of dealing with them (she repeated the need for issue specificity over and over in her interview with me). For her and like-minded colleagues, this meant revising the SOFA.[67] For the more radical leaders, the explanations of the moderates boiled down to mere "reformism" (*kaeryang chuŭi*), whereas what they wanted was to "change the foundation" of the nation's relationship with the United States through collective action (*ponjil chŏk undong*).

The much-publicized protests at Maehyangni (Kunni strafing range) in spring 2000 proved to be a field test for which side—ideological or issue-oriented—would win. According to Kim Yonghan, it came down to *ch'ŏlsu* (withdrawal) versus *hwan'gyŏng* (environment). The former group argued that Maehyangni would not even be a problem if it weren't for the presence of U.S. bases. For the moderates, there were other ways to interpret and diagnose the problems at Maehyangni; they emphasized environmental concerns—for the land, people's health, and their livelihood. In a sense, the two opposing sides engaged in what one PAR-SOFA leader called the "spirit of competition" and agreed that "whoever yells the loudest will win over Maehyangni [as an issue]."[68] Apparently, during the protests, some of the pro-environment activists complained that the pro-withdrawal participants were "ruining" the demonstration.[69] Reconciliation of these opposing views could not be achieved. Kim Yonghan admitted that after all the hours of heated debate and mutual attempts to persuade the other side, it was better just to agree to disagree. "No conclusive agreement (*kyŏllon*) was possible, and fighting was just not worth it."[70]

For the National Campaign, Maehyangni represented the very kind of issue-orientation that they prioritized when setting their own organizational agenda: specificity of grievance and the verifiability of damage and loss to camp town civilians. Lee Sohŭi emphasized that Maehyangni and the revision of the SOFA were two big national issues—which were happening simultaneously—for *kiji* activists. Maehyangni in particular fit her criteria of a viable issue for movement politics: (1) evidence of specific and serious harm/damage to victims, (2) representative of other locales or communities facing problems related to the U.S. military, (3) potential to leave a "legacy" for *kiji* activism, (4) possibility of societal support (mobilization), and (5) possibility of achieving practical change or results (e.g., reparations for damage, apology from the U.S. side, change in military practice, and so on). For activists like Lee, the point was to raise an issue only if it reflected the real needs and experiences of the *hyŏn'jang* (real-life arena). She emphasized that it is the lived experiences and grievances of the local camp town people that give legitimacy to the organizational activity by Seoul-based groups and CSO elites.

O Tuhŭi, another veteran activist who worked closely with Father Mun in the bases movement, characterized the *changjŏm/tanjŏm* (strength/weakness) of Korean *undong* culture as *hŏhŏ silsil*. That is, when there is a big issue, people flock in numbers and exert their collective passion and voice, but just as quickly, they can disperse and dissipate. She referred to this as a "unique trait" among Koreans and commented that the peaks-and-valleys dynamic made sustained and focused activism on a given issue difficult.[71] But Korean social movements are not unique in this regard. As John McCarthy states, "The looseness of membership attachment to coalitions" versus the "tightness of attachment" (through bureaucratic control as well as contractual relationships) might be regarded as a "weakness of the coalition form giving it a transitory, more fragile character."[72]

Moreover, there was a significant divide between the interests of the periphery (*chibang* or regions/locales) and the center (Seoul-based activists) and between activists who saw their role as responding to the needs of individuals whose lives are most closely affected by the U.S. bases and those who saw their role as prescribing the interests of the nation. Multiple strands of political experience and intentions, commitment to the collective and particularistic causes (SOFA revision, environmental preservation, or other improvements in camp towns), organizational capacity, and protest styles encountered one another in the bases movement. And along with them, interwoven were various personality conflicts, past bonds of cooperation and/or contention among groups, and other such baggage. Instead of uniformity, most activist leaders eventually had to accept that serious differences of opinion cannot and should not be wiped away.

The *kiji undong* also became more appealing to earlier skeptics as the social movement grew and diversified its coalition membership and increased political momentum. In the initial stages of the bases movement, organizers like Father Mun and O Tuhŭi never imagined working together with the conservative Federation of Korean Trade Unions (FKTU). The progressive Korean Confederation of Trade Unions (KCTU) was a more natural and willing ally. And FKTU itself was wary about *kiji* activists' seemingly anti-American views and vocal demands to reform the SOFA. But to the PAR-SOFA initiators' surprise, the FKTU reached out to them and actively joined in the spring of 2000 and contributed funds to the PAR-SOFA movement. O stated during our interview that the FKTU was concerned about the KCTU's prominent position in the coalition, especially given that the fledgling *Woegi nojo* (U.S. Base Korean Union), which had been formed to advocate for the labor rights of Korean nationals working for the U.S. military, was formally a part of the FKTU.[73] In short, as resource mobilization theory suggests, interest-driven motives—to maintain organizational influence and not lose ground to its competitor—apparently spurred the conservative union into solidarity action with radicals, progressives, and others.[74]

As a coalition, the *kiji undong* became a large tent "under which disparate groups and interests can share organizing methods, bridge differences, moderate radical tendencies, coordinate action, draw a following, and achieve greater public impact both within and outside South Korea."[75] It adopted the *simin undong* trait of institutional engagement, such as attention to procedural reform, legal activities, and formulation of policy alternatives. In contrast to the anti-U.S. movements of the 1980s, which tended to be heavy on radical (nationalist and anti-imperialist) rhetoric and adopted violent means of protest, the bases movement has sought to raise public awareness and persuade public opinion and government policy. They follow in the tradition of watchdog groups familiar in the West, whose self-identified role is to check the misinformation, secrecy, and cover-ups that their governments may engage in.

Nevertheless, social movement actors do not transform their identities or approach to political life in a snap. Even while adopting new identities, resources, goals, and methods, old habits die hard. In this regard, the *kiji* movement also reflects the legacy of the student/democracy movements of the 1970s and 1980s, whose ranks included the likes of Father Mun and Chŏn'guk Yŏnhap leaders. Elsewhere, I have written that the activists

> grew adept at tujaeng (struggle, fight) as the one reliable resource and method of influence in a military-authoritarian society. Because they come from such a protest tradition, [these activists] target the remaining "big guns" in their country, namely, the USFK. Their political access and their influence on U.S. security policy and practice are limited, and so they rely on their comparative advantage: public demonstrations and [provocative] media coverage.[76]

There is also the reality that CSO leaders, even if they want to work through institutional channels of government—to gather information, different perspectives, and to get their concerns on the government's agenda—confront the problem of "saving face" when dealing with their own constituencies. For example, both Korean and American government representatives lamented that it is difficult and frustrating to meet and discuss grievances rationally with some of the *kiji* CSOs. In some instances, the more diehard *kiji* activists like Father Mun sometimes refused to meet with U.S. embassy or Korean officials. At other times, meetings turned into recrimination sessions such that the U.S. or Korean side gave up and wrote off hard-line activists as impossible to work with. At other times, progress was made through information-sharing and discussions of government priorities and constraints with activists. One senior researcher of the Korean Institute for Defense Analysis (KIDA), a Mr. Kim, observed that even after constructive discussions were held and that CSOs expressed appreciation for information, the per diem paid by his institute, and the incorporation of some of their grievances into government positions, the same CSO leaders would "change their language as soon as they walked out the door" and adopt a confrontational front when addressing their constituents.[77] They did not want to look like "sell-outs" after having dealt with government representatives. The media would make the meetings seem more dramatic than they were, which in some cases, *kiji* activists wanted for the sake of getting attention and positioning themselves for more leverage. Mr. Kim was particularly concerned that activists and the general public tended to get misinformation from the media, and so he took seriously the task of providing accurate data and contextual analysis for the CSOs he engaged with.

Mr. Kim, who was one of the most well-informed and analytically astute and fair-minded thinkers about the politics of *kiji* activists in alliance politics, mentioned that lawyers and other professionally trained individuals were easier to work with. He also stated clearly that the Korean government at times benefited from the activists' vocalism because they raised issues that might disfavor the Korean side, which the Ministry of National Defense or the Ministry of Trade and Foreign Affairs then could "use for negotiations" with the United States. U.S. embassy officials corroborated, noting that *kiji* activists/protesters were an "unseen presence" at the negotiation table.[78] Mr. Kim, who seemed to lean toward the conservative side of politics, articulated that *kiji* activists "are not necessarily anti-American and not pro–North Korea." Rather, they were "just pro–South Korea" and *wanted the government to act in that way* (emphasis added).[79]

Scholars of social movements accept that past episodes or cycles of contention shape future movements. Relevant to this discussion, Doug McAdams writes about the connections between "collective memory" and "legacy anti-Americanism."[80] He encourages scholars "to look beyond the immediate episodes that typically command attention and analyze the ways in which the constructed legacies of these struggles increase or decrease the likelihood of later conflict."[81] Here, McAdam is correct in looking to the past to understand the present and future. In the Korean case, the tendency to engage in "street democracy" and aim for maximalist rhetoric and goals is a habit from the past. But the past has its limits. There are current inadequacies in terms of access to institutional channels, familiarity with debating different points of view, acceptance of the need to negotiate with the opposition, and understanding that all of these practices and compromise are essential in strengthening and sustaining democratic life. This holds true for CSO activists as well as the political establishment. Moreover, domestic path dependence is of limited influence when new opportunities for political engagement and identity-transformation within and outside the society are available. They make impossible any predictable trajectory from past to present and future. In the case of the *kiji* movement, as the next chapter will show, social movement trends outside Korea highly influenced the framing of issues and the diffusion of ideas, methods, coalitions, activist identities, and goals.

NOTES

1. Kyŏngsu Hwang, "Kulyok hyŏbsang hanŭni ch'arari Kunsan konghang p'aesoehaja" (Rather than submit to negotiations, better to get rid of the Kunsan airport), *Mal chi* (Mal magazine), January 1998, 147.

2. Chuhan Migun munje haegyŏl undongsa (Korean People's Movement for Solution of US Forces Korea Issues), *Nogunri esŏ Maehyangni kkaji* (From Nogunri to Maehyangni) (Seoul: Doseo Publishing, 2000), 146.

3. On the use of the terms *kiji undong* and "bases movement," see the introduction to this volume.

4. The tendency in both Korean society and American political circles to view left-leaning or progressive politics in Korea as monolithic is a curiosity, given the existence of good scholarship by progressive scholars that explicitly documents internal competition and contention over ideology, goals, strategy, tactics, leadership and more. In English, see Namhee Lee, *The Making of Minjung: Democracy and the Politics of Representation in South Korea* (Ithaca, NY: Cornell University Press, 2007); Insook Kwon, "Militarism in My Heart: Women's Militarized Consciousness and Culture in South Korea," Ph.D. diss., Clark University (2000).

5. Chuhan Migun munje haegyŏl undongsa, *Nogunri esŏ Maehyangni kkaji*, 7.

6. Author interview with Ch'a Migyŏng, Ilsan, Korea, June 18, 2002.

7. See Sunhyuk Kim, "State and Civil Society in South Korea's Democratic Consolidation: Is the Battle Really Over?" *Asian Survey* 37, no. 12 (1997); and "Civil Society in South Korea: From Grand Democracy Movements to Petty Interest Groups?" *Journal of Northeast Asian Studies* 15, no. 2 (1996).

8. Author interview with Kim Yonghan, Korea, May 13, 2002.

9. Suzanne Staggenborg, "Coalition Work in the Pro-Choice Movement: Organizational and Environmental Opportunities and Obstacles," *Social Problems* 33, no. 5 (June 1986), 388.

10. Sunhyuk Kim, "State and Civil Society in South Korea's Democratic Consolidation," 1142.

11. Also see Sunhyuk Kim's *The Politics of Democratization in South Korea: The Role of Civil Society* (Pittsburgh, PA: University of Pittsburgh Press, 2000), chapter 6.

12. Sunhyuk Kim, "Civil Society in South Korea: From Grand Democracy Movements," 94–95.

13. Sunhyuk Kim, *Politics of Democratization in South Korea*, 128.

14. Ibid., 130.

15. Robert D. Putnam, *Making Democracy Work: Civic Traditions in Modern Italy* (Princeton: Princeton University Press, 1993), chapter 6.

16. *Korea Herald*, February 28, 2001.

17. Ibid.

18. Fred Rose, *Coalitions across the Class Divide: Lessons from the Labor, Peace, and Environmental Movements* (Ithaca, NY: Cornell University Press, 2000), 205.

19. Ibid., 155. Although Rose uses the term "movements" to specify organized action around a single issue, I use the term more liberally to refer to social movements in general, including coalitions.

20. Robert D. Putnam, "Bowling Alone: America's Declining Social Capital," *Journal of Democracy* 6, no. 1 (January 1995), 71.

21. Sunhyuk Kim, *Politics of Democratization in South Korea*, 125–126.

22. Larry Diamond, *Developing Democracy: Toward Consolidation* (Baltimore: Johns Hopkins University Press, 1999), 242, 223.

23. For example, see "South Korea's Filmmakers Roll into Action to Protect Foreign-Movie Quota," *International Herald Tribune*, December 11, 1998. www.iht.com/articles/1998/12/11/seoul.t_0.php (accessed April 2, 2008).

24. Author interview with Mun Chŏnghyŏn, Iksan, Korea, May 4, 2002.

25. John D. McCarthy, "Velcro Triangles: Elite Mobilization of Local Antidrug Issue Coalitions," in *Routing the Opposition: Social Movements, Public Policy, and Democracy*, ed. David S. Meyer, Valerie Jenness, and Helen Ingram (Minneapolis, MN: University of Minnesota Press, 2005), 90.

26. See John D. McCarthy and Mayer N. Zald, "Resource Mobilization and Social Movements: A Partial Theory," in *The American Journal of Sociology* 82, no. 6 (May 1977), 1212–1241; McCarthy and Zald, "Social Movement Industries: Competition and Cooperation among Movement Organizations," in *Research in Social Movements, Conflicts, and Change*, vol. 3, ed. Louis

Kriesberg (Greenwich, CT: JAI Press, 1980); William Gamson, *The Strategy of Social Protest* (Homewood, IL: Dorsey Press, 1975).

27. McCarthy, "Velcro Triangles," 90.

28. Author interview with Kim Yonghan, Korea, May 13, 2002.

29. Agence France Press, June 22, 1999 (Lexis-Nexis; accessed July 25, 2001).

30. Kyung-Taek Oh, "Transnational Cooperation of NGOs in Northeast Asia: Campaign against Shipment of Taiwanese Nuclear Waste to North Korea," paper presented at the annual meeting of the American Political Science Association, August 29–September 1, 2002.

31. Author interview with PAR-SOFA leader, June 18, 2002.

32. Author interview with Kim Yonghan, Korea, May 13, 2002.

33. Author interview with Ch'a Migyŏng, Ilsan, Korea, June 18, 2002.

34. Su-Hoon Lee, "Korea's Environmental Movement," in *Asia's Environmental Movements: Comparative Perspectives,* ed. Yok-shiu F. Lee and Alvin Y. So, (Armonk, NY: M. E. Sharpe, 1999), 109.

35. Su-Hoon Lee et al., "The Impact of Democratization on Environmental Movements," in *Asia's Environmental Movements,* 233.

36. Ibid.

37. Yok-shiu F. Lee and Alvin Y. So, introduction to *Asia's Environmental Movements,* 5, 11. For similar observations regarding the Philippines, see Francis A. Magno, "Environmental Movements in the Philippines," in *Asia's Environmental Movements.*

38. Su-Hoon Lee et al., "The Impact of Democratization on Environmental Movements," in *Asia's Environmental Movements,* 235.

39. Author interview, Korea, June 18, 2002.

40. Jane Dawson, *Eco-Nationalism: Anti-Nuclear Activism and National Identity in Russia, Lithuania, and Ukraine* (Durham, NC: Duke University Press, 1996), 169.

41. Heather S. Gregg, "Divided They Conquer: The Success of Armenian Ethnic Lobbies in the United States," working paper 13, Inter-University Committee on International Migration, Massachusetts Institute of Technology (2002), 20.

42. Miranda A. Schreurs, *Environmental Politics in Japan, Germany, and the United States* (New York: Cambridge University Press, 2002), 67–68.

43. Ibid., 68.

44. Lee and So, introduction to *Asia's Environmental Movements,* 290.

45. The Status of Forces Agreement between the United States and the Republic of Korea is the executive agreement defining and regulating the legal and procedural terms of the deployment of U.S. forces in accordance with the U.S.-ROK Mutual Defense Treaty of 1953. Negotiations began in 1962 and ended in 1966, with the agreement taking effect in February 1967. It underwent a revision process from 1988 to 1991 and again in 1995–2001.

46. For example, in the case of custody upon arrest by the Korean side, both a U.S. representative and a lawyer representing the accused must be

present at the interrogation of the accused; statements taken without the presence of the U.S. representative and the lawyer are not admissible in court. Due process provisions also include the right to release on bail.

47. *Korea Herald,* June 19, 2000, www.koreaherald.co.kr.

48. *SOFA Inducement,* a document of the PAR-SOFA and Korean House for International Solidarity (KHIS). The quote is taken from the conclusion of the section entitled "The Korea/U.S. Status of Forces under Scrutiny / Where Stands Korea—A Comparison with the German and Japanese SOFA." I obtained the document from a leader of the KHIS and PAR-SOFA. The *Inducement* was compiled during the campaign for the revision of the SOFA in 2000.

49. *Korea Herald,* May 19, 2000 (accessed May 20, 2000).

50. Ibid.

51. *Korea Herald,* November 8, 2000, quote from the preface of the "white paper" (accessed July 12, 2001).

52. Ibid.

53. *Korea Herald,* April 15, 1999.

54. *SOFA Inducement;* see the section entitled "Civil Society Demand and Position on the Direction and Substance of SOFA Amendment, Subsection, Facilities and Areas: The Free and Uncontrolled Land Use by the U.S. Armed Forces."

55. Ibid.

56. Ibid.

57. Ibid.

58. U.S. Senate Armed Services Committee, *Department of Defense Authorization for Appropriations for Fiscal Year 2002: Hearings on S. 1416,* 107th Cong., 1st sess., March 27, 2001, 160, available at www.gpo.gov.

59. Center for Strategic and International Studies (CSIS), *The U.S.-ROK Status of Forces Agreement Revision Process: Path to an Agreement* (Washington, DC: CSIS, 2001), 5.

60. Article IV of the 2001 U.S.-ROK Status of Forces Agreement states that the "Government of the United States is not obliged, when it returns facilities and areas to the Government of the Republic of Korea on the expiration of this Agreement or at any earlier date, to restore the facilities and areas to the condition in which they were at the time they became available to the United States armed forces, or to compensate the Government of the Republic of Korea in lieu of such restoration."

61. Kyoung-Ryung Seong, "Delayed Decentralization and Incomplete Democratic Consolidation," in *Institutional Reform and Democratic Consolidation in Korea,* ed. Larry Diamond and Doh Chull Shin (Stanford, CA: Hoover Institution Press, (2000), 101.

62. Chŏn'guk Yŏnhap, "Paljach'wi" (History), www.nadrk.org/intro/his.html.

63. Ibid., www.nadrk.org/intro/sub-rule.html.

64. Author interview with Kim Yonghan, Korea, May 13, 2002.

65. NIMBY stands for "Not In My Backyard."
66. Author interview with Kim Yonghan, May 13, 2002.
67. Author interview with Lee Sohee, Seoul, Korea, March 27, 2002.
68. Author interview, May 13, 2002.
69. Author interview, May 13, 2002.
70. Author interview with Kim Yonghan, May 13, 2002.
71. Author interview, Iksan, Korea, May 4, 2002.
72. McCarthy, "Velcro Triangles," 101.
73. Author interview, Iksan, Korea, May 4, 2002.
74. For a discussion of competition among social movement organizations, especially in coalitions, see Will Hathaway and David S. Meyer, "Competition and Cooperation in Movement Coalitions: Lobbying for Peace in the 1980s," in *Coalitions and Political Movements: The Lessons of the Nuclear Freeze*, ed. Thomas R. Rochon and David S. Meyer (Boulder, CO: Lynne Rienner, 1997); Suzanne Staggenborg, "Coalition Work."
75. Katharine H. S. Moon, "Korean Nationalism, Anti-Americanism and Democratic Consolidation," in *Korea's Democratization*, ed. Samuel S. Kim (New York: Cambridge University Press, 2003), 137.
76. Katharine H. S. Moon, "Civil Society Organizations and Alliance Politics," in *Strategy and Sentiment: South Korean Popular Opinion and the U.S.-ROK Alliance*, ed. Derek Mitchell (Washington, DC: Center for Strategic and International Studies, 2004), 53.
77. Author interview, Seoul, spring 2002.
78. Author interviews, U.S. Embassy, Seoul, spring 2002.
79. Author interview, Seoul, spring 2002.
80. Doug McAdam, "Legacies of Anti-Americanism: A Sociological Perspective," in *Anti-Americanisms in World Politics*, ed. Peter J. Katzenstein and Robert O. Keohane (Ithaca, NY: Cornell University Press, 2007), 258.
81. Ibid.

4. Made in Korea and Beyond

Regional and International Activism

In late 2002 and early 2003, while the United States government gathered ammunition and readied itself for war in Iraq, people around the world mobilized to fight the United States government through public protests. In Australia, on one October Sunday alone during a month of protests, "more than 30,000 took to the streets, voicing their opposition to the U.S. war and the unconditional support given to it by Australian Prime Minister John Howard. A sea of banners and placards condemned the Bush and Howard governments: 'No blood for oil' and 'Regime change begins at home.'"[1] Across Asia, similar voices were raised, and in Seoul, students filled the streets, carrying placards that read, "We oppose U.S. war against Iraq." They also chanted, "Let's drive out U.S. troops [from Korea]" and stomped on "two large American flags with skulls drawn on them."[2] Protests also took place in Pusan, Taegu, Taejŏn, Kwangju, and Wŏnju. Across the Pacific, Americans prepared for the October 26 march on Washington, DC, which was reported as the largest protest in DC since the Vietnam era.[3] Act Now To Stop War and End Racism (ANSWER) was prominent among organizers of the national effort. This was part of a global day of protests coordinated with other cities around the world.

The international momentum against the United States grew in 2003. The sole superpower was spurned at the United Nations by its longtime European friends, France and Germany. On February 15, 2003, an estimated 16 million people who "follow[ed] the sun around the world . . . , marched, demonstrated, sang songs of peace, and occasionally . . . clashed with the police" to protest the U.S.'s plans to invade Iraq.[4] England exhibited the largest demonstration in London's history, with 1.75 million, and in Italy, around 2.5 million joined in solidarity. "The banners [that the Italians] waved and the death masks some of them wore symbolized their outrage at American aggression and indifference to international law."[5] According to Sidney Tarrow, the international protests "involved an enormous range of participants, from grizzled veterans of the 1960s to religious groups and young people who had been inducted into political life during the global justice protests of the previous years."[6]

The anti-war and anti-globalization protests were part of the trend toward a wider and intensified transnationalization of civil society organizations and activism. Based on research by Jackie Smith,[7] Tarrow observes that transnational activism since the 1970s has expanded in almost all sectors (issue areas), but that organizing around human rights, environment, and peace, in addition to "development and empowerment," and multi-issue groups, had grown most significantly by 2000.[8] These transnational trends correspond with the growth of human rights, women's rights, and environmental NGOs in Korean civil society in the 1990s.[9]

The *kiji*/bases movement in South Korea, including the outpouring of criticism toward the United States and the alliance in the winter of 2002–3, needs to be understood in the global social movement contexts of the time. Many Korean civil society leaders were influenced by and participated in the various transnational movements of the late 1990s and early 2000s, among them, the global justice movements that traveled around the globe, which started in Seattle, Washington (November, 1999), and traversed Porto Allegre, Brazil (2000, 2002, 2003), Prague (September, 2000), Göthenburg, (June, 2001), Genoa (July, 2001), Washington, DC (2001), and Florence, Italy (November, 2002). Spain, Greece, Germany, and Switzerland also have been venues of global protest, as has Mumbai, the host of the first Asian Social Forum in 2004. Organizers and participants targeted international organizations such as the World Trade Organization, the International Monetary Fund, and the World Bank, in addition to the G-8 summits and the World Economic Forum in Davos, Switzerland. In principle, the protesters opposed neoliberalism and globalization from above and advocated social justice platforms that emphasized (economic and social) equality, human rights, and environmentalism. In practice, protesters mixed a variety of grievances and discontents, especially against their own national governments. For example, the Italian anti-war protesters in February 2003 were not only protesting U.S. policy and the Italian government's support for the war but also for "a host of domestic claims, ranging from pension reform to unemployment to the legal problems of Prime Minister Berlusconi."[10]

This tendency to conflate domestic grievances, criticize U.S. policy, and appeal to universal norms is also characteristic of the Korean bases movement. As Margaret Keck and Kathryn Sikkink write in *Activists Beyond Borders,* transnational advocacy networks necessarily blur the line between domestic and international political spaces and activities.[11] Moreover, the transnational context of domestic activism is critical because "[t]ransnational movement organizations and networks play an especially crucial role in translating international norms of human rights and democracy into local contexts. By doing so, they alter the opportunities for domestic movements and, consequently, the likelihood of movement success."[12]

The multi-issue orientation of the *kiji* movement benefits from and contributes to the parallel development at the transnational level. According to Jackie Smith, "the number of [transnational] groups adopting multi-issue organizing frames doubled between 1993 and 2000."[13] For *kiji* activism, this meant more organizations, campaigns, and audiences to ally with or from which to gain support and/or sympathy. It meant diversified resources in terms of information gathering and dissemination, joint projects, and international exposure that could translate into recognition, media coverage, and political leverage back home. Moreover, for organizations that seek international experience and/or impact, multi-issue activism increases the opportunity to access regional and international institutions, such as the European Union and the United Nations. Indeed, based on their in-depth study of anti-globalization movements, della Porta and her coauthors are clear that the diversity of issue areas or heterogeneity of "bloc affiliation encourages more participation by nonaffiliated individuals: difference attracts."[14]

The Korean bases movement has roots in the Asia-Pacific network of transnational activism that linked together people from Okinawa, Japan, the Philippines, Australia, Canada, the United States, and Vieques, Puerto Rico. Tarrow describes transnational activists as "individuals and groups who mobilize domestic and international resources and opportunities to advance claims on behalf of external actors, against external opponents, or in favor of goals they hold in common with transnational allies."[15] Indeed, Korean activists physically traveled to various places where U.S. bases have been located and the local activists have been willing to discuss comparable experiences. The Koreans also publicized their local and national issues and campaigns externally and educated their own constituencies about related conditions and activism abroad.

Understanding these national-regional-transnational connections is important for the following reasons. First, activists from these countries exchanged information about one another's organizational activities, agendas, political strategies, mobilization of resources, and methods of political expression. They compared and assessed national policies and organizational progress. Second, transnational networks helped broaden the audience for each national movement. Third, the transnational solidarity provided a kind of international legitimacy to each national movement, even if domestic support was scant or skeptical. Fourth, international interaction provided framing devices and diffusion of protest repertoires. In particular, the regional and global context helped broaden Korean *kiji* activism from the narrow frame of nationalism and anti-imperialism once pushed by radical student activists in the 1980s to a broader, inclusive frame of democracy and political participation, human rights, and the environment in the 1990s and 2000s.

WOMEN'S MOVEMENTS AGAINST U.S. MILITARISM

Recent enactments of contentious politics around civil-military relations between U.S. bases and Asian societies emerged from trans-Pacific solidarity movements for women's rights in the late 1980s and early 1990s. For decades, leaders like Takazato Suzuyo of Okinawa and Matsui Yayori, the well-known Japanese journalist and feminist activist, raised issues related to Asian women, gender politics, and women's human rights at various international meetings of government officials and NGOs. Together with Filipina counterparts like Aida Santos and leaders of GABRIELA, the umbrella organization of numerous women's groups in the Philippines, they raised awareness of and forged collective interests around issues concerning East Asian women and the U.S. bases. Specifically, they built networks of individuals, information, and cooperation on both sides of the Pacific Ocean. Moreover, their networks were both broad yet tightly knit together, engaging cross-cutting issues such as the international women's movement, peace movement, labor and human rights movements, environment, economic development, the political empowerment of women, and more.[16]

Even under authoritarian rule in the 1970s, Filipinas did not hesitate to speak up and campaign nationally and internationally against the Philippines authorities and the United States military for abetting and condoning the physical, sexual, and economic exploitation of and violence against women who worked in the R&R industry along Olongapo and Subic Bay, where U.S. forces had been stationed until the early 1990s.

Sister Mary Soledad Perpinan, GABRIELA, and other progressive leaders played a catalytic role in this regard. For example, Filipina activists wrote a letter opposing sex tourism and included an emphasis on U.S. military prostitution, "specifically the whoredoms created by the presence of the U.S. Naval Base in Subic and Clark Air Base in Angeles City. The letter was handed to Pope John Paul II during his visit to Manila and copies were given to the heads of the United States, Japan, and the Philippines."[17]

They also drew comparisons between the compromised sovereignty of the Philippines government in its relationship with the more powerful U.S. government and the compromised rights and dignity of Filipinas who "serviced" American (male) military personnel. Aida Santos, a long-time activist against the U.S. military bases in the Philippines (and later the Visiting Forces Agreement) wrote in the early 1990s that in the Philippines, "[r]acism and sexism are now seen as a fulcrum in the issue of national sovereignty."[18] Such activists made the case that the personal is indeed political and international.[19]

Progressive women's rights activists were some of the first in East Asia to voice what they perceived to be the negative social impacts of housing U.S. forces. A. Lin Neumann wrote, "The US Naval Base presence and commercialized prostitution in Olongapo has spawned several subsidiary institutions which are unsanctioned but which continue to exist: streetwalking, racket and extortion, pickpocketing and snatching, drug pushing, illicit dollar trading, smuggling of PX goods, and sidewalk vending."[20] Since the 1970s, these themes, placed in the larger context of imperialism, sexism, and racism, have been echoed in Korea, Okinawa, and Thailand (which had been used as major R&R bases for American troops in the Vietnam War).[21]

In South Korea, Yu Pognim, a Korean democracy activist, and Faye Moon, an American missionary, activist, and wife of the Korean democracy leader Rev. Mun Tonghwan were the first to focus attention on the plight of the Korean *kiji ch'on* women. Together with the assistance of a handful of student activists and the financial support of some Protestant churches, they established Durebang (My Sister's Place) in 1988 as a counseling center, shelter, and later bakery (to generate income for older women who had left the sex business and younger women who wanted to get out).

Yu and Mun were mavericks even in the progressive world of democracy and human rights activism to which they belonged, for they were the first to recognize *kiji ch'on* women as legitimate Korean citizens—not pariahs—in need of public attention and welfare assistance. But despite their efforts to raise awareness of the relationship between the U.S. bases and this underclass of women and their Amerasian children, most of Korean society continued to ignore the women and their needs. Rather, Yu and Mun found increasing solidarity with their activist counterparts from the Philippines, Okinawa/Japan, and the United States as women organized around issues of sexual violence and slavery, militarism, and human rights in the Asia-Pacific.

In 1988, women from the Philippines, Korea, Japan, the United States, Canada, England, Taiwan, and Thailand met on the Korean island of Cheju "to share information on related issues and problems from different parts of the world, especially Asia, to forge women's solidarity as activists and criticize the role of governments and businesses in fostering the trade in women's sex work."[22] At that conference, Professor Yun Chŏng Ok, formerly of Ewha Womans [sic] University in Seoul and a founding member of the movement for redress on behalf of former "comfort women" (*chŏngsindae*), gave her first public presentation of her groundbreaking research on militarized sexual slavery under Japanese control. At the same conference, a Korean woman also gave her own testimony of the ordeals she experienced as a sex worker catering to U.S. servicemen in Korea.[23]

The women's human rights movement that developed political momentum in the 1990s[24] helped shed light on the exploitation and abuse of *kiji ch'on* women and others in the sex trade around the world. In Asia, the "comfort women" movement, which demanded official apologies, historical accountability, and compensation from the Japanese government for the sexual violence committed against Korean and other women by Japanese troops during the Pacific War, helped establish political abuses long regarded as "private mishaps" into recognized violations of human rights and therefore in need of official accountability.

In Korea, it took the brutal murder in 1992 of "bargirl" Yun Kŭmi by a U.S. soldier and the rising organizational power of both local activists and those from Seoul, following the democratic transition in Korea, to piece together some understanding of the social and political costs of the U.S. military presence. For the towns housing the U.S. installations, this crime coincided with the start of decentralization measures in South Korea, and the protests and media coverage around Yun's murder in Tongduch'ŏn helped boost what soon became a movement for local autonomy and residents' rights (see chapters 2, 3, and 5).

But unlike the 1995 gang rape of a Japanese girl on Okinawa by three U.S. Marines, the death of Yun Kŭmi did not itself spark a national debate about the presence and prerogatives of the U.S. forces or a crisis in the alliance relationship. For one, the death of a prostitute did not draw as much sympathy as the rape of a twelve-year-old schoolgirl who had been kidnapped and violated by three young men. For another, the crisis over the North Korean nuclear program and the difficult negotiations over the Agreed Framework of 1994 occupied most of the attention in the media and among the elites who managed the alliance. By contrast, the 1995 rape case galvanized widespread outrage and political activism in Okinawa, including a prefectural referendum on the presence and size of the U.S. bases.[25] Civic activism in response to the rape generated severe tensions in the U.S.-Japan alliance, and government officials in Tokyo and Washington sprung into action to repair the relationship and reform the alliance.

Within weeks of the rape incident, the two governments established the Special Action Committee on Okinawa (SACO) with the explicit intent "to reduce the burden on the people of Okinawa and thereby strengthen the US-Japan alliance."[26] The most significant agreement was to close and return Futenma Air Base to Okinawa, "a top priority for Okinawans."[27] Additionally, the SACO resolved to reduce by 20 percent the total acreage of land used by the U.S., employ noise reduction measures, and increase information and transparency about U.S. military-related activities (including policies and accidents). Then Prime Minister Ryutaro Hashimoto not only understood that local sentiment on Okinawa could be a deal maker or breaker for the Japan-U.S. alliance, but also "believed that the "resolution of the Okinawa issue was critical to the longevity of his government."[28] While pushing executive privilege to rein in Okinawa's (and Governor Ota's) assertion of local power, Hashimoto "acknowledged that the central government had not been sensitive to Okinawan interests and offered the prefecture a variety of economic benefits."[29]

Japanese activists who had just returned from the UN Conference on Women in Beijing responded immediately to the rape and established organizations and networks that later became key players in regional and international activism dealing with U.S. bases, violence against women, human rights, and peace for the next decade. In October 1995, about a month after the rape, Okinawan women established the Rape Emergency Intervention Counseling Center to support and assist rape victims, and soon thereafter on November 8, established Okinawa Women Act against Military Violence (OWAAMV). Composed of a diverse group of people, including activists, housewives, working women, university students, elected officials, and municipal and prefectural officials, OWAAMV staged protests and signature campaigns in front of the Okinawa Prefectural Office. They traveled to Tokyo to meet with the prime minister and officials at the Foreign Ministry and the U.S. Embassy, "and to hand over 55,000 signatures protesting the rape and U.S. military presence in Okinawa."[30]

Wanting broader support for their cause at home, OWAAMV organized "peace caravans" in 1996 and in 1998 to major U.S. cities in order to meet with a broad spectrum of American civic and religious organizations and members of the U.S. government, Congress, and the United Nations Commission on Human Rights. Their goals ranged from investigating abuses against Okinawan women and children by U.S. personnel to revising the U.S.-Japan Security Treaty and SOFA, cleaning up the environmental damage caused by the U.S. military, educating the U.S. military personnel serving in Okinawa and other overseas venues on cultural awareness and human rights, and reducing and ultimately removing U.S. forces from the island.[31]

In Japan, Korea, and the Philippines, women's activism has influenced the popular perception of each SOFA with the U.S. as weak when it comes to protecting the rights and safety of the host nation's citizens, especially women and children living near the U.S. bases. And in all three countries, women have campaigned to include women's rights and welfare needs in the SOFA. For example, in the Philippines, sex workers in Olongapo, together with GABRIELA and health organizations, pressured the Philippine government to "obtain a guarantee that all U.S. service personnel coming into the Philippines be tested for HIV."[32] In 1988, the Philippines Immigration Commissioner required all U.S. servicemen entering the Philippines to present certificates verifying that they were AIDS-free.[33] More recently in Korea, women's groups tried to push particular concerns regarding *kiji ch'on* women and children into the revised SOFA which took effect April 2, 2001. Their demands were mostly unmet, significantly due to the framing of issues and leadership conflict among *kiji* activists, as the next chapter will explain.

In 1997, OWAAMV joined with advocacy groups from Korea such as Durebang and Saewoomtuh, as well as the Philippines, the United States, and mainland Japan to establish the East-Asia-U.S. Women's Network against Militarism. Their purpose was to exchange information about the negative impact of U.S. military bases in these societies, particularly on women and children, and to educate and campaign against militarism and military values. Their first international gathering took place in Okinawa in1997 (and again in 2000), followed by one in Washington, DC

(1998), and South Korea (2002). In 2000, the group expanded to include members from Vieques, Puerto Rico, who were also engaged in protest against the U.S. installations there, and thereby changed its name to East Asia-U.S.-Puerto Rico Women's Network against Militarism.

Through such networks and gatherings, Asian-Pacific women's groups helped to educate one another and broaden the scope of their work from local and national to regional and international concerns. As a result, the role and impact of the Asian women's movement against U.S. troops have grown larger than their original focus on women, because these political actors did not stick to a narrow agenda. Okinawan women, in particular, have resisted parochial tendencies and incorporated environmental issues and global networking as integral aspects of their work. During a 1998 visit to Washington, DC, which had been sponsored by the DC-based Asian Pacific Center for Justice and Peace (APCJP) and the Institute for Policy Studies (IPS), Asian members of the East-Asia-U.S. Women's Network against Militarism "expressed an interest in making common cause with other regional groups facing the consequences of the US military presence on their home soil."[34] The Washington-based organizations helped link some of these women's groups with those organized around environmental issues and base cleanup, such as the People's Task Force for Bases Cleanup of the Philippines. In October, 1999, a representative from the OWAAMV, together with the Okinawa Environmental Network, traveled to Washington, DC, to participate in the International Grassroots Summit on Military Base Cleanup (of which more below).

American CSOs have played a key role in bringing disparate individuals and national issues together and helping to "cross-fertilize" them. In particular, church groups helped initiate bases-related activism as part of the larger solidarity around pacifism and anti-militarism or anti-imperialism that emerged in the 1960s and 1970s. Progressive and/or global ministry-oriented Presbyterians, Methodists, Lutherans, Mennonites, Quakers, and various Catholic groups became the "champions" of anti-bases activism. (Many of them came from missionary backgrounds and had lived abroad, for example, in the Philippines or Korea). They formed international networks and sponsored training, financial assistance, and moral support to many like-minded individuals and organizations outside the United States.[35]

Secular organizations also played key roles, helping foreign activists "navigate" the landscape of American politics, especially Washington, DC. Miriam Young, who served as the director of the APCJP and organized the women's conference in 1998, explicitly stated during an interview with me that her organization's intention was to help both East Asian and American activists understand how Washington works because "they need to know what is and isn't possible, what's worth working on," how legislation in the U.S. works, who's on important congressional committees, how the different bureaucracies function, and so on. She observed that some of the anti-militarist women's groups she had met, especially American ones, were "extremely idealistic" (perhaps because they were in their formative stages of development, as she noted) and "operated in a totally separate world from *realpolitik*—the military, National Security Council, etc." She found the fact that such activists "didn't ever interact with the other side" highly problematic and encouraged the participants to talk to people who are opposed to one's own thinking and "not just to those who are on your side." Her emphasis was on dialogue among like-minded *and* unlike-minded actors.[36]

ANTI-MILITARISM AND PEACE ACTIVISM

Such transnational peace activism has been indispensable to defining and shaping the social movement regarding U.S. bases in Asia. Korean and Okinawan activists in particular have exchanged and coordinated information, agendas, and "personnel" particularly since the 1995 gang rape of the Okinawan teenage girl by U.S. marines. In August 1996, Kim Yonghan, the co-leader of the National Campaign in the early-mid 1990s and later of the return-of-land movement and the PAR-SOFA (see chapter 3), went to Japan at the invitation of Japanese peace activists. He participated in activities commemorating the fifty-first anniversary of the bombing of Hiroshima, learned about the particularities of the U.S. presence in Japan, namely the "private" leasing of land and "rent" paid by the Japanese government. Arriving before the Okinawa referendum, he inquired about the procedures and details of the return-of-land movement in Japan. He also enlisted the Okinawans' help in the Korean *panhwan* (return-of-land) movement and proposed an international, collective demonstration (with activists in Okinawa, the Philippines, Australia, Germany and other NATO countries) for the following spring.[37] In an article for the Korean *Mal* magazine (*Mal chi*), he emphasized the impressive diversity and dynamism of peace and anti-base activism among the Japanese.[38]

In 1997, Okinawans visited Seoul to participate in the weekly Friday demonstration in front of Yongsan Garrison that was organized by the National Campaign for the Eradication of Crimes by U.S. Troops. In 1998,

Okinawans formed the Han-Oki People's Solidarity with the purpose of educating themselves about U.S. military-related problems affecting Koreans and to network with peace activists in Korea, Taiwan, the Philippines, and Puerto Rico.[39] The international affairs representative of this group acknowledged the Korean activists' goal of revising the Korea-U.S. SOFA but also advised them to be mindful of the ongoing damage and other negative impacts that persist with the troops that are already stationed on their land.[40] His point was that revision was not the end-all and be-all. Also in 2000, an Okinawan folk singer came to Korea to participate in a memorial observance of the Kwangju massacre and was reported in the Korean press to have "apologized" to the residents of Maehyangni for contributing to their affliction—apparently because some of the U.S. aircraft that engaged in strafing exercises at the Kunni range flew over from Okinawa, where they were based.[41]

Koreans and Okinawans also organized the Full Moon Festival in July, 2000, a simultaneously staged and regularly held gathering in both Korea and Okinawa for the purpose of promoting peace.[42] *Hankyore Sinmun* featured one of the Okinawan organizers, Dakaesu Ayano, who was also active in the movement against the U.S. construction of a heliport in Henoko (as a replacement for Futenma heliport). The article emphasized her transformation from a "typical housewife" into a bases activist and her special commitment to organizing on behalf of Okinawans and Maehyangni residents. The message to the reader was clear: any common citizen, duly inspired by a sense of justice, can become an effective bases activist.

Okinawans did not focus only on the bases issue in their solidarity efforts with Koreans. In the spring of 2000, Masahide Ota, the then governor of Okinawa, led a delegation of about 130 Okinawans, including Kina Shokichi, a famous musician, to North Korea to "promote grassroots exchanges in an effort to ease regional tensions."[43] Kina also promoted the "Arirang Movement," an effort to send rice to North Koreans, and participated in a fundraising concert—"Change All Arms into Musical Instruments"—with other Japanese musicians to aid North Koreans.

In contrast to the conventional view of Korean-Japanese antipathy and Korean nationalist sentiments against Japan, the cooperation and solidarity between Korean and Okinawan *kiji* activists reveal a genuine empathy and admiration for one another. Chŏng Yujin, a co-founder and early leader of the National Campaign, is an example of how directly and profoundly transnational activism—centered on the Okinawan peace movement and bases activism—transformed her own nationalistic mindset and "anti-American" stance. In a candid and highly reflective essay on her initiation into the world of peace activism, she describes how Okinawans introduced to her novel concepts about the positive substance of peace (as contrasted with a mere oppositional stance, such as anti-Americanism) and the mental transformation that is required to engage in genuine solidarity work.

In an article entitled "Why Is There No 'Yankee Go Home' in Okinawa?" Chŏng describes key lessons learned: (1) above all, the preciousness of human life is the foundation and goal of peace activism, not "national interest," sovereignty, or nationalist ends; (2) systems and cultures of militarism, not U.S. bases or troops per se, are the problem; (3) seeking peace means not demonizing and dehumanizing "the other" ("Yankee Go Home" demonizes and degrades individual Americans); and (4) solidarity requires acceptance of difference and the recognition of mutuality among participants (e.g., responsibility, assistance, accountability). Chŏng then uses what she learned to critique sharply Korean civil society, particularly those *kiji* activists who are motivated by nationalism and anti-American sentiments than any genuine desire for peace between societies and the improved welfare of the individuals who live near the bases. She challenges her fellow Korean activists to consider: What have Koreans learned from their own history, particularly the Korean War? She laments that Koreans have received a legacy of anger and the desire to "create enemies," rather than the will to make peace, from both the war and the student democracy movement of the 1980s (in which she participated).[44]

The regional and transnational networks of peace activism and anti-militarism/bases movements were squarely in place by the time of the armored vehicle accident that killed the two Korean school girls in June 2002. Okinawan activists offered moral support by publicizing at home Koreans' grievances toward U.S. bases and by extending gestures of solidarity across national boundaries. Kuwae Teruko, an Okinawan peace activist who later went on a hunger strike in front of the U.S. Consulate in Naha to protest the U.S. war in Iraq, visited Korea in December 2002 as part of Asian Peace Alliance (APA). This delegation came to Korea to offer moral support against the acquittal of the U.S. soldiers responsible for the deaths of the two schoolgirls and to join the tens of thousands of Koreans participating in candlelight vigil protests.[45] During a candlelight vigil on January 18, 2003, that was organized by the Korean Pan National Committee for Two Girls Killed by U.S. Military Vehicle, solidarity messages from the APA and the East Asia-U.S.-Puerto Rico Women's Network against Militarism were read to the public.

Support also came from as far away as Vieques, Puerto Rico. Ismael Guadalupe Ortiz, leader of the anti-bases movement in Vieques sent a message of "solidarity with the people of Korea," condemning and protesting the U.S. troops' role in the deaths of the two teenage girls: "This is one more abuse added to those crimes perpetrated by the U.S. military against the Korean people since the Korean War. These crimes committed by the U.S. are awaiting the repudiation of the world community."[46] This message was delivered not only to Koreans but also to netizens (Internet citizens) around the world, made available by various websites.

Although Koreans and Puerto Ricans do not have a "natural" affinity toward one another in terms of geography, culture, or trade, the presence of U.S. bases in both societies—and activism criticizing them—has created networking and bonding opportunities since the late 1990s. In July, 1999, just a few months after David Sanes of Vieques had been killed by an errant U.S. Navy bomb, the anti-bases activist Ismael Guadalupe visited Maehyangni (Kunni bombing range) to learn about the conditions in Korea and to seek solidarity. He expressed alarm at how much worse he found the conditions that the Korean villagers endured, compared to their Vieques counterparts, given the former's closer proximity to the strafing area.[47]

In turn, representatives of the Korean *kiji* movement supported Puerto Rican activists' fight to remove U.S. forces from Vieques. When Father Mun Chŏnghyŏn led a delegation of activists in September 2000 to the United States to campaign for the revision of the U.S.-Korea SOFA, his first public appearance was in front of the White House to participate in a protest organized by Puerto Rican activists against the U.S. presence in Vieques. In his speech, he demanded that the U.S. leave Puerto Rico, and in an essay that he penned soon thereafter, Mun expressed how deeply he was moved by the experience of international solidarity with the Puerto Ricans' cause. He realized that although of different nationalities, the people of Vieques and of Maehyangni had much in common because of what they suffered at the hands of the U.S. bombing facilities. He also witnessed the similarities between protest repertoires across national boundaries, including fear of police and the possibility of arrest.[48]

In early October 2000 Mun Chŏnghyŏn and representatives of KHIS traveled to Vieques to learn about the impact of the U.S. installations on local residents, to exchange information about Maehyangni and Vieques, and to participate in peace activism with local and international participants. In an essay describing the visit, Pyŏn Yŏnsik, a member of the delegation, noted how strange and unfamiliar he was to that part of the world, how beautiful he found the island, and how similar he found the issues between—and the activists' commitment to—Vieques and Maehyangni. Closing his essay with a plea for peace in Vieques and in Maehyangni, Pyŏn quotes the words of a Vieques priest: "Just as family and friends come to visit someone who is ill, we all are part of one family. In all corners of the global village, people share our suffering."[49]

Around the same time, women's organizations also extended their trans-Pacific networks on base-related matters. In 2001, representatives of the East Asia-U.S.-Puerto Rico Women's Network against Militarism traveled to Puerto Rico to learn about the activist work of Vieques women.[50] In 2002, activists from Korea and the Philippines conducted collaborative investigation and research into the situation of Filipinas who work in camp towns around U.S. bases in Korea. In 2004, the Philippines would play host to women's groups from East Asia collaborating on base-related issues.[51]

While activists traveled to one another's sites of contention and publicized their common grievances against the U.S. military, Korean media outlets publicized the transnational connections. In the summer of 2000, *Hankyore Sinmun* published a series called "Another Look at the U.S. Bases," which featured grievances and protest movements against the U.S. military presence in different parts of the world. From Vieques, one reporter described the history of the U.S. naval presence on the island and the locals' grievances and protest methods, such as break-ins into and encampments within the U.S. installations, sit-ins, and environmental and health surveys. The comparison between Vieques and Maehyangni was explicit: poverty, lack of arable land, environmental damage, and health hazards caused by the bombing range.[52]

The U.S. war in Iraq became a rallying point for Asian peace activism in the early 2000s and made obvious to the activists the linkage between the presence and conduct of U.S. troops in Asia and the U.S. military presence in Iraq and Afghanistan. For example, Japanese—with Okinawans playing a central role—staged protests against the war in twenty-three major locales around the country in solidarity with about twenty-five countries that coordinated protests on January 18, 2003.[53] Okinawans sponsored and engaged in multinational and multicultural activities, including musicians and performers from Okinawa and Korea, as well as more serious forms of protest, such as hunger strikes and demonstrations in front of the U.S. Kadena Air Base. About a hundred protesters chanted "No war on Iraq" at the American GIs on base, and according to the Asian Peace Alliance, Takazato Suzuyo, the well-known feminist and anti-bases leader, reported that some GIs came out to show their support for the protesters.[54] Additionally, about 300 Okinawans participated in the hunger strike against the war, while the Okinawa Peace Liaison Council sent a seven-member peace delegation to Iraq in mid-January.[55]

The Asian Peace Alliance was established in September 2002 with representatives from Bangladesh, Cambodia, Hong Kong, India, Indonesia, Japan, Korea, Malaysia, Nepal, Pakistan, the Philippines, Sri Lanka, Thailand, Australia, the United States, and Britain gathering in the Philippines to address the U.S. war on terror and its particular impact on Asia, including Afghanistan. From the outset APA took an anti-militarist stance, with special emphasis on protesting U.S. plans to invade Iraq.[56] Another transnational organization, the Asia Partnership for Human Development (APHD), consisting of twenty-two Catholic development agencies from Asia (including Caritas Coreana), Europe, Canada, Australia, and New Zealand, also conjoined their peace activism and other programs (including sustainable agriculture, human rights, women's rights, local empowerment, interfaith dialogue, and more) with the bases movement in Okinawa and Korea. In 2003, the East Asia Regional Assembly of the APHD met in Okinawa. In their assembly statement, the participants committed themselves to "solidarity with the people from Asia-Pacific nations who suffer from the presence of foreign military bases in their territories and intend to join their peace-building efforts by providing a platform for them."[57] And they added a sharp rebuke: "The US military bases strip the local people of their dignity and contribute to the loss of land and the destruction of the environment."[58]

In 2004, the APHD followed up by holding the Inaugural Peace Building Seminar in Seoul on September 10, which focused on the impact of the U.S. military presence on Korean society.[59] Civil Network for a Peaceful Korea (CNPK) was a participating organization at the seminar. In an interview by APHD's *Mosaic* magazine, Chŏng Usik of CNPK criticized U.S. dominance in the alliance with Korea and stated "his dream for a three-way civil society network of peace groups in the ROK, USA, and Japan" to resolve the tensions on the peninsula.[60] His emphasis on the need for a close Korea-Japan partnership—an "alliance of communication and advocacy"—is particularly interesting, given the commonly assumed nationalistic animosity of Koreans, progressives included, toward Japan and the assumption held by Korean conservatives that the CNPK is anti-American.

We learn from these developments that *kiji* activists in Korea and elsewhere increasingly understand the complex nature of networking and mobilizing. Korean activitists appreciate the opportunities brought to their social movements at home by working with like-minded Americans and Japanese, despite or regardless of the ideological cynicism or hostility their political allies or co-workers may feel toward U.S. or Japanese government policies. The bottom line is a practical understanding that they cannot afford to alienate potential supporters, no matter the nationality. More important from an academic perspective is the growing identity among such actors as professional activists and self-conscious builders of social movements within and outside of their country.

Furthermore, Japanese-Korean cooperation through Peace Boat programs exemplifies the multi-issue aspect of transnational activism in the region and the facility with which *kiji*-related issues get translated into other activist arenas. Since 2005, "Peace and Green Boat" cruises annually have brought together hundreds of Japanese and Koreans interested in building an "'East Asian Bio-community' built on peace and environmental sustainability" and reducing tensions between the two countries.[61] The 2005 trip included travel to areas of historical conflict and tension for Korea (Panmunjom and the DMZ) and for Japan and its neighbors (Nanjing Massacre Museum and Nagasaki). Two years later, the trip had expanded in geographical and issue coverage to include ports in Russia, including Sakhalin (to which Koreans in World War II had been forcibly moved by Japan), energy resources, global warming, antinuclear reprocessing, Korean survivors of the Hiroshima and Nagasaki bombings, indigenous rights and local empowerment, eco-tourism, and the democracy movements of Korea.[62] Such a potpourri of issues lends itself to extending solidarity networks beyond single issues and diversifying the numbers and types of CSOs that later can be expected to support specific campaigns and projects.

THE ENVIRONMENTAL MOVEMENT

Since the mid- to late 1990s, among the different types of transnational activism, environmental activism targeting U.S. bases has become the most significant driver in the Korean bases movement. For the two major organizations, Green Korea United (GKU) and the Korea Federation of Environmental Movements (KFEM), transnational networking has shaped issue content and organizational activities and alliances, and has multiplied the reach of disparate environmental groups within and outside Korea. In particular, environmental CSOs in Korea, Japan, and the Philippines have engaged in information-sharing, comparative analysis, face-to-face meetings at conferences, and collaboration on specific projects.

Both KFEM and GKU took organizational shape as environmental consciousness and activism were spreading internationally and transnationally. KFEM, which formally was established in 1993 by merging the Korea Anti-Pollution Movement Association (KAPMA) with several local environmental groups, has become the leading environmental organization in Korea. It adopted an internationalist and transnationalist outlook from the beginning. Having participated in the UN Conference on Environment and Development in Rio de Janeiro in 1992, KFEM's leaders incorporated global environmental issues, such as the depletion of the ozone layer, deforestation, biodiversity, and climate change into the organization and engaged in transnational cooperation from the start. Since its establishment, KFEM allied with Greenpeace on various campaigns, including a national anti-nuclear campaign in 1994, a project opposing 1995 French nuclear tests in the South Pacific, and the 1997 effort (with GKU) to prevent the dumping of nuclear waste from Taiwan to North Korea. It also participated in major international meetings such as the UN Framework Convention on Climate Change, the 1995 UN Conference on Women, and the World Social Forums (1995, 2000). KFEM also has led or participated in seminars for information sharing and skills development for environmental activists and organizations in Asia and abroad.

GKU also engages in mainstream campaigns, sometimes with KFEM and transnational groups, but of the two, GKU more aggressively pursues anti-militarist and anti-hegemonic campaigns. GKU has participated in a range of international gatherings and campaigns, for example, the 2001 World Conference against A&H Bombs (Hiroshima and Nagasaki) and the 2004 Japan Peace Conference in Sasebo (home of a U.S. naval base), which campaigned against foreign bases. GKU also participated in Word Social Forum meetings that opposed foreign military bases around the world.[63] At the Mumbai WSF in 2004, representatives from thirty-four countries,[64] including Korea, met to educate one another on local perspectives and to coordinate and campaign together as the International Network against Foreign Military Bases. The network's report states that "[b]oth the speakers from Korea and Japan detailed the long history of a large and damaging US military presence in their countries. There, military abuse of civilian populations has gone largely unpunished; Land has been confiscated and contaminated. The history of local resistance was also shared."[65] It is clear that the forums provided new and expanded opportunities for networking and audience recruitment to the cause for GKU and other bases activists in Asia and that their participation provided concrete evidence and political momentum to the international anti-bases movement.

GKU, like KFEM, has engaged in conventional transnational and international activism, working with non-governmental organizations and international organizations on issues such as climate change, biodiversity, and the protection of wetlands. Such participation of course provides new institutional and alliance frameworks as well as normative platforms on which to organize, including bases activism. For example, GKU emphasized the strategic aspects of the UN Environmental Program's adoption of Montevideo III, which includes military accountability for environmental problems in its general mission to have states develop, codify, and enforce international environmental law. GKU hoped that the UNEP's planned "global survey on the application of environmental norms by military establishments," would become a "milestone to publicize U.S. military base-related environmental pollution all around the world."[66] These specific stipulations in the document bear particular relevance to the work of Korean *kiji* activists in the early 2000s:

> Study the feasibility of developing legal mechanisms for mitigating damage caused by military activities, especially concerning:
>
> (i) The removal of military hardware that harms the environment;
>
> (ii) The restoration of the environment damaged by military activities.[67]

In the late 1990s and early 2000s, Korean activists took particular interest in environmental issues affecting foreign communities that housed U.S. bases, particularly the Philippines and Vieques, Puerto Rico. In addition to meeting one another at international meetings, they visited one another's communities to engage in fact-finding and solidarity. For one, the Korean activists wanted to take lessons learned from foreign lands and apply them to the SOFA revision process. Second, they found strength in numbers and gained credibility through parallel cases. Third, for Koreans, this period coincided with high drama around environmental problems in Korea that were associated with the U.S. bases, heightening activist and public interest over similar situations around the world. For example, a GKU representative visited Vieques in August 2000 and wrote a detailed summary report of its environmental issues and forms of activism. It stated that "[o]n the other side of the earth in Puerto Rico there was another Maehyangni." (As mentioned, the KHIS representative who had visited Vieques later in the fall made similar comparisons.) The GKU report highlighted the challenge of getting the United States to take responsibility for environmental cleanup. Relaying what the GKU representative had learned from Edward Makanani, and activist who had worked for thirteen years for the cleanup of a former U.S. Marine bombing area on the Hawaiʻian island of Kaholabi, the report concluded:

> If there aren't any environmental articles in SOFA the tremendous amount of recovery cost will have to be relied on [sic] the Korean government, [sic] eventually the people will be burdened for the financial cost. As it is seen in the Kaholabi case, the polluted land caused by [U.S.] military operations will take tremendous amount of money and time. Maehyangni should not make the same mistakes as Viequez nor the Kaholabi. . . . Peace in Vieques (Paz Para Viequez!), Peace in Maehyangni! (Paz Para Maehyangni!).[68]

Although the U.S. forces withdrew from the Philippines in 1991, Filipino activists continued their bases movement with an environmental focus. Established in 1994, the Philippines Task Force for Bases' Cleanup (PTFBC) worked closely with the U.S. Working Group for the Philippine Bases' Cleanup, which became part of the Filipino/American Coalition of Environmental Solutions (FACES), to pressure the U.S. government into taking moral responsibility and providing financial and technical assistance for the cleanup of the bases. These and other affiliated NGOs that worked on peace, anti-militarism, environmental protection, health, sustainable development, human rights, and women's rights met at international conferences to exchange information and strategies. In 1996, the PTFBC convened representatives from the Philippines, Okinawa/Japan, Korea, Panama, Puerto Rico and the United States "for the first time to discuss the environmental and national sovereignty issues associated with hosting American military bases."[69] Participants compared notes on the type and scope of environmental problems, the role of the U.S. military in creating them, and the need for accountability by both the U.S. and home governments.

By the second international summit, held in Washington, DC, in 1999, the number of sponsoring organizations grew to include not only the PTFBC, but also Arc Ecology (U.S.), Asia Pacific Center for Peace and Justice (U.S.), Fellowship of Reconciliation on Latin America and the Caribbean, Institute for Policy Studies (U.S.), and the Committee for the Rescue and Development of Vieques (Puerto Rico). Their policy goals became more specific: U.S. development of overseas cleanup standards consistent with domestic requirements; transparent disclosure of environmental information to the host society and government by the U.S. military; negotiation and implementation of base-closure cleanup agreements by the U.S. and the host nation; and appeals to the United Nations, the European Union and other international bodies to pressure the United States into observing international norms and conventions on environmental responsibility and human rights.[70]

Martha Honey, who was a key IPS organizer, had found that various country groups were working on base-related matters in isolation, unaware of conditions and political work in other places. She recalled that an Okinawan activist she had met at a meeting in the late 1990s taught her a lot about the need to bring together people to make comparisons; she came to realize that they are part of a global movement rather than lone rangers in their homelands. And for her, base-related issues were American issues, especially since environmental cleanup of nuclear waste sites in Hawai'i and other states, as well as environmental damage, especially in Vieques, were salient concerns among some political and religious activists at the time (Quakers, for example, were active in the Hawai'ian movement) (author interview, Washington, DC, April 24, 2009).

The U.S. Government Accounting Office (GAO) itself had investigated environmental damage in overseas settings, which added firepower to foreign activists' claims. In 1992, its report, *Military Base Closures: U.S. Financial Obligations in the Philippines,* documented various problems and served to legitimate the grievances that activists in the Philippines, as well as Korea and Vieques, later pursued. According to the report, "[e]nvironmental officers at both Clark Air Base and the Subic Bay Naval Facility have identified contaminated sites and facilities that would not be in compliance with U.S. environmental standards."[71] They include underground storage tanks and fire-fighting facilities that have leaked fuel and chemicals into the soil and water, landfills that have lead and other heavy metals, PCBs and other untreated pollutants buried in the ground, and untreated sewage waste in the Subic Bay area. [72] In 1994, a team of U.S. investigators, basing their analysis on documents already released by the U.S. Department of Defense, found hundreds of different contaminants that are known to cause harm to humans, marine life, and land ecosystems.[73]

The PTFBC, together with a broad array of Filipino and international activists, scientists, public health officials (including the World Health

Organization and the Philippine Department of Health), and the media, compiled data on contaminated sites and raised political awareness of the incontrovertible evidence of damage to human life and the environment near the former U.S. military sites. In particular, the former Clark Air Force Base Command (CABCOM), which had been converted into a temporary refugee camp to accommodate numerous Filipino families whose homes had been destroyed by the eruption of Mount Pinatubo in 1992, became notorious for causing serious illnesses among the refugees and those born in the camps. In 1996, a health survey of 761 families living in 13 communities around Clark Air Base, conducted by the Canadian epidemiologist Dr. Rosalie Bertell and the Canadian Institute for the Concern of Public Health, found a "'startlingly high' level of kidney diseases and kidney problems," as well as central nervous system damage that were "apparently connected with both water and air exposures" in and around the base.[74] In the Subic area as well, local residents and activists documented the location, extent, and type of environmental problems left behind by U.S. forces. In July, 2000, 200 Filipinos filed a class action suit against both their own government and the United States, demanding compensation and cleanup.[75]

Korean activists and the media were quick to pick up on the toxic waste and health problems associated with the U.S. military in the Philippines, Vieques, Okinawa, and Germany. In 2000, during the time of the SOFA negotiations, PAR-SOFA activism, and the *panhwan* movement, *Hankyore Sinmun* featured a series of comparisons. Based on investigation in the Philippines, *Hankyore* documented the environmental and health problems attributed to the U.S. presence, referred to both the GAO report and the class action lawsuit, and concluded that the Philippines case clearly shows that problems associated with the U.S. presence do not end with the withdrawal of the military.[76] The article lamented the lack of U.S. accountability—since according to the U.S.-Philippines SOFA, the United States is exempt from any responsibility for environmental damages discovered after it has returned facilities to the host government or the restoration of the environment to its original state at the start of U.S. occupancy. The same stipulation applies to the SOFA with Korea and Japan. The bottom-line warning was that Koreans, like the Filipinos, would be stuck with whatever environmental damage came to light after any U.S. reversion of land or withdrawal.

By contrast, the newspaper featured the positive steps that the U.S. seemed to take in Germany to address both the environmental damage around the U.S. installations and the demands by the local populations.

For instance, it reported that since 1986, the U.S. government funded 75 percent of a water purification project to remedy problems emanating from Camps Taylor and Sullivan in the Mannheim region and that the city government and the U.S. military established a committee to investigate environmental problems on a regular basis.[77] Moreover, according to *Hankyore*, since 1990, the U.S. had responded to Kaiserslautern's demands to address water and soil damage by submitting investigative reports and working with the locals to clean up the problems.[78] Since the end of the Cold War and the return of land used by the U.S. military back to Germany, 218 of the 504 installations were assumed to pose some environmental danger and that because of the 1993 U.S.-German environmental addendum, the U.S. committed to abiding by German environmental laws and to funding much of the cleanup. [79]

Although the focus was on Germany, the lessons Koreans should learn were clear: (1) the U.S. treats some allies better than others; (2) the U.S. can and does take financial, practical, and moral responsibility for damage if citizens and their government, backed by law, insist on holding the U.S. accountable; (3) as evident in the Philippines, the return of land to the host country is not the end-all and be-all but can come with environmental problems that are costly; and (4) the strength of the SOFA—whether it is "fair" to the host country or not—determines U.S. accountability. In Korea in the summer of 2000, these were critical issues, given that both the revision of the SOFA with the U.S. and the return of land through the Land Partnership Program were under negotiation.

Just as Koreans paid attention to the post-U.S. withdrawal activism in the Philippines and developments in Germany, they followed environmental issues associated with the U.S. military in Japan, which became salient in the 1990s (e.g., PCB leakage accident at the Kadena Air Base in Okinawa, heavy metal pollution at the Yokosuka Naval Base, and PCB stockpiling at the Sagami Depot in Kanagawa Prefecture). Since the mid- to late 1990s, the relocation of Futenma Marine Air Station developed into a heated contestation over the interests of local Okinawan citizens, the U.S. military, the local Okinawan authorities, and Tokyo. Local citizens had long protested the disruptive presence of Futenma Station, located in Ginowan City, a densely populated area. As part of a base consolidation and reduction package, the Japanese and U.S. governments had agreed to move the facilities to the coast of Nago City in northern Okinawa. When Tokyo committed itself to building a new heliport on massive landfills, local citizens and national environmental groups aggressively protested such construction. They argued that the landfills and the military operations would pose serious danger to the area's marine life and flora, particularly the rich coral reefs and an endangered marine mammal species called the dugong.[80] Citizens and local officials pressured the Japanese government and the U.S. military to conduct various environment impact assessments and engaged in independent investigations as well.

GKU, a member of the People's Action for the Revision of the SOFA (PAR-SOFA), claims to be the first Korean CSO to have conducted an independent environmental survey of more than thirty U.S. base areas, covering eleven regions, in 1996. They documented a variety of problems, including serious noise pollution from military helicopters and fighter planes, oil spillage, improperly treated waste, and the disposal of depleted uranium in ordnance without proper safeguards.[81] They called on the U.S. government to investigate environmental damage; share information with Korean citizens, NGOs, and experts; and duly compensate for damage or restore the environment in Korea and in all "the nations where the Forces are stationed."[82] They also called for the future observance of strict environmental standards by U.S. forces in overseas areas.

Environmental concerns over U.S. military activities became headline news in 2000, when Yongsan Garrison, the headquarters of the Eighth U.S. Army, admitted to dumping 75.7 liters of toxic chemicals into the Han River in February 2000. It was GKU that first discovered and publicized the incident at a press conference on July 13, 2000. The group charged that the Yongsan mortuary had poured 228 liters of embalming fluid, including formaldehyde and methanol, into the river, which serves as the main source of water supply for Seoul residents. Calling the incident an "inhumane and uncivilized crime against the environment"[83] and "an exemplar for how the U.S. and U.S. military is [sic] deceiving, purposefully or not, Korea and its people,"[84] GKU and its partners demanded full investigation and transparency; the resignation of General Thomas Schwartz, the commander of the USFK; a formal apology from the United States (and its then ambassador, Stephen Bosworth); revision of the SOFA to include mandatory environmental inspections inside the U.S. bases (by U.S. and Korean governmental authorities and NGOs); the mandatory restoration of the environment to its original state; and "payment of the U.S. to Korea for the cost of their environmental damage."[85] In numerous documents and press interviews, GKU reiterated the potential of these environmental issues to raise the temperature of anti-American ire among Koreans.

On July 14, 2000, the U.S. military admitted that 75.7 liters of hazardous chemicals containing formaldehyde and methanol were drained into the Han River but that it was a minimal amount that had been duly processed before being released into the river and posed no danger to the environment. But the Korean media and civic groups portrayed the incident as paradigmatic of U.S. abuses of the Korean environment and people and campaigned aggressively on the web, in the media, at government offices, and on the streets for a formal apology and redress. On July 24, Lieutenant General Daniel Petrosky, commander of the Eighth U.S. Army, issued a written apology and statement from the U.S., stating a commitment to investigate the incident and to prevent similar incidents. Many Korean newspapers emphasized that it was the "first official apology by the commander of the 8th U.S. Army to the Korean people since 1945, when U.S. troops were first stationed in South Korea."[86]

Despite the near fifty-year presence, the impact of U.S. installations and facilities on the local environment—in terms of damage, safety, safeguards, conservation, and restoration—was never a policy issue before the second half of the 1990s. But the environmental movement made up for lost time by pushing its concerns and demands for accountability to the top of the agenda for the revision of the SOFA (chapter 5). In a sense, the environmental movement in Korea, particularly GKU, rose in public prominence due to its leadership role in PAR-SOFA. Even though environmental consciousness and activism had just taken root in the post-democratization period of the early to mid-1990s, within a few years, the environment became a major framing device for the *kiji* movement.

For students of social movements, frames are key to the success or failure of a movement to attract participants, allies, supporters, and media attention and to influence political discourse and change. One can have the most compelling concern, but without an effective "schemata of interpretation"[87] that draws upon existing and familiar cultural and discursive experience, organizing and mobilizing people and institutions become almost impossible. Tarrow states that "[a]ctivists are thus both consumers of existing cultural materials and producers of new ones. Proposing frames that are new and challenging but still resonate with existing cultural understandings is a delicate balancing act."[88] Tactically, too broad a frame can render a movement incoherent and disorganized, but too narrow a frame can limit participants, supporters, and target audience. The framing of social movements entails adapting to political opportunity structures—including new institutions and networks—understanding issue context, and negotiating among different participant groups and competing frames. According to della Porta and her colleagues, heterogeneity of a frame "triggers an ongoing process of identity building, open to continual renegotiation" because "movements built by interconnecting organizations that differ in their logic of action, type of identity, and country of origin, if they want to succeed in mobilizing and creating a new collective identity, must engage in an intense activity of negotiation with the purpose of building collective frames to be shared by the individual and structural potential mobilizations."[89]

All three movement types or blocs involved in *kiji* activism—women's rights, peace/anti-militarism, and environment—have distinct frames that resonate among each of the bloc's adherents, both domestically and internationally. But of the three, environmentalism has had the most traction in attracting broader public support and getting institutional responses from the Korean government and the U.S. military. Simply put, environmentalism is "hot," and "green" in vogue. Both the Korean government and people started to take a keen interest in recycling, sustainable energy, and green technology in the mid-1990s.[90] Moreover, there are structural transformations stemming from democratization, such as the empowerment of local governments and communities, that have fostered a sense of ownership and self-direction over environment conditions, land use, and planning (see chapter 2). Also, in some cases, the decentralization of government converged with international norm-setting and organizing around the environment. Since the institutionalization of decentralization in 1995, Koreans began incorporating "Local Agenda 21" into local government and community planning. Agenda 21, which recognized the vital need for local government participation, was adopted at the U.N. environment conference in Rio in 1992 as a sustainable development action plan for the twenty-first century. As of March 2004, 226 local Korean governments out of 250 (90.4 percent) were adopting and implementing the agenda.[91]

Korean environmentalists also successfully pursued electoral politics to get their agendas on the policy table. In 1995, when the first local elections in about thirty years were held as a consequence of democratization and decentralization, KFEM solicited "environmental candidates" to run for various positions. Thirty-two of the forty-six that KFEM had supported actually won, with two gaining mayoral seats. Moreover, as Su-Hoon Lee and his coauthors write,

> [m]any political leaders selected environmental movement leaders as their policy advisers or full-time aides, sponsored conferences . . . , and even maintained close personal ties with environmental activists. During elections, the environment becomes a popular issue and virtually every candidate claims to be pro-environment. In this respect,

> democratic consolidation has empowered the environmental movements in South Korea.[92]

Certainly, the Korean political establishment has not been willing to ally so closely with activists for women or for peace. This would not resonate with the larger public that, despite profound transformations toward gender equality and aspirations for peace, continues to privilege males and military definitions of national security.

But national ascendance in politics alone cannot explain the rise of environmental activists in the *kiji* movement. The regional and international social movement contexts were highly conducive to environmentalism as a useful framing device. In Korea, Japan, and the Philippines, environmental activism pertaining to the U.S. military presence (or legacy) gained momentum in the 1990s. Until then, awareness or concern had been sporadic and contained. But decentralization of government during that period in all three countries definitively provided new opportunity structures. In the Philippines, the Local Government Code of 1991, which explicitly requires NGO participation in local governance, allowed "local coalition-building efforts [to] assume a critical space in the environmental movement's menu of strategic concerns."[93] While Filipino post-democracy environmentalists advocated for a notion of "natural security" in contrast to "national security,"[94] Korean activists were emboldened by a "convergence of the radical democratic pursuit of citizen empowerment and the environmentalist demand for sustainable development."[95] Okinawa, which had developed a stronger peace movement and environmental consciousness by the 1990s than its neighbors, under Governor Ota Masahide, became the most well-known case of direct, sustained challenge to the central government by prefectural authorities and citizens.[96] These developments added energy and synergy to environmental activism in the region.

The environment as a major frame in the *kiji* movement reflects trends that social movement theorists have observed since the 1990s. For one, the environment has become a useful "venue" for activists who were less effective in mobilizing support or achieving their goals through other frames. Keck and Sikkink offer the example of indigenous rights activists, "who found the environmental arena more receptive to their claims than human rights venues had been."[97] In the Korean case, peace and women's rights continue as relevant frames, but the environment frame brought bases activism to the mainstream public, facilitated the incorporation of *kiji* issues into policymaking, and developed transnational resources in a way that the other frames were unable to do. The appeal of the environment frame may have something to do with the fact that it is not as nebulous and utopian as peace and not as radical as ending sexism toward women.

But calls for environmental consciousness alone would not have promised much effect, especially since the problems encountered by the localities housing U.S. bases generally do not affect the larger population. (As stated in chapter 2, these areas also have been on the periphery of national politics and policymaking.) According to Keck and Sikkink, "[e]nvironmental campaigns that have had the greatest transnational effect have stressed the connection between protecting environments and protecting the often vulnerable people who live in them."[98] In Korean and transnational bases activism, the environment and the local populations living near U.S. bases get framed as victims. Specifying victims, both individuals and communities, helps activists and the public grasp onto a problem whose causes might be more complex and out of reach to most people. Such specificity also parallels the Korean *kiji* watchdog National Campaign's emphasis on taking up issues that have specific causes and victims (see chapter 3) rather than sweeping ideologies and generalized finger-pointing. Additionally, specifying environmental problems related to the U.S. bases allows direct, measurable comparisons with other overseas settings (for example, level of soil contamination from specific toxins, decibels of noise pollution from jets and helicopters) and government redress, if any.

The fact that the two major Korean environmental organizations were receptive to joining the *kiji* movement is also important in understanding frame alignment. As mentioned in chapter 3, GKU was eager to work on *kiji* issues, providing both personnel and an affiliated ideology of protecting the sovereignty and preservation of Korean soil (*paedal*). And although KFEM joined later, the organization had a variety of interests, programs, and network connections that facilitated participation in the multi-issue activism surrounding U.S. bases. Although it emerged as the premier environmental organization by the mid-1990s, KFEM has included a diverse array of issues in its work: poverty, human rights, women's rights, and peace issues, as mentioned earlier. It participated in the UN NGO Forum on Women in Beijing and various World Social Forums, as well as the UN Conference on Human Settlements in Istanbul (1996).[99] Such heterogeneity of issues—also evident in the Japanese peace and environmental organizations and the Okinawan women's movement—allowed "frame bridging"—"the linkage of two or more ideologically congruent but structurally unconnected frames regarding a particular issue or problem"[100]—to occur in the Korean *kiji* movement.

And although systematic "frame transformation" among the different movement blocs and actors—"the planting and nurturing of new values, jettisoning old ones, and reframing erroneous beliefs and 'misframings'"—did not take place among every constituent group in the *kiji* movement (as the next chapter will show), key participants, like KFEM, and key individuals such as Chŏng Yujin indeed experienced frame transformation in their thinking and political orientation. In Chŏng's case, access to transnational peace and women's activism enabled her to jettison the old frame of Korean nationalism and anti-Americanism and adopt new values and activist aspirations: peace and mutual understanding among nationalities and historical enemies. If not for her transnational exposure, especially to Okinawan activists, her world view regarding the U.S. bases and *kiji* activism might have remained unexamined and stuck in anti-American antipathy.

Even the die-hard veteran "anti" activist Father Mun Chŏnghyŏn—anti-Korean government, anti-U.S., anti-hegemony, anti-compromise with the establishment—tempered his nationalism with the desire and need for transnational solidarity and cooperation. The recognition that one's national case is not the only pressing one, that one is not a unique victim of U.S. power, becomes available when activists cross borders in body and mentality. It also accompanies the sense that one is contributing to the improved welfare of those in distant places. This is part of what it means to be a "rooted cosmopolitan," whom Tarrow defines as "people and groups whose relations place them beyond their local or national settings without detaching them from locality."[101] To be a rooted cosmopolitan does not require the relinquishing of national identity or nation-promoting intent. Tarrow cites Kwame Anthony Appiah's observation that "rooted cosmopolitanism" and "cosmopolitan patriotism" are interchangeable.[102] Indeed, "[w]orking transnationalism reveals cosmopolitans without cosmopolitan ideology in the capacity of quite ordinary people, moving back and forth between the local and the translocal and among a variety of (not necessarily compatible) identities."[103]

NOTES

1. National Network to End the War Against Iraq, "Anti-War Protests Begin in Asia-Pacific," October 15, 2002, www.endthewar.org/features/asia pacific/htm (accessed November 19, 2003).

2. Ibid.

3. *Washington Post,* October 27, 2002, www.commondreams.org/headlines02/1027-07.htm (accessed January 14, 2009).

4. Sidney Tarrow, *The New Transnational Activism* (New York: Cambridge University Press, 2005), 15.

5. Ibid.

6. Ibid., 16.

7. Jackie Smith, "Exploring Connections between Global Integration and Political Mobilization," *Journal of World-Systems Research* 10 (2004), 255–285.

8. Tarrow, *The New Transnational Activism,* 44. With specific reference to anti-globalization movements, Donatella della Porta and her coauthors observed the following: "More or less everywhere, competition and tensions between institutional and more radical unions [in North America and Europe] have shifted into cooperation and to dialogue in the ESF [European Social Forum]." See Donatella della Porta, Massimiliano Andretta, Lorenzo Mosca, and Herbert Reiter, *Globalization from Below: Transnational Activists and Protest Networks* (Minneapolis, MN: University of Minneapolis Press, 2006), 35.

9. See Hyuk-Rae Kim," The State and Civil Society in Transition: The Role of Non-Governmental Organizations in South Korea," *Pacific Review* 13, no. 4 (2000), 603.

10. Tarrow, *The New Transnational Activism,* 15.

11. Margaret E. Keck and Kathryn Sikkink, *Activists beyond Borders: Advocacy Networks in International Politics* (Ithaca, NY: Cornell University Press, 1998).

12. Dawn Wiest and Jackie Smith, "Regional Institutional Contexts and Patterns of Transnational Social Movement Organization," *Korea Observer* 37, no. 1 (spring 2006), 99.

13. Tarrow, *The New Transnational Activism,* 73.

14. Della Porta et al., *Globalization from Below,* 44.

15. Ibid., 43.

16. Some of the observations in this section are informed by interview discussions with Takazato Suzuyo, April 21, 2004, Naha City, Okinawa.

17. Sister Mary Soledad Perpinan, R.G.S., "Confronting Prostitution Tourism," *Canadian Women's Studies* 7, nos. 1–2 (1986), 127.

18. Aida Santos, "Gathering the Dust: The Bases Issue in the Philippines," in *Let the Good Times Roll,* ed. Saundra Sturdevant and Brenda Stolzfus (New York: New Press, 1992), 40.

19. Cynthia Enloe *Bananas, Beaches and Bases: Making Feminist Sense of International Politics* (Berkeley, CA: University of California Press, 1990), chapter 9.

20. A. Lin Neumann, "Hospitality Girls in the Philippines," *Southeast Asia Chronicle* no. 66 (January–February 1979). I found this article in a packet entitled "Tourism and Prostitution" (November 1979), 13, at the office of ISIS, Geneva, Switzerland in 1989.

21. Thanh-dam Truong, *Sex, Money, and Morality: Prostitution and Tourism in Southeast Asia* (Atlantic Highlands, NJ: Zed Books, 1990), 161–167.

22. Katharine H. S. Moon, "South Korean Movements against Militarized Sexual Labor," *Asian Survey* 34, no. 2 (March–April 1999), 312.

23. Korea Church Women United (KCWU), "Women and Tourism: International Seminar Report" (Seoul: KCWU, April 20–23, 1988).

24. Elisabeth Friedman, "Women's Human Rights: The Emergence of a Movement," in *Women's Rights, Human Rights: International Feminist Perspectives,* ed. Julie Peters and Andrea Wolper (New York: Routledge, 1995).

25. See Robert D. Eldridge, "The 1996 Okinawa Referendum on US Base Reductions: One Question, Several Answers," *Asian Survey* 37, no. 10 (October 1997), 879–904; Sheila A. Smith, "Challenging National Authority: Okinawa Prefecture and the U.S. Military Bases," in *Local Voices, National Issues: The Impact of Local Initiative in Japanese Policy-Making,* ed. Sheila A. Smith (Ann Arbor, MI: University of Michigan Press, 2000), 102–103. Among voters, 89 percent desired a reduction of bases, but the turnout was relatively low and the ballot questions ill-phrased. Nevertheless, the referendum had symbolic political implications about local preferences and autonomy.

26. Japan Ministry of Foreign Affairs, "Japan-U.S. Special Action Committee (SACO) Interim Report," April 15, 1996, www.mofa.go.jp/region/n-america/us/security/seco.html (accessed July 13, 2009).

27. Mike M. Mochizuki, "A New Bargain for a Stronger Alliance," *Toward a True Alliance: Restructuring U.S.-Japan Security Relations,* ed. Mike M. Mochizuki (Washington, DC: Brookings Institution, 1997), 15.

28. Ibid.

29. Ibid., 25.

30. Carolyn Bowen Frances, "Women and Military Violence," in *Okinawa: Cold War Island,* ed. Chalmers Johnson (Cardiff, CA: Japan Policy Research Institute, 1999), 192–193.

31. Ibid., 193. Also, Yoko Fukumura and Martha Matsuoka, "Redefining Security: Okinawa Women's Resistance to U.S. Militarism," in *Women's Activism and Globalization: Linking Local Struggles and Transnational Politics,* ed. Nancy A. Naples and Manisha Desai (New York: Routledge, 2002), 253.

32. Saundra Sturdevant and Brenda Stolzfus, "Disparate Threads of the Whole: An Interpretive Essay," in *Let the Good Times Roll,* 311.

33. Cynthia Enloe, *Bananas, Beaches, and Bases,* 89. Enloe refers to the *Christian Science Monitor,* February 18, 1988.

34. "The International Grassroots Summit on Military Base Cleanup: A Healthy Environment Is a Human Right," (conference report, Trinity College, Washington, DC, October 25–29, 1999), 2, www.webcom.com/ncecd/basecleanup.htm (accessed April 27, 2006).

35. Author interview, Miriam Young (director of the U.S. Non-Government Organization Forum on Sri Lanka, Washington, DC), April 24, 2009.

36. Ibid.

37. Yonghan Kim, "Okinawa Migun kiji panhwan undong e sŏ paeunda" (Learning from the return of U.S. military base movement in Okinawa), *Wŏlgan Mal* (Monthly Mal magazine), September 1996, 92–95.

38. Ibid.

39. *Hankyore Sinmun,* August 2, 2000, www.hani.co.kr (accessed March 4, 2002).

40. Ibid.

41. Ibid.

42. *Hankyore Sinmun,* August 6, 2000, www.hani.co.kr (accessed March 4, 2002).

43. *Asian Political News,* March 13, 2000. Also in 1997, Shina, together with other Japanese musicians, had staged a fundraising concert to promote food aid and later released a DVD entitled "Swap All Weapons for Musical Instruments," www.findarticles.com/p/articles/mi_mo@DP/is_2000_March_13/ii_60067278/print?tag (accessed October 13, 2008).

44. Yujin Chŏng, "Okinawa e nŭn woe 'yangki go hom' guho ga ŏbssŭlgga?" (Why in Okinawa is there no "Yankee Go Home" slogan?), *Tangdae P'ipyŏng* 14 (spring 2001).

45. Asian Peace Alliance, *Occasional Newsletter,* no. 01-2003, www.human.mie-u.ac.jp/~peace/APA-03.htm (accessed November 12, 2008).

46. Base21, "Puerto Rican Solidarity with Korean People," http://base21.jinbo.net/show/show.php?p_cd=0&p_dv=0&p_docnbr=21475 (accessed October 2, 2002).

47. Chaejun Ch'oe, "Miguk, Hanguk, kŭrŏna uri," in Korean House for International Solidarity, special feature: "Do You Know about SOFA?" (Nŏhiga SOFA rŭl Anŭnga?), *Saram i saram ege* (People to people), October–November 2000, 25.

48. Chŏnghyŏn Mun, in ibid., 30–32.

49. Yŏnsik Pyŏn, in ibid., 40.

50. "East Asia-U.S.-Puerto Rico Women's Network against Militarism," blog post, People's Solidarity for Participatory Democracy, November 8, 2003, blog.peoplepower21.org/English/7533 (accessed November 10, 2008).

51. Interview with Takazata Suzuyo, Okinawa, April 21, 2004.

52. *Hankyore Sinmun,* August 20, 2000, www.hani.co.kr/section-00300/003004011200008202210004.htm (accessed March 2, 2004).

53. Asian Peace Alliance, *Occasional Newsletter,* no. 01-2003.

54. Ibid.

55. Ibid.

56. Max Lane, "Philippines: Asian Peace Alliance Formed," *Green Left Online,* www.greenleft.org.au/2002/508/27508 (accessed December 3, 2008).

57. Asia Partnership for Human Development, *Annual Report 2003* (Bangkok: APHD Secretariat), 4, www.aphd.or.th/annual-report/pdf/aphd-annual-report-2003.pdf (accessed November 12, 2008).

58. Ibid.

59. Asia Partnership for Human Development (APHD), *Mosaic* magazine, April–August 2004, www.aphd.or.th/mosaic/pdf/mosaic_4.pdf (accessed December 19, 2008). This issue focused on conflict and peace on the Korean peninsula and the presence and impact of U.S. forces in Korea and Okinawa.

60. Ibid., 9.

61. Peace Boat, "Japanese-Korean Historic Peace Voyage Marks 60 Years since World War II," April 26, 2005, www.peaceboat.org/english/nwps/pr/arc/050426/index.html (accessed December 12, 2008).

62. Peace Boat, "Regional Voyage 2007," October 28, 2007, www.peaceboat.org/english/voyg/61/index.html (accessed December 12, 2008).

63. Bal Pinguel, Herbert Docena, and Wilbert van der Zeijden, "No Bases," in *Report on the Strategy Meetings of the International Network against Foreign Military Bases,* World Social Forum 2005, Brazil, January 27 and 31, 2005, www.tni.org/acts/wsf5bases.pdf (accessed December 12, 2008).

64. They included Argentina, Australia, Belgium, Brazil, Canada, Chile, Cuba, Ecuador, France, Germany, Greece, Hong Kong, India, Indonesia, Italy, Japan, Korea, Kyrgyz Republic, Mauritius, Netherlands, New Zealand, Norway, Pakistan, Philippines, Puerto Rico, Seychelles, South Korea, Switzerland, Thailand, Turkey, UK, and the U.S.

65. Andres Conteris, Ben Moxham, Herbert Docena, and Wilbert van der Zeijden, "Report of the International Anti-US Bases Conference World Social Forum," Mumbai, India, January 17 and 20, 2004, www.tni.org/detail_page.phtml?page=acts_wsf4usbases (accessed January 16, 2009).

66. Green Korea United, "Forbidden Rights to Pollute the Korean Peninsula: U.S. Military Activities and Environmental Disaster," January 31, 2003, blog.peoplepower21.org/English/8505 (accessed January 15, 2009).

67. United Nations Environment Program, "The Programme for the Development and Periodic Review of Environmental Law for the First Decade of the Twenty-first Cenutry," Decision 21/23 of the Governing Council of 9, February 16–17, 2001, www.unep.org/law/PDF/GC22_2_3_add2_Montevideo%20III.pdf (accessed January 16, 2009).

68. Green Korea United, "Do Not Trust the US Military," October 2, 2000, www.greenkorea.org/zb/print_innerHTM.php (accessed April 12, 2007).

69. "The International Grassroots Summit."

70. Ibid. Also see John Lindsay-Poland and Nick Morgan, "Overseas Military Bases and Environment," *Foreign Policy in Focus* 3, no. 15 (June 1998), www.fpif.org/briefs/vol3/v3n15mil_body.html (accessed January 28, 2006).

71. U.S. General Accounting Office, Report to Congressional Requesters, "Military Base Closures: U.S. Financial Obligations in the Philippines" (Washington, DC, January 1992), 27.

72. Ibid, 27–28.

73. Republic of the Philippines Third Judicial Region, Regional Trial Court, *Zambales, Wilfredo Mesiano, et al. v. The Department of Defense of the United States, et al.* (2000), 59–70, www.yonip.com/main/articles/Clark.html (accessed March 5, 2004).

74. Republic of the Philippines Third Judicial Region, Regional Trial Court, *Pampanga, Karen Lacson, et al. v. The Department of Defense of the United States of America, et al.* (2000), www.yonip.com/main/articles/Clark .html (accessed March 5, 2004).

75. Ibid.

76. *Hankyore Sinmun,* September 3, 2000, www.hani.co.kr (accessed February 26, 2002).

77. *Hankyore Sinmun,* August 27, 2000, www.hani.co.kr (accessed February 26, 2002).

78. Ibid.

79. Ibid.

80. The dugong became a central rallying point for anti-bases activists and local officials in the Henoko area and Okinawa in general. See "Statement of the Japan Environment Lawyers Federation Regarding the Dugong Population of Okinawa," August 1, 2001, jca.apc.org/JELF/English/JELF-stateD.html (accessed November 13, 2003); Love Dugong Network, "Survey and Preservation of the Dugongs and Habitat in Okinawa and a Message for World Peace," 2nd ed., March 11, 2000, www.okinawa-u.ac.jp/~tsuchida/Save-Dugong/love/messageE.html (accessed November 12, 2003).

81. Green Korea United, "A Korean Environmental Report on the U.S. Bases," June 16, 1999, 7–8, www./A%20Korean%20Environmental%20Report%20on%20the%20U.S.%20Bases.htm (accessed July 25, 2001).

82. Ibid., 6.

83. Green Korea United, "Petition Statement to the ROK Ministry of Defense," August 8, 2000, www.greenkorea.org/sub_board/way-board.cgi?db=eng_statement&j=v&no=2&pg=1 (accessed August 8, 2001).

84. Green Korea United, "Protest Statement," August 8, 2000, 1, www.greenkorea.org/sub_board/way-board.cgi?db=engl_statement&j=v&no=3&pg=1 (accessed August 8, 2001).

85. Green Korea United, "Petition Statement," 1.

86. *Korea Herald,* July 25, 2000, www.koreaherald.co.kr/SITE/data/html_dir/2000/07/25/200007250010.asp (accessed July 25, 2000).

87. David A. Snow, E. Burke Rochford, Jr., Steven K. Worden, and Robert D. Benford, "Frame Alignment Processes, Micromobilization, and Movement Participation," *American Sociological Review* 51 (August 1986), 464.

88. Tarrow, *The New Transnational Activism,* 61.

89. Della Porta et al., *Globalization from Below,* 89–90.

90. For example, since 1995, households and commercial building owners are required to purchase specifically designed plastic bags for garbage disposal and recycling, with a high rate in the increase of recycling. Major dailies such as the *Chosun Ilbo* and the *Dong-A Ilbo,* as well as broadcasting companies, launched various environmental campaigns in the 1990s. In 1999, environmental and other civic groups successfully mobilized the public against a dam construction project in East Sea (Korea's east coast), causing President Kim Dae Jung to cancel the project in June 2000.

91. R.O.K. Ministry of Environment, "Local Agenda 21 in Korea," October 17, 2003, eng.me.go.kr/docs/news/hotissue/hotissue_view.html?topmenu=E&cat=520&seq=19&page=4 (accessed January 20, 2009).

92. Su-Hoon Lee, Hsin-Huang Michael Hsiao, and Hwa-Jen Liu et al., "The Impact of Democratization on Environmental Movements," in *Asia's Environmental Movements: Comparative Perspectives,* ed. Yok-shiu F. Lee and Alvin Y. So (Armonk, NY: M.E. Sharpe, 1999), 235.

93. Francisco A. Magno, "Environmental Movements in the Philippines," in *Asia's Environmental Movements,* 173. On decentralization in the Philippines, see Terrence R. George, "Local Governance: People Power in the Provinces?" in *Organizing for Democracy: NGOs, Civil Society, and the Philippines State,* ed. G. Sidney Silliman and Lela Garner Noble (Honolulu: University of Hawaiʻi Press, 1998).

94. Su-Hoon Lee et al., "Impact of Democratization," 242.

95. Ibid., 243.

96. Sheila A. Smith, "Challenging National Authority."

97. Keck and Sikkink, *Activists beyond Borders,* 18.

98. Ibid., 27.

99. Korea Federation of Environmental Movements, "About Us," english.kfem.or.kr/aboutus/aboutus1.htm (accessed March 23, 2007).

100. Tarrow, *The New Transnational Activism,* 62. See David A. Snow et al., "Frame Alignment Processes," 467.

101. Tarrow, *The New Transnational Activism,* 42.

102. Ibid.

103. Ibid., 46.

5. Winners and Losers in Civil Society Politics

On October 28, 1992, Yun Kŭmi, a young bar hostess and sex worker, died in Tongduch'on at the hands of Kenneth Markle, a private in the U.S. Army. She was found "naked, bloody, and covered with bruises and contusions—with laundry detergent sprinkled over the crime site. In addition, a Coke bottle was embedded in Yun's uterus and the trunk of an umbrella driven 27 cm into her rectum."[1] Before her death, she was called, like the thousands of other *kiji ch'on* (camp town) women who have sexually serviced U.S. soldiers since the 1950s, *yanggalbo* (Western whore) by Korean society.[2] After her brutal murder, she was extolled as a *sunkyŏlhan ttal* (pure daughter of Korea) by her compatriots. Before her murder, the life of a camp town prostitute was understood and accepted as nasty, brutish, and short, a necessary cost of maintaining the tens of thousands of U.S. service personnel (overwhelmingly male) who helped safeguard South Korea's national security. Soon after her death, the National Campaign for the Eradication of Crimes against Korean Civilians by U.S. Troops (Undong Ponbu), the first national organization formed to uncover, monitor, and demand official accountability for U.S. military crimes and abuses against Koreans, was established. (See chapter 3 for further discussion of Undong Ponbu.) Yun's death gave organizational shape and political focus to the criticisms of Korea's relationship with the United States that had been floating around in the general public for decades.

The advocacy groups for *kiji ch'on* women were what Sidney Tarrow calls "early risers" in the bases movement, individuals and organizations that gave momentum to the "diffusion of a propensity for collective action . . . to both unrelated groups and to antagonists."[3] In this regard, the *kiji ch'on* women's groups put the connections among gender discrimination, violence against women, and national security on the national political map, a marked change since the period of authoritarian rule, when national security issues were off-limits to independent public criticism and when personal costs for the sake of national security were assumed to be "natural." They helped introduce new issues such as anti-militarism and peace activism to Korean civil society. Moreover, as we have seen in chapter 4, women's groups helped forge transnational networks that benefited the work of other bases activists. Last, they facilitated a change in the balance of power between the capital and the regions, prompting local governments and residents to articulate and press their interests with the central government and Seoul-based civil society organizations (CSOs).

Yet, the early birds were not able to lead the People's Action for the Reform of the SOFA (PAR-SOFA) coalition or to move their concerns to the top of the policy agenda during the revision of the SOFA. The case of militarized prostitution demonstrates the openings for and limitations to civil society participation. There are winners and losers, issues that gain salience and others that get eclipsed or silenced in any social movement. The *kiji undong* in general and the SOFA revision movement (PAR-SOFA) in particular are no exceptions. The diversification and mainstreaming of women's issues in the national women's movement left the *kiji ch'on* movement practically orphaned, while a "masculinist-nationalist" group of CSO leaders—concerned primarily with rapid reunification, complete withdrawal of U.S. troops, and a fuller assertion of Korean sovereignty—used and subordinated these women's grievances. This latter group sought to "instrumentalize" (*toguhwa*) the plight and suffering of prostituted women for its own political gain. Focusing on militarized prostitution also shows that nationalistic ideology, rather than being a nebulous or monolithic phenomenon, persists or dominates in specific issue areas of the bases movement. *Kiji* activists came to acknowledge local interests and environmental concerns as legitimate issues in their own right, but women-oriented issues were considered less than legitimate unless tied to the symbolic power and fate of the "nation."

KIJI CH'ON UNDONG: THE "EARLY BIRDS"

Although the violence and suffering endured by Korean women who sexually "service" American servicemen are not the sole causes of the *kiji undong* (bases movement) in Korea, these women's lives and deaths have captured the public's attention and galvanized collective outrage against both real and perceived U.S. military abuses of power and privilege in their host country. Private Markle's murder of Yun Kŭmi in 1992 is a case in point. Later, in 1995, the Korean media and public were up in arms over the alleged sexual molestation of a Korean woman by a U.S. serviceman and the ensuing violence between Koreans and U.S. personnel inside a Seoul subway train. The media generated much heat and misinformation about the couple and the incident without noting the particulars of their relationship—the man and woman were married and engaging in a public display of affection (usually frowned upon in Korean society).[4]

In 2000, the murder of another prostitute, Kim Sŏnghui, by Private Christopher McCarthy generated more criticism of U.S. troops and the command's bungled handling of the case. McCarthy admitted to strangling Kim in February 2000, although he stated that he had not intended to kill her. The Korean court tried, convicted, and sentenced him to eight years in prison. His appeal led to a two-year reduction. While under U.S. military custody (in accordance with the SOFA in force at the time), McCarthy escaped on the day of his trial before the South Korean court. He was recaptured about eight hours later. Citizens were outraged by the bungling of the case and exerted more pressure to revise the SOFA so as to strengthen Korean legal authority and custody over alleged American perpetrators.

The general public's sense of anger and affront in these cases reflected a sensitivity to a history of sexual privilege over Korean women by foreign men in uniform, whether Japanese during the colonial period or American since the military occupation and the stationing of permanent bases under the Mutual Defense treaty of 1953. Not only activists but also officials and analysts for the Korean Ministry of Foreign Affairs and Trade have acknowledged the undeniable link between the abuses and violence (both alleged and proven) against Korean women, especially camp town prostitutes, and anti-bases sentiments and activism.[5]

As early birds on the camp town scene, advocates for *kiji ch'on* women tended to the day-to-day welfare needs of the bar women and their children, elderly women who could not earn regular income from the sex industry, as well as those seeking to free themselves from bar owners and pimps. Since 1986, they established shelters and counseling centers like My Sister's Place (Durebang, opened in 1988) and worked to put issues like violence against women, debt bondage, police brutality, and militarism on civil society's political agenda. In the immediate aftermath of Yun's death, Tongduch'on civic groups, such as the Tongduch'on Citizens' Committee, taxi union, teachers' unions, student associations, as well as various advocacy groups from Seoul, joined forces to protest GI brutality, the neglect of local police in investigating and pushing for custody, and the lack of investigative work and pressure by the mass media.[6] They staged large demonstrations at the front gates of the U.S. Second Infantry Division (2ID) and initiated petitions against violence by U.S. troops against civilians and for the fair investigation and redress of the murder. In particular, they demanded that the Korean government should have jurisdiction over the case and the custody of Markle.

Even strangers to Tongduch'on, like Kim Yonghan of P'yŏngtaek (who, in the early 1990s, was interested in blocking a potential transfer of U.S. personnel from Yongsan to P'yŏngtaek), traveled to the infamous camp town that had long hosted the U.S. 2ID in order to learn how to "do activism" regarding U.S. bases.[7] He became a leader of the new National Campaign and later helped lead the *panhwan* (return-of-land) movement and the PAR-SOFA (see chapter 3).

Many other CSO leaders in contemporary Korean society had their start or substantive grassroots training in Tongduch'on and other camp towns through the women's counseling and advocacy centers that grew throughout the 1990s such as Saewoomtuh (established in 1996). Chŏng Yujin, who had been a staff member of Durebang in the early 1990s, helped found and lead the National Campaign. Throughout the late 1990s, working closely with Okinawan activists, Chŏng helped develop peace activism in South Korea (discussed in chapter 4), and in the early 2000s joined the newly created National Human Rights Commission. (The commission is the first-ever independent governmental body established to oversee human rights issues in South Korea.) Moreover, several active members of Women Making Peace, a major feminist peace organization that was established in 1997, and Magadalena House, a shelter for women working in the general sex industry, began their work on women and violence at Durebang or at Saewoomtuh.

All of these centers have sponsored Korean and international scholars, artists, religious leaders, political activists, elected officials, and members of the media, who, through their interactions with prostituted women and their advocates, have helped raise awareness of camp town concerns, gender relations, sex trafficking and the sex industry, human rights, and alliance politics. Advocacy groups like Durebang and Saewoomtuh also sponsored university students who came to the camp towns to conduct their "Membership Training" (MT) or field experience.[8] These students, most of whom never had had exposure to *kiji ch'on* life and politics, would serve as volunteers at the centers, participating in community programs, administrative work, outreach, daycare and tutoring for the children of prostituted women, and sharing meals and conversation with various camp town women. In this way, people outside the *kiji ch'on* came to know something about the living conditions, abuses, stresses, hopes, and survival skills of the camp town women and other residents. Consciousness-raising about the relationship between militarization and women and the trade-offs between national and human security were two key lessons learned through these camp town classrooms.

Although Korean society generally has viewed camp towns as pariah towns and has politically marginalized or ignored their issues, grassroots persistence and dedication have fostered and transformed the development of local civic leaders and women's issues into national and international leaders and issues. Moreover, without the lives and deaths of camp town women to serve as witness to the social and psychological cost of housing U.S. troops in Korea, and without the pioneering work of the women's advocacy groups and residents' organizations, the contemporary social movement criticizing U.S. bases would lack moral authority. The head of the National Campaign in 2002 emphasized that local grievances and complaints prompt organizational activism and offer legitimacy to the social movement.[9]

However, the role and status of the *kiji ch'on* advocacy movement within the larger bases movement confirms Sidney Tarrow's observation that "the power to trigger sequences of collective action is not the same as the power to control or sustain them." Tarrow goes on:

> Internally, a good part of the power of movements comes from the fact that they activate people over whom they have no control. This power is a virtue because it allows movements to mount collective action without possessing the resources that would be necessary to internalize a support base. But the autonomy of their supporters also disperses a movement's power, encourages factionalization, and leaves it open to defection, competition, and repression.[10]

Furthermore, Georgina Waylen finds that "there is no necessary connection between playing an important part in any stage of the process of democratization and having any particular role during the period of consolidation."[11] Taken together, Tarrow's and Waylen's comments illustrate that, ironically, the very success of early risers in motivating citizen action and transforming larger political processes and agendas may lead to less and less leverage over the direction of political action and policy outcomes in a democratic society.

Additionally, the *kiji ch'on* movement's inability to play a prominent role in the larger coalition movement is attributable to the fact that social movements in Korea, including the women's movement, have been moving away, both ideologically and structurally, from a focus on *minjung* (common, downtrodden masses) toward *simin* (citizen, usually middle-class) since the mid-1990s[12] (see chapter 3). The emergence of hyper-marginalized camp town women as a focus of political concern in the early 1990s occurred within a civil society context that still held on to its *minjung* legacy. According to Namhee Lee,

> the shift from minjung to simin displaced the poor and the marginalized in the social and political discourse. The true minjung who could not revert back to their non-minjung identity in the changed sociopolitical reality of South Korea would have to construct their emancipatory narrative on a different terrain, that of articulating the issues largely on the basis of interest (as a right-bearing and right-claiming citizen, for example).[13]

But with democratic deepening and greater institutionalization of civil society issues, the emphasis on the *minjung,* including the *kiji ch'on* women, declined while mainstream women's issues received increased political interest and attention.

WOMEN, GENDER, AND CIVIL SOCIETY

Environmental conditions for violence against women and other abuses existed prior to Yun's murder. The following memorandum by a civilian official of the U.S. Forces in Korea reveals that the military was aware of the potential for politicization as early as the 1960s: "It is easily conceivable that the large number of assaults by US personnel against Korean national females, no matter what the provocation might have been given for these assaults, could be made into a major article condemning American brutality."[14] In contrast to the public treatment of Yun's death, *kiji ch'on* women who had lost their lives to GI violence in the 1950s, 1960s, 1970s, and 1980s almost always remained unacknowledged and unclaimed by the larger Korean society.

For example, on July 13, 1977, a brutal and egregious murder comparable to that of Yun Kŭmi took place near Kunsan Air Force base and was barely noticed by the larger public. The official U.S. Air Force investigation report of the murder records the following:

> Victim was possibly rendered unconscious either by a blow above the right eye, or by restricting the flow of oxygen to the brain with the scarf tied around her neck. . . . At some point Victim was conscious enough to grasp hair from her assailant's body with her right hand,

> which should have caused pain to her assailant. Due to the amount of Kleenex forced into her mouth, Victim again lost consciousness. Victim's assailant then apparently proceeded to stab Victim in the chest, stomach and vaginal area, while standing over her. It appeared that the assailant kneeled over Victim, pulled Victim's head up towards his chest and then stabbed Victim in her back . . . , breaking the knife on the third thrust, leaving the knife blade imbedded in Victim's back.[15]

But in the context of limited rights and protections for regular citizens prior to democratization in the late 1980s, those regarding *kiji ch'on* prostitutes were close to nonexistent. Generally, the government viewed military prostitution as a necessary evil to accommodate the social and sexual needs of U.S. servicemen and began to regulate the women systematically in the early 1970s,[16] and the general public regarded these women as social and moral refuse. However, democratization, decentralization, and the growth of "NGO-ism" in the 1990s created a political context in which the localized, marginalized, and "privatized" taboo reality of *kiji ch'on* women's lives could become a public issue.

In addition to the usual demonstrations, pamphleteering, petitions, and so on, citizens began testing the legal system to address personal grievances and demand public redress, even on behalf of prostitutes. For example, on July 19, 2000, the Citizens Coalition for Economic Justice (CCEJ) challenged the legality of the Status of Forces Agreement in South Korea's Constitutional Court. The brief alleged that the agreement "violates the Korean Constitution's provision on human dignity, equal rights, the right of criminal victims to testify in court, environmental rights, and the right to the pursuit of happiness."[17]

The case is striking for two reasons. First, it was the first institutional challenge seeking to de-link national security agreements between governments from the protection of individual civil and human rights. Or in other words, national sovereignty no longer could trump individual rights, and Koreans were willing to put their legal system to the test. Second, the claim was filed on behalf of common people living near the U.S. bases who had suffered loss or damage. Attorney Lee Sokyŏn, secretary-general of CCEJ, registered the claim specifically on behalf of the parents of the murdered sex-worker Kim Sŏnghui.[18] Again, like Yun Kŭmi, Kim became a posthumous standard-bearer for the rights of all Korean citizens vis-à-vis the U.S. military.

Democratization and civil society development are not gender-neutral processes. Recent feminist examinations of gender, women, and civil society in South Korea focus on two contrasting perspectives. The first emphasizes the limited participation of women and the marginalization of women's issues since democratization began in 1987. For Lily Ling, it is the invariability of masculinized cultural norms and political practices in state-society relations—despite the rapid socioeconomic changes in much of East Asia—that compromises the development of democracy and civil society.[19] In particular, she criticizes the "hyper-masculine" developmental state for dominating society.[20] For Seungsook Moon, not only Confucianist political culture but the more immediate legacy of androcentric and masculine practices under authoritarian rule and the resistance movements to it limited women's access to and the insertion of gender-specific issues into the political arena.[21]

The second perspective takes a more optimistic approach, namely, that women and women-oriented organizations have played a significant role in developing civil society and furthering democratic consolidation. This perspective highlights the contributions of women's movements to create institutional changes in government, especially legal prohibitions against discrimination and the extension of new rights and protections, as well as women's increased access to government bureaucracies and funding for women's issues.[22]

Other scholars emphasize how the inverse is also true: civil society can be good for facilitating women's political participation. According to Larry Diamond, "[b]ecause of the traditional dominance by men of the corridors of power, civil society is a particularly important base for the training and recruitment of women (and members of other marginalized groups) into positions of formal political power."[23] Aili Mari Tripp bears witness to this, based on her research in Africa, observing that "[p]olitical openings of the early 1990s changed the face of the women's movement . . . , making it possible for the formation of new nonpartisan organizations geared toward lobbying, civil education, and leadership training, emboldening women to run for office."[24] Indeed, many prominent South Korean women in politics and government in recent years got their political start as leaders of CSOs and educational institutions.[25]

Both the optimistic and pessimistic interpretations are partially correct. Women's activism and women-oriented issues in Korea have greatly increased and benefited from civil society activism since 1987, yet women continue to be the "weaker sex" in terms of economic and political power and influence in Korea's fast-changing democracy. What both perspectives share in common is their overemphasis on the state as the agent of exclusion and marginalization (for pessimists) or of inclusion and empowerment (for optimists). This tension reflects the current tendency in research on women and democracy to position women between two extremes of insider or outsider, institutional mainstreaming versus autonomy on the margins.[26]

From the optimists, we tend to learn about the successful issues but not those that were neglected or pushed out by civil society actors and therefore never given the chance to contend for serious state attention. Understanding how and why some women's issues and organizations become insiders or remain outsiders *within the world of CSOs* is important for understanding how disparate concerns become issues for collective social action and appear on the policy agendas of the state. Studying actors and issues that are less successful in achieving institutional attention may shed light on the uneven and variable nature of democratic consolidation and civil society development. Jongryn Mo observes that "different levels of democratic consolidation can exist in different political areas within a given type of democracy. The rules of one policy area may be widely accepted while the rules of another policy area may lack such consensus."[27] I would add that this observation applies also to politics within civil society. The legitimacy of an issue, goal-orientation, pluralism, cooperation, and the building of social capital may be more developed in some issue areas among some organizations (and members) but lagging in others.

How and why certain organizations' agendas and political interests rise from the grassroots to the institutional level and, conversely, how and why the agendas and interests of others fail to do so is a key question in understanding the politics of social movements in general and the PAR-SOFA in particular. This especially is important with respect to civil society movements in Korea, which are dominated by coalition activism. With respect to women's issues, prior to negotiations between government and women's groups, they must be negotiated among civil society groups. In the process, we may find that "early risers" do not necessarily get to shape the political and policy content of the movement, that conflict over what constitutes legitimate issues and actors, and gender biases among what are commonly perceived as "progressive" groups hinder the progress of sub-movements, like the *kiji ch'on* movement.

DIVERSIFICATION AND "MAXIMALISM" IN CIVIL SOCIETY

In the PAR-SOFA coalition, women's organizations and human rights groups were not the primary players, despite the fact that women's activism on behalf of camp town women in the late 1980s and early 1990s served as a foundation for CSO criticism of U.S. power and privilege in Korea. Rather, since the mid- to late 1990s, organizations and activists who focused on environmental, legal, and reunification interests, in addition to local officials and residents' groups, have shaped the movement's policy concerns and political rhetoric and the course of government action. Specifically, among the CSOs, Green Korea United (GKU), Korea Federation of Environmental Movements (KFEM), Citizens' Coalition for Economic Justice (CCEJ), Lawyers for a Democratic Society (Minbyun), and the National Alliance for Democracy and Reunification of Korea (NADRK/Chŏn'guk Yŏnhap), local *panhwan* (return-of-land) activists, and local governments and residents' associations have played key roles. The National Campaign has continued to serve as the main watchdog group and clearinghouse for many of the issues related to USFK conduct affecting Korean civilians, but with a small staff, the organization has had to rely on the human resources, organizational infrastructure, mobilizational power, and constituent reach of other CSOs.

The variety of—and competition among—these and other organizations reflects the multifaceted nature of the bases movement, but it also reflects two salient trends in civil society activism. The first is the proliferation and diversification of women's organizations throughout the 1990s, which have made the coordination of issues, goals, and methods of action among them more complicated and difficult. Simply, the challenges and obstacles to achieving solidarity on specific issues have increased with the growth of civil society. Whereas women's activism in the military-authoritarian period of the 1970s to the late 1980s focused mainly on labor rights, opposition to sex tourism by Japanese men, and the struggle against authoritarian regimes, the post-1987 period is characterized by a wide and ever-growing array of issues: equal employment, environmental concerns, consumer rights, electoral participation, political reform, human rights, disability rights, sexual harassment and violence, anti-militarism, peace, reunification, welfare provision, maternal care and development of daycare, abolishment of the patrilineal family registry system, and more. Some of these issues had been around in the earlier period, but the momentum, mobilization of resources, and media attention around these issues were made possible in the new democratic environment.

Within the larger women's movement, there is also a tendency toward less radical, more mainstream issue representation.

> In particular, the imperative to reach out to diverse groups of women in largely conservative local communities often means that these organizations start with less controversial matters such as the environment, consumer rights, and childcare, rather than issues such as sexual/domestic violence that speak directly to power relations between gendered individuals.[28]

This is a function of both the ascendance and dominance of the middle class and the increasing institutionalization of women's political roles and women's issues in the new political environment.[29] This is in contrast to the earlier generation of the women's movement, which focused on working-class women and socioeconomic inequalities, and gave rise to female leaders from factories, slums, and farms.[30] And although some highly visible female politicians and government officials had received the bulk of their political training and experience through radical activism in the 1970s and 1980s, once they assume national public office, the need to respond to and reflect a wider spectrum of political ideology and interests became necessary. Under these conditions, spearheading the cause of prostituted women is not the way to win friends and influence in the overwhelmingly male-dominated and rough-and-tumble political establishment in South Korea.

The diversification and mainstreaming of issues have been coupled with competing perspectives on the sex industry that are not easy to reconcile. For example, the debate about victim/agent and prostitute/sex worker that has become salient in Western academic and activist circles[31] has also been taking place in Korea in recent years, making agreement on how to address the trafficking of women, the sex trade, and camp town prostitution more difficult.[32] In particular, with regard to foreign sex workers, Sea-ling Cheng emphasizes that "[i]n spite of their structural vulnerabilities as migrant women in *gijichon,* they cannot be flattened into a singular identity as either 'victims' or 'agents.'"[33]

In fall 2001, Korean women's groups and the government-sponsored think tank on women's issues, the Korean Women's Development Institute, made first-time efforts to draft and propose a "Special Act on the Prevention of Sex Trafficking" to the National Assembly. Initially, the proposed bill emphasized harsher punishment for pimps, traffickers, and bar owners and the provision of protection and welfare services for victims of trafficking, particularly foreign nationals. It also de-emphasized the punishment of prostituted women. But there was disagreement among the different women's organizations over the criminal status of prostituted women and the need for state-regulated sexual commerce. Many of the advocates for camp town women generally opposed the treatment of prostituted women as criminals and particularly opposed their institutional detention/imprisonment, while more mainstream women's representatives advocated some type of detention and the retention of state-designated and regulated prostitution zones.[34] Contradictory provisions advocating both the punishment and protection of women resulted, together with feelings of rancor among the participating activists.

Related is the fact that the "comfort women" (*chŏngsindae*) movement became the focal point in the 1990s of aggressive activism against militarism and sexual violence and for women's human rights. Although the leaders of the comfort-women movement and those of the *kiji ch'on* movement initially attempted to join forces and work together for women's human rights, their differences over the moral legitimacy of women in each category—former "comfort women" and their advocates saw the *chŏngsindae* as chaste women who were forced into prostitution and slavery, while viewing the camp town women as unchaste, voluntary participants in prostitution—ultimately split them apart. They "lost the opportunity to promote an expanded understanding of human rights that incorporates issues around human trafficking, sexual exploitation and violence into the mainstream of the women's movement."[35] As the comfort women issue gained ground nationally and internationally, it overshadowed the fledgling movement for camp town women's rights and welfare.[36] These cases of conflict and competition are particularly regrettable since human, financial, and institutional resources available to address marginalized women's concerns in Korea have been scarce in the first place.

The second characteristic is the tendency of some Korean CSOs toward maximalist strategies and zero-sum conflict.[37] Although Kyoung-Ryung Seong attributes this trend particularly to interest-based associations (e.g., labor and professional groups), the trend also applies to some leaders of the *kiji* movement. Maximalist thinking gets expressed at various moments (depending on the internal politics) in terms of foreign policy goals, such as the withdrawal of U.S. troops, a total overhaul of the Status of Forces Agreement, resistance to U.S. hegemony, the signing of a peace treaty between North and South, and/or the reunification of the Korean peninsula. As discussed in chapter 3, this reflects the continuing legacy of the anti-authoritarian/pro-democracy struggles of the 1970s and 1980s, during which many in the CSO/activist community had tested their mettle or come of political age. Their political environment was characterized by *t'ujaeng* (struggle/fight) and zero-sum stakes: life and liberty versus death or imprisonment; military versus civilian rule; dictatorship versus democracy.

Those who espouse maximalist strategies regarding U.S. troops tend to be male. They have disparaged and disregarded the calls by some female activists to focus attention on individual human suffering, particularly that of camp town women who live with day-to-day forms of exploitation, social marginalization, and various kinds of violence. Chŏng Yujin, the co-founder and former leader of the National Campaign, recounts conversations and debates with male anti-base activists who argued that withdrawal is the "fundamental" issue and that rape, murder, sexual exploitation, and abandoned Amerasian children are "minor," "personal" issues. They charged that the National Campaign was merely reformist, neglecting to put national reunification first and to lead the cause for withdrawal. They also blamed women's "reformism" and the assertion of gender and sex issues into the policy debates for causing a split in the collective movement.[38]

Under such masculine nationalism, women's suffering becomes a symbolic currency detached from their actual lives and needs. Chŏng, a long-time activist with her "field start" at Durebang, passionately criticizes these men's tendency to create a pecking order of importance and value among activist causes, "ranking" issues like withdrawal of troops and national reunification at the top and individual human rights at the bottom.[39] In her written critiques, Chŏng offers a biting challenge to those who value the withdrawal of U.S. troops above all else:

> With no clarity about the timetable and method of a withdrawal, what are individuals who suffer the consequences of U.S. military misconduct supposed to do? Does it mean that only the imperialist U.S. military and the Korean government that shields it are to blame for the crimes (by the U.S.) that occur until the time of withdrawal? And that as long as progressive activists keep denouncing the U.S. military, they bear no responsibility [for allowing crimes to continue]?[40]

Here she squarely places moral and political responsibility for the conditions that engender crimes by U.S. troops against civilians not only on the U.S. and Korean authorities but also on those activists who disregard and disparage the human rights of camp town residents, especially the prostituted population.

According to Chŏng, of all the concerns raised among anti-troop CSOs during the 1990s, those regarding camp town women's rights and welfare encountered the most resistance among the predominantly male-led leadership. Male leaders revealed their sexist biases, blaming *kiji ch'on* women for "volunteering" to consort with U.S. soldiers and thereby invite danger upon themselves. They questioned the need for society to protect such "impure" women, even when they were victims of crimes, and accepted as inevitable the lack of societal attention to their needs.[41] Kim Hyunsun, the head of Saewoomtuh and a leading figure in the *kiji ch'on* advocacy movement, stated that such moralistic and dualistic thinking abets the tendency among even progressive human rights activists to categorize individuals as "deserving of human rights protection," "deserving less protection," or "deserving no protection."[42]

This maximalist tendency manifested itself in the nationalist inclination to subsume women's bodies and sexuality as collective property. Since "fundamental," collective concerns like reunification and national sovereignty rank at the top on the masculinist agenda, private, "individual" concerns become important only if they are useful for advancing the former. Chŏng condemns this kind of "instrumentalization" (*toguhwa*)[43] of individual and human rights among progressive activists as politically hypocritical and morally cruel. She condemns what some of her male colleagues have uttered—that the larger the number of victims (of U.S. servicemen), the more power for the nationalist cause[44]—arguing that this ultimately reveals the emptiness of the nationalist promise for women: Whether it is the nationalism of the right or of the left, "nation" is not an inclusive concept. In both instances, women are excluded.[45]

Masculinist nationalism is manifested in yet another way in activism against U.S. troops: the question of who is the legitimate actor for the nation. Again, Chŏng notes from her extensive movement experience that male colleagues repeatedly emphasized that in activism concerning the nation and national sovereignty, men should be the leaders. This was their way of criticizing her organization, the National Campaign, for their all-female leadership. The gender-biased message was that men should be taking on the "important work on behalf of the nation" and that an organization that was run by women would not be able to be maximally effective in the nationalist cause.[46]

The tendency for nationalist (and internationalist) movements to subsume and delegitimize expressly feminist or women-centered interests has long existed in Korea and elsewhere.[47] Both the anti-colonial independence movement and the socialist movement of the 1920s and 1930s exhibited such tendencies, despite their progressive rhetoric to emancipate women. Kenneth Wells discusses the way in which male nationalist and socialist leaders regarded the *Kunuhoe*, the socialist-nationalist women's organization active in 1927–31, as a subsidiary movement and how female leaders themselves came to uphold the view that national liberation was the "fundamental" issue rather than gender relations or specific women's issues. Women working for nationalist objectives "were hindered in their pursuit of an independent agenda by lack of support from other women, hostility from Korean men, the nationalists' stranglehold on the debate, and the subsumption of women's liberation under the socialist agenda."[48]

Feminist scholars of Korean history and society have remarked on the pattern of "androcentric citizenship"[49] that continues to marginalize or dismiss women-specific standpoints and agendas at both the state and societal levels. Chungmoo Choi notes that Korea's colonial and anti-colonial experiences gave rise to a national subjectivity "[that] has been exclusively a male subjectivity."[50] In critiquing the masculinist political culture of Korea's military authoritarianism post independence, Seungsook Moon describes how official or state nationalism under Park Chung Hee emphasized the androcentric national subject as a citizen-soldier, with the "militaristic tint" stronger during the 1970s as military authoritarian rule became more severe.[51] The progressive democracy movement of the 1980s was no different, as Insook Kwon cogently describes the bitter gender politics within the student movement as male-dominated and masculinist in thought and organization.[52] When in 1989 the Korean Women's Association United (KWAU) joined the National Federation of Nationalistic and Democratic Movements—the "center of all democratization and reunification movements"[53]—women faced familiar criticism from the predominantly men's organizations for being "passive and formal." For the men, real politics was assumed to take place on the streets through demonstrations and confrontations with the government rather than the gradual improvement of rights and interests that KWAU was promoting through legislation and system reform.[54] Jane Jaquette's prediction that women's political participation in new democracies does not necessarily promise equality and empowerment holds true in *kiji ch'on* politics, because "nationalism and identity politics can 'capture' gender politics."[55]

But despite the persistence of masculinist-nationalist thinking and strategizing, today there is more room in the political arena for gender-specific concerns than was the case in the early part of the twentieth century or in the pre-democratic 1980s. For one, men and masculinist politics do not have a stranglehold on the bases debate. The bases movement in general and the PAR-SOFA in particular are neither ideologically monolithic nor violence-prone. They do not seek to revolutionize or fundamentally change Korean society, and as mentioned earlier, it is a coalition movement that serves as an "umbrella" or clearinghouse for many types of political, social, and economic grievances and criticisms.[56] By definition and structure, it cannot claim to be one thing or another for a significant period of time. Rather, its very fluidity—in personnel, leadership, agenda priorities, goals, movement tactics, and interdependent relationship between the center and the localities—has created room for the gender debates. Consequently, women and women-specific issues have not been purged from the movement but rather have found varied ways to articulate and activate their concerns. Gender, as one of several factors in the internal political contestation of the *kiji* movement, has had to vie for frame alignment, policy influence, and public following. PAR-SOFA efforts did include *kiji ch'on* women and children's rights and welfare, but in the end, gender-specific issues did not gain prominence.

KIJI CH'ON WOMEN AND THE SOFA

Although many in the PAR-SOFA coalition were disappointed with the 2000–2001 SOFA revisions (discussed in chapter 3) and demanded another round of revisions for more change to their liking, a comparison of environmental and women-related issues reveals that the politics of "issue salience" *among* CSOs affects agenda-setting at the policy level. Environmental interests had their issues addressed and pushed by the Korean negotiators, debated by both the U.S. and Korean negotiating teams, and ultimately incorporated into the revisions, whereas women-related issues received barely any attention at the official policy level. Green Korea United (GKU) and the Korea Federation of Environmental Movements (KFEM) were established only in the mid-1990s, compared with camp town women's centers, which had been organized years earlier. And environmental issues gained serious public attention and popularity only in the 1990s, whereas the plight of camp town women has been synonymous with the fifty-plus-year history of the U.S. presence in Korea. But the symbolic contrast is stark: environmental issues quickly rose to the surface of public consciousness and came to represent anew the degradation and destruction of Korea by U.S. forces, while *kiji ch'on* women and the degradation they represented were pushed to the margins of political consciousness and of policy.

In contrast to the concerted, aggressive efforts made by environmental activists and officials of the Ministry of Environment (MoE) to push environmental issues onto the SOFA agenda, no such concerted effort was made on behalf of *kiji ch'on* women and issues. The Ministry of Gender Equality did not treat *kiji ch'on* women's issues as a priority. Moreover, organizational leadership within the PAR-SOFA was a significant factor: GKU assumed the first coordinating role and housed the coalition headquarters in its office at the outset of the movement. Although camp town women as victims of U.S. troop abuses served as a rhetorical catalyst and source of activist training for the larger bases movement, their interests did not rise to the top of CSO agendas. In turn, they barely received attention from policymakers.

Some women's organizations, including Saewoomtuh, did try to emphasize camp town women and children's interests in the CSO debates even as late as July 2000, just before the last round of SOFA negotiations between the Korean and U.S. governments was about to take place that fall and winter.[57] Noting that the public and bases activists all were overlooking the very population most physically and historically affected by American servicemen's behavior—the *kiji ch'on* women—*kiji ch'on* activists criticized not only the U.S. military but also the prejudices and ignorance within Korean society toward these women. They endorsed SOFA provisions that would give the Korean government greater power over troop-related crime cases, especially over investigation of cases involving Korean civilians. They also demanded the incorporation of protections for camp town women and children: job-training and funding of social welfare programs for the women; elimination of the government-sponsored examinations for sexually transmitted diseases (STDs), which have been mandated for all women who work in camp town bars and clubs; financial support by U.S. authorities for living and educational costs of Amerasian children in Korea who have been abandoned by their American fathers; women's and their Amerasian children's needs to be incorporated into economic development plans of local towns following any future U.S. troop withdrawal or base consolidation; enforcement of HIV/AIDS tests for U.S. service personnel in Korea; and sexual violence and crime-prevention training programs for U.S. troops.[58] But unlike most of the PAR-SOFA activists, they were emphatic that the SOFA is neither the sole source of nor the answer to *kiji ch'on* women's problems. These women leaders called for legal and institutional accountability by both U.S. and Korean government authorities to recognize and protect women's human rights.[59]

The revised SOFA, which took effect April 2, 2001, reflects two of these concerns but in ways that the women had not bargained for. It outlined twelve major crime categories, including murder and "egregious rape," whereby Korean authorities could take a U.S. service member into custody at the time of arrest and indictment rather than after the conclusion of all legal proceedings. But even in such cases, a number of conditions would have to be met.[60] Concerned Korean women's organizations took issue with the revised provisions, officially offering their position to oppose the ratification of the SOFA at a hearing before National Assembly members.

First, they argued that the notion of "egregious rape" is confusing and nonsensical, questioning the very possibility of non-egregious rape. They also argued that the particular conditions for custody upon indictment made it nearly impossible for American rape suspects to be apprehended and detained by the Korean police because of the usually witness-free and "he said/she said" nature of the crime. In addition, they challenged, how would authorities determine what kinds of evidence would qualify a rape as "egregious"? From their perspectives, these revisions would continue the history of ignoring sexual violence and crimes against camp town women, leaving the burden of proof upon them, offering loopholes for U.S. servicemen, and allowing camp town women to suffer injustice.[61] Their demand for the creation of articles mandating regular examinations of servicemen for HIV/AIDS—as a way to protect the health of camp town women—was met part way. The revised SOFA does not stipulate that the U.S. military will conduct regular check-ups, but it promises to share quarterly statistical information on troops with HIV/AIDS with the Korean government.[62]

Finally, the bilateral framing of camp town issues, including those affecting *kiji ch'on* women, is itself an obstacle to improving women's rights and human rights in general. Given that the SOFA is a bilateral document, such a framing is necessary and inevitable. However, it fails to reflect current realities: Foreigners have increasingly constituted the civilian population of camp town residents. In terms of *kiji ch'on* women, since the mid-1990s, women from the Philippines and the former Soviet countries migrated (or were trafficked) into these areas to serve as cheap labor in the sex and entertainment industries around the camp towns. At the same time, the number of Korean women in the sex industry declined considerably. In Kyonggi Province, where 65 percent of the 34 major U.S. military installations have been based, the number of Korean women working in the bars and nightclubs declined drastically from 1,269 in 1999 to 386 by 2001.[63] Since the 2000s, the majority of women coming into contact with U.S. soldiers are foreign nationals, often "illegal" (undocumented) and therefore lacking legal agency and political legitimacy in Korean civil society.

In addition to the women, male migrant laborers from abroad, particularly from Southeast and South Asia, work and reside in or near some camp towns. They also patronize the local camp town bars and clubs. Yet Korean activists' focus on the revision of the SOFA as a way to increase the protection of Korean citizens' rights and welfare assumes that only Koreans and Americans reside in the same locality and that only Korean civilians become victims of crimes and misconduct by U.S. personnel. And despite the increasingly multinational, multicultural, and multilayered legal (and illegal) arrangements hosted by the *kiji ch'on* areas, Korean activists have continued to criticize the U.S. for degrading and/or violating *Korean* women's dignity and human rights. Nationalistic symbolism and rhetoric that in this case presupposes both a gendered and a monoethnic subject cloud the changing demographic reality of camp towns.

In some ways, *kiji ch'on* women and related issues have become less invisible and marginalized since the 1990s. Through the "nationalization" of *kiji ch'on* realities that once had been eschewed as private and peripheral, murders and other types of violence against prostituted camp town women have become *causes célèbres* for the revision of the Status of Forces Agreement. The women also have been interviewed on national and international television, and documentary films and academic studies about their lives have been publicized in mainstream society. Some local governments housing the U.S. bases have helped fund social welfare projects for camp town women through the counseling and advocacy centers.[64]

The agency of camp town women to describe and define their needs and develop constructive skills has also improved. Kim Yŏnja, a madam and sex worker for nearly three decades, became an outspoken speaker and activist for *kiji ch'on* women, their children, and their human rights and needs. She also published a memoir in 2005.[65] Other women have been encouraged and trained by staff members of the *kiji ch'on* counseling centers to participate in peer outreach and counseling, in research on local conditions, and at international conferences. In a bold attempt at inclusiveness, staff members at Saewoomtuh also conducted a survey of thirty *kiji ch'on* women to gather their views on the main issues addressed in the proposed bill for the prevention of sex trafficking. The vast majority opposed the detention/institutionalization of the women themselves and supported harsher punishment for pimps, traffickers, and the consumers of sex. Noting that "[t]here has been no instance where the opinion of the sisters were reflected in the law-making and revision processes of the enactment of the law against sex trafficking," Saewoomtuh had hoped to have the voices of camp town women—"sisters"—reflected in legislation.[66]

However, despite the new public attention and NGO efforts to empower camp town women, violence—verbal, economic, psychological, and physical—has remained a daily phenomenon in many of these women's lives. Alleged violence against these women by U.S. personnel continue to be uninvestigated or underinvestigated. Camp town women's advocates contend that for every one case that receives media attention and legal redress, there are many others that never even reach the stage of initial police investigation.[67] Moreover, most elderly women who have left the sex trade confront poverty and social abandonment. And the stigma of camp town women, children, and their localities as pariahs still resounds in larger society.

Despite the spread of democracy to the camp town areas, residential empowerment has not reversed the marginalization or exclusion of these women. The enhancement and assertion of local power through democratization and decentralization have allowed local residents with some type of recognizable resource such as capital, development ideas, legal expertise, and/or political backing or following to shape policy agendas. *Kiji ch'on* women do not possess such resources. Moreover, for local politicians, there is little political caché in advocating for these women's rights and needs, although in the context of bases activism, highlighting negative social consequences of the U.S. troop presence can generate valuable political capital. Even those who have led protests on behalf of murdered women like Yun Kŭmi or Kim Sŏnghui or have been elected into local office riding on the protests have not looked into or advocated for the camp town women who are still living, even though the latter are *bona fide* constituents.[68]

Students of democratic consolidation point out that a maturing democracy is one in which civil and political society (elected officials) work together to channel, articulate, and institutionalize disparate, parochial, or free-floating ideas and concerns among the public. For example, Juan Linz and Alfred Stepan state that "political society—informed, pressured, and periodically renewed by civil society—must somehow achieve a workable agreement on the myriad ways in which democratic power will be crafted and exercised."[69] But how hypermarginalized groups like the prostituted women in camp towns are to inform, pressure, and periodically renew political society remains an unanswered question.

One could argue that the dearth of female public officeholders has helped perpetuate the marginalization of camp town women's issues. According to Pippa Norris and Ronald Inglehart,[70] anti-egalitarian political culture appears to be the strongest obstacle to women's political participation in elected office. And Korea is no exception. As of 2000, Korean women represented the lowest percentage of national legislators among the non-Communist countries of East Asia at 5.9.[71] Even decentralization and local autonomy—which many women had hoped would facilitate easier access to elected office because of lower levels of competition and entry barriers than in national politics—yielded minimal political representation for women. In the first local election in 1991, "women won only 0.9 percent of the seats at both the county and provincial levels, and the number of women victors increased to only about 1.5 percent in the 1995 elections. Given the all-out efforts that women made to gain local representation, these results [we]re extremely disappointing."[72] Of course, there is no certainty that under more egalitarian conditions, female politicians at any level would have been more likely than men to address issues concerning camp town women, since prejudice against "taboo constituents," like *kijich'on* women, limit the ways in which "democratic power will be crafted and exercised" by women, for women.

Rather than being an open marketplace of political interests and ideas, civil society has great power to decide who belongs or not, whose grievance and pain are worthy of collective attention, and whose case presents organizations and their leaders with enough potent capital with which to challenge state authorities. This presents a problem for expanding the boundaries of civil society and political participation in general, for those who lack the educational, political, economic, and social resources to claim and exercise rights are left out in the cold. Moreover, Roy Grinker observes that when the purpose of civil society activism transforms into an assertion of national identity and a claim for collective liberation from victimization by greater forces, it is relatively easy to "establish symbolic linkages between the nation and sexuality, the divided people of Korea and the trespassed and violated [woman's] body."[73] In such a context, a *yanggalbo*, or "Western whore," like Yun Kŭmi might be rehabilitated posthumously to command reverence and sympathy from the surviving members of the national body. But reverence and sympathy do not necessarily translate into rights and equal access and protection under law for the living.

NOTES

1. Rainbow Center, *Rainbow Newsletter,* no. 3 (Flushing, NY, 1994), 8.

2. Korean activists use the term *kijich'on yŏsŏng* (*kijich'on* women) to refer to the Korean women who work in the R&R (rest and relaxation) industry in the U.S. military camp towns.

3. Sidney Tarrow, *Power in Movement: Social Movements and Contentious Politics,* 2nd ed. (New York: Cambridge University Press, 1998), 144–145.

4. *New York Times,* August 24, 1995; *Dong-A Ilbo,* August 25, 1995, english .donga.com (accessed February 1, 2002).

5. Based on author's interviews with officials and researchers from the ROK government and a review of internal government documents in Seoul, Spring 2002.

6. Yi Kyochŏng, "Chuhan migun ui Yun Kŭmi-ssi salhae sa'gŏn kwa Tongduch'ŏn simindŭl ui tujaeng" (The case of the USFK murder of Yun Kŭmi and Tongduch'ŏn citizens' struggle), September 17, 2002; Chŏn Usŏp, "Saraitnŭn ddang, huimang ui ddang" (Land that lives, land of hope), in *Nogŭnri to Maehyangni* (History of the Korean people's movement for solution of U.S. Forces Korea issues) (Seoul: Kip'ŭn Chayu Publishing, 2001), 100–103.

7. Author interview with Kim Yonghan, Seoul, May 13, 2002.

8. On Membership Training (MT), see chapter 2.

9. Author interview with Lee Sohui, director of the National Campaign, Seoul, March 27, 2002.

10. Tarrow, *Power in Movement,* 23.

11. Georgina Waylen, "Women and Democratization: Conceptualizing Gender Relations in Transition Politics." *World Politics* 46 (1994), 329.

12. Sunhyuk Kim, "State and Civil Society in South Korea's Democratic Consolidation: Is the Battle Really Over?" *Asian Survey* 37, no. 12 (1997), 1142.

13. Namhee Lee, "The South Korean Student Movement: Undongkwŏn as a Counterpublic Sphere," in *Korean Society: Civil Society, Democracy, and the State,* ed. Charles K. Armstrong (New York: Routledge), 156.

14. John A. McReynolds, "Community Relations Advisory Council (CRAC), Bupyong (ASCOM)," U.S. Forces Korea, memorandum, November 1, 1968.

15. U.S. Department of the Air Force, District 45 (AFOSI), Report of Investigation, File #7745D6-206, August 5, 1977 (obtained through the U.S. Freedom of Information Act).

16. Katharine H. S. Moon, *Sex among Allies: Military Prostitution in U.S.–Korea Relations* (New York: Columbia University Press, 1997).

17. Citizens' Coalition for Economic Justice, "SOFA Constitutional Review/Claim Request," July 19, 2000.

18. Ibid.

19. Lily H.M. Ling, "The Limits of Democratization for Women in East Asia," in *Democracy and the Status of Women in East Asia,* ed. Rose J. Lee and Cal Clark (Boulder, Colorado: Lynne Rienner, 2000), 169–182.

20. Ibid.

21. Seungsook Moon, "Carving Out Space: Civil Society and the Women's Movement in South Korea," *Journal of Asian Studies* 61, no. 2 (2002), 473–500.

22. Rose Lee, "Democratic Consolidation and Gender Politics in South Korea," in *Democracy and the Status of Women in East Asia,* 123–141; Hyun-back Chung, "Together and Separately: 'The New Women's Movement' after the 1980s in South Korea," *Asian Women* 5 (1997), 19–38; Seungsook Moon, "Carving Out Space," 489–492.

23. Larry Diamond, "Rethinking Civil Society: Toward Democratic Consolidation," *Journal of Democracy* 5, no.3 (1994), 9–10.

24. Aili Mari Tripp, "Women and Democracy: The New Political Activism in Africa," *Journal of Democracy* 12, no. 3 (2001), 146.

25. For example, Yi Mikyŏng, a second-term national legislator, and Han Myŏngsuk, the first Minister of Gender Equality (since 2001) and former legislator. She also became the first female prime minister in 2006–7 and then became a presidential candidate but failed to win the top seat. With the election of Roh Moo Hyun as president in 2003, Han became the new Minister of Environment, and Chi Uihui, another long-time women's activist, the new Minister of Gender Equality. Kim Sukhui, an academic from Ewha Womans [sic] University, served as the Minister of Education under former president Kim Young Sam.

26. Jane Jaquette, "Women and Democracy: Regional Differences and Contrasting Views," *Journal of Democracy* 12, no. 3 (2001), 115–117.

27. Jongryn Mo, "Political Learning, Democratic Consolidation, and Politics of Labor Reform in South Korea," in *Democratic Consolidation and Globalization in Korea: Assessments and Prospect,* ed. Chung-in Moon and Jongryn Mo (Seoul: Yonsei University Press, 1999), 310.

28. Seungsook Moon, "Carving Out Space," 490.

29. Rose Lee, "Democratic Consolidation," 123–141; Seungsook Moon, "Overcome by Globalization: The Rise of a Women's Policy in South Korea," in *Korea's Globalization,* ed. Samuel S. Kim (New York: Cambridge University Press, 2000), 141.

30. Hyun-back Chung, "Together and Separately," 30.

31. See part I of Kamala Kempadoo and Jo Doezema, eds., *Global Sex Workers: Rights, Resistance, and Redefinition* (New York: Routledge, 1998).

32. These tensions and debates are reflected in Sea-Ling Cheng, *On the Move for Love: Migrant Entertainers and the U.S. Military in South Korea* (Philadelphia: University of Pennsylvania Press, 2010). Jae Hee Baek, "I'm

Entertainer, I'm Not Sex Worker," in *Yonggamhan Yŏsŏngdŭl* (Women of courage), ed. Magdalena House (Seoul: Sam-in Publishing, 2002), 191–228, portrays the different identifications of self and other women as "prostitute," "sex worker," or "entertainer" among various women in camp towns.

33. Cheng, *On the Move for Love,* 194.

34. Myung-hee Kim, "Saewoomtuh for Prostituted Women and Their Children," in *Sex Trafficking Eradication Project: Networking against the Asian Sex Industry and Promoting Anti Sex Trafficking Legislation* (conference report, Seoul, Saewoomtuh for Prostituted Women and Their Children/ Human Rights Solidarity for Women and Migration in Korea) (October 9–11, 2001), 26–27; author interviews, June 14, 2002, P'yŏngtaek.

35. Katharine H. S. Moon, "South Korean Movements against Militarized Sexual Labor," *Asian Survey* 39, no. 2 (1999), 326.

36. Ibid.

37. Kyoung-ryung Seong, "Civil Society and Democratic Consolidation in South Korea: Great Achievements and Remaining Problems," in *Consolidating Democracy in South Korea,* ed. Larry Diamond and Byung-Kook Kim (Boulder, CO: Lynne Rienner, 2000), 101.

38. See also Yujin Chŏng, "'Minjok' ui irŭmŭro sunkyŏlhaejin ddaldŭl" (Daughters who have become pure in the name of the "nation") *Tangdae Pip'yŏng* 11 (2000), 228, 229, 231.

39. Ibid., 231; Yujin Chŏng, "P'yŏnghwarŭl mandŭn danŭn kŏt" (To make peace), in *Ilsang ui ŏgapkwa sosuja ui inkwŏn* (Daily oppression and the human rights of minorities) (Seoul: Saram Saeng'gag, 2000), 94.

40. Yujin Chŏng, "'Minjok' ui irŭmŭro sunkyŏlhaejin ddaldŭl,"233 (translation mine).

41. Yujin Chŏng, "P'yŏnghwarŭl mandŭn danŭn kŏt," 106.

42. Hyunsun Kim, "Juhan migun kwa yŏsŏng in'kwŏn" (The U.S. military in Korea and women's human rights), paper presented at the Jeju Academic Conference on Human Rights, 2001.

43. Yujin Chŏng, "P'yŏnghwarŭl mandŭn danŭn kŏt," 92–96.

44. Ibid., 92, 95.

45. Ibid., 96; telephone conversations with Chŏng, May 2002, Seoul.

46. Yujin Chŏng, "P'yŏnghwarŭl mandŭn danŭn kŏt," 99–100.

47. See M. Jacqui Alexander and Chandra Mohanty, introduction to *Feminist Genealogies, Colonial Legacies, Democratic Futures,* ed. M. Jacqui Alexander and Chandra Mohanty (New York: Routledge, 1997). For an argument supporting the coexistence and synergy of nationalist and feminist movements, see Geraldine Heng, "'A Great Way to Fly': Nationalism, the State, and the Varieties of Third-World Feminism," in *Feminist Genealogies, Colonial Legacies, Democratic Futures.*

48. Kenneth M. Wells, "The Price of Legitimacy: Women and the Kŭnuhoe Movement, 1927–1931," in *Colonial Modernity in Korea,* ed. Gi-Wook Shin and Michael Robinson (Cambridge, MA: Harvard University Press, 1999), 193.

49. Seungsook Moon, "Carving Out Space."

50. Chungmoo Choi, "Nationalism and the Construction of Gender in Korea," in *Dangerous Women: Gender and Korean Nationalism,* ed. Elaine H. Kim and Chungmoo Choi (New York: Routledge, 1998), 14.

51. Seungsook Moon, "Overcome by Globalization," 143–144.

52. See Insook Kwon, "Militarism in My Heart: Women's Militarized Consciousness and Culture in South Korea" (Ph.D. diss., Clark University, 2000), on the masculinization of the student/democracy movement.

53. Hyun-back Chung, "Together and Separately," 28.

54. Ibid., 29.

55. Jaquette, "Women and Democracy," 121.

56. Katharine H. S. Moon, "Korean Nationalism, Anti-Americanism, and Democratic Consolidation," in *Korea's Democratization,* ed. Samuel S. Kim (New York: Cambridge University Press, 2003), 135–158.

57. Saewoomtuh Counseling Center, "SOFA kaejŏng e daehan uri e ipjang" (Our position on the SOFA revision), July 27, 2000.

58. Ibid.; PAR-SOFA, *SOFA Inducement; Ohmynews,* July 26, 2000 (accessed March 26, 2002).

59. Saewoomtuh, "SOFA kaejŏng"; *Ohmynews,* July 26, 2000.

60. The Agreed Minutes to the Agreement under Article IV of the Mutual Defense Treaty between the Republic of Korea and the United States, Status of U.S. Armed Forces in the Republic of Korea, as amended January 18, 2000, Article 22, 5c:2, states: "In cases where the Republic of Korea authorities have arrested an accused who is a member of the United States armed forces or the civilian component, or a dependent at the scene of the crime, in immediate flight there from or prior to the accused's return to U.S. control and there is adequate cause to believe that he has committed a heinous crime of murder or an egregious rape, and there is necessity to retain him for the reason that he may destroy evidence; he may escape; or he may cause harm to the life, person, or property of a victim or a potential witness, the United States military authorities agree not to request transfer of custody unless there is legitimate cause to believe that a failure to request custody would result in prejudice to an accused's right to a fair trial."

61. Hyunsook Lee Kim, "So'pa kaejŏng, muŏtsi munje inga? Yŏsŏng e kwanjŏm esŏ" (SOFA revision, what are the problems? Women's perspectives), statement , Seoul, February 8, 2001.

62. Understandings to the Agreement under Article IV of the Mutual Defense Treaty between the Republic of Korea and the United States of America, regarding Facilities and Areas and the Status of United States Armed Forces in the Republic of Korea and Related Agreed Minutes, as amended January 18, 2001, Article 26:3.

63. Shin-mook Jung et al., "The Sisters' Position on the Special Law against Sex Trafficking," in *Sex Trafficking Eradication Project: Networking against the Asian Sex Industry and Promoting Anti Sex Trafficking Legislation* (conference report, Seoul: Saewoomtuh for Prostituted Women and Their

Children/Human Rights Solidarity for Women and Migration in Korea, October 9–11, 2001), 77.

64. Saewoomtuh staff, in meetings with author, summer 1999 and spring 2002.

65. Yŏnja Kim, *Amerika T'aun Wang Ŏnni* (The King Sister of America town) (Seoul: Sam-in Publishing, 2005).

66. Shin-mook Jung et al., "The Sisters' Position," 77–86.

67. Saewoomtuh, "SOFA kaejŏng"; Saewoomtuh staff, in conversation with author, July 7, 2002, Pyŏngtaek.

68. Author interviews, July 7, 2002, Pyŏngtaek.

69. Juan Linz and Alfred Stepan, "Toward Consolidated Democracies," *Journalof Democracy* 7, no. 2 (1996), 18.

70. Pippa Norris and Ronald Inglehart, "Women and Democracy. Cultural Obstacles to Equal Representation." *Journal of Democracy* 12, no. 3 (2001), 126–140.

71. Jaquette, "Women and Democracy," 118.

72. Mikyung Chin, "Self-Governance, Political Participation, and the Feminist Movement in South Korea," in *Democracy and the Status of Women in East Asia,* ed. Rose J. Lee and Cal Clark (Boulder, CO: Lynne Rienner, 2000), 102.

73. Roy Richard Grinker, *Korea and Its Futures: Unification and the Unfinished War* (New York: St. Martin's Press, 1998), 100.

Conclusion

Democracy and Discontents

The Cold War changed the meaning of old enmities and alliances, facilitating the active exploration among East Asian nations for new configurations of cooperation and neighborliness with one another even as wariness about China's growth and changing power dynamics in the region have weighed on people's minds. The large majority of Japan's trade is with its regional neighbors, and of course, China is now Korea's top trading partner. Numerous cooperation schemes have been spawned to advance simultaneously national and regional interests and to ensure against an overbearing U.S. regional hegemony; the East Asia Summit was one such attempt.

Without doubt, the anti-Communist "glue" that once held together the military and political commitments between the United States and its East Asian partners and helped prop up American cultural hegemony in the region has lost much of its adhesive power. South Koreans, who had for decades imitated nearly everything American and set aside things Korean, now buy and view more homemade music and films/videos than American imports. Anthony C.Y Leong marks 1999 as

> a watershed year for South Korean cinema, [one in which] the latest "Korean New Wave" became a creative force to be reckoned with. After spending many years taking a backseat to big-budget Hollywood imports, Korean filmmakers reclaimed the country's movie screens as nine homegrown productions earned a place in the box office top 20, such as 'Shiri,' 'Attack the Gas Station,' and 'Tell Me Something,' which occupied the number 1, 3, and 8 positions among all the top-grossing films that year. South Korea's film industry no longer needed to rely solely on the country's quota system for financial viability.[1]

In the new millennium, according to the Korean Film Council, Korean cinema's domestic market share rose to more than 50 percent in 2001, 2003, 2004, and 2005.[2]

Moreover, in the 2000s Korean pop culture (*hallyu*, or the "Korean Wave") has been a commodity with a fast-growing audience in Japan, China, and Southeast Asia. And even with Western imports to East Asia, Japan has played a leading role in introducing concepts and techniques to "Asianize" Western culture, thereby forging an eclectic but distinct Asian system and aesthetic for media entertainment and pop culture.[3] In this dynamic cultural, social, economic, and political context, the role of the United States in East Asia has become ambivalent and open to question by Asian publics, generating what John Ikenberry calls a "legitimacy deficit" that stems from the changing distribution of global and regional power.[4]

But without understanding the changes in the internal distribution of power in Asian countries, explaining the impact of external relations and outcomes remains limited. If authoritarian rule had remained the dominant trend in much of Asia, the crisscrossing transnational linkages between private actors, the experimentation with entrepreneurial and cultural risk-taking, the exchange of information and political opinions across borders, the willingness to construct new political interests and identities, and the freedom to challenge the official framing and justification of policy priorities would not characterize today's East Asia. Without the freedom to scrutinize U.S. policies and their respective government's relations with the United States, Asian societies could have kowtowed to elite perceptions and explanations of foreign policy and national security and harnessed more tightly U.S. power and protection in the face of rapid change and accompanying uncertainty in the region. But democratization (and social liberalization) since the late 1980s has challenged the domestic political power structures and the established versions of the relationship with the United States that had been the *modus operandi* for much of the authoritarian period in Cold War Asia. Here, Samuel Kim's critique of realist approaches to Northeast Asian security is worth emphasizing: "[D]ifferences in internal constructions and resulting domestic politics have a greater impact on how states or their decision makers define threats and vulnerabilities [as well as opportunities], and therefore on the whole security problematic, than does the structure of the international system."[5]

The United States is good at invoking democracy in its foreign policy, but not good at responding to it during the tough times. Ironically, it is the very success of post–World War II American hegemony that has gotten the U.S. into the recent predicament of having to struggle with both enemies and friends who are resentful of its power and policies. The very fact that the U.S. believed it was able to fashion the world according to its own image abetted a type of liberal myopia regarding the process and progress of democracy. As revealed by the United States' rather painful attempts to "rally" its European and Asian allies behind its cause in Iraq in the early 2000s, democratic nations do not simply fall into line. They don't easily play follow-the-leader, and their own leaders contend with the wrath of public opinion as much as, if not more than, the wrath of the United States. The soil that the United States helped make hospitable for the seeds of democracy in Western Europe and East Asia have yielded fruit that is both sweet and bitter. On the one hand, democracy promotion can serve the U.S. national interest by advancing the rule of law and human dignity, stability, and peace, but it also risks the creation of democratically elected regimes that can be hostile to U.S. interests[6] or a democratization process that degenerates into civil strife and regional instability.[7] Along these lines, Fareed Zakaria has criticized aggressive democracy promotion for begetting political strongmen and "illiberal democracies."[8]

Democratic realities in South Korea, Japan, and the Philippines, which all have housed U.S. bases long-term, are not prone to extremes in terms of hostility toward the United States or abetting strongmen or civil strife (the Mindanao region being the exception), but U.S. attempts to push for internal democratization abetted a liberalization process and foreign policy repercussions that it did not bargain for. The example of U.S.-Philippines relations in the mid- to late 1980s is most obvious. Following the fraudulent presidential election victory of Ferdinand Marcos in early February 1986, the Reagan administration put a dent into decades of U.S. economic and military support for the corrupt, authoritarian Marcos regime. President Reagan warned the dictator "against suppressing the independent poll-watching group, NAMFREL; vigorously challenged the election's credibility; and finally told Marcos it was time to go."[9] The U.S. shared the credit for enabling "people power" to transform the Philippines nearly overnight into a political democracy, but within a few years that very democracy also enabled the Philippines legislature to "kick out" the U.S. bases.

Even though President Corazon Aquino tried to overturn the Senate's decision by appealing to "people power" through a national referendum, she backed down because of the political and legal battle she would have had to wage against constitutionalists: Aquino's populist move was sure to "set off a series of time-consuming court challenges by lawmakers and others who [would] assert that the Constitution permits voters to overrule a vote by the Senate on a regular law, but not on a treaty."[10] Even if nationalism served as a motivation for the Senate's decision against the U.S. military, it was constitutional authority that was served and advanced through the political struggle over the bases.

GENERATIONAL GAP

In the U.S. National Intelligence Council East Asia report of September 2000, Scott Snyder states:

> Perhaps the most significant factors that are likely to influence the medium-to-long-term future of US-ROK relations are social and political changes resulting from generational transitions in Korean attitudes toward the United States. These demographic changes are also stimulating political pluralization and social change in South Korea. It appears that the strong bonds of the US-ROK relationship initially forged through the Korean war are gradually weakening as a younger generation without direct experience of the war itself replaces sentimental views of the United States based on direct knowledge of American sacrifice on behalf of South Korea during the war with a more pragmatic view of the relationship based on a cold, hard assessment of where shared interests may lie in the future."[11]

In any society, it is inevitable that as generations change and history grows distant that the public's policy perceptions, interpretations, and preferences change. American college students of today can make only scant reference to World War II, the Korean War, and the Vietnam War. Even more recent events, like first Gulf War or the fall of the Berlin Wall (Cold War) occupy little space, if any, in their minds. To expect young Koreans to live actively with the history of the 1950s and the American and UN roles when their daily lives are defined by instant-messaging, cramming for university entrance exams, and competing for good jobs is unrealistic and unfair unless we hold high historical standards for all youth around the world. And Snyder's prediction that interests, rather than sentiment, will guide Korea's youth in the future accords with the fundamentals of realist theory, despite the strong identity politics among Koreans.

Korean youth are not the only ones blamed for resurgent nationalism, historical amnesia, and naïveté; misunderstanding Asian youth has been a trend in the 2000s. Among Japan watchers, there is a similar tendency to describe younger generations of Japanese as more nationalistic, ahistorically minded, and anti-American than their older cohorts.[12] But there is no neat linear connection between age and love of nation or support of Japan-U.S. relations. Although there is evidence in recent years that the majority of younger political elites favors constitutional revision and expanded regional and international roles for Japan, the younger generations' sense of national pride and the desire for regard by the international community is "not narrow, xenophobic, and inward looking such as the nationalism prevalent in pre-World War II Japan."[13]

Among common Japanese youth, surveys conducted throughout the 1990s show that they view themselves as decisively less patriotic than older Japanese: For example, only 26 percent in the twenty to twenty-four age group in 1998 (versus 21 percent 1986) had a "strong sense" of patriotism, compared to over 70 percent of the over-sixty-five group in both years.[14] Additionally, younger Japanese (ages twenty to thirty-nine) identified with ambivalence toward patriotism (i.e., "don't know") in higher percentages (over 50 percent) than strong or weak patriotism in 1986, 1988, and 2002. By contrast, only 20.4 percent of Japanese males and 26.4 percent of Japanese females seventy years and older had an ambivalent sense of patriotism in 2002. 73.4 percent of the men felt "strong" patriotism versus 6.2 percent "not strong."[15]

Moreover, high-school students have challenged the government's efforts to mandate the singing of "Kimigayo," the Japanese national anthem, at graduation and other such ceremonies. Students from the Saitama Prefectural Tokorozawa High School in 1998, in 2001 from the West Hiroshima Municipal Takaya School, and in 2002 from the Sapporo Minami High School filed pleas with human rights attorneys that the raising of the flag or the enforced singing of the national anthem violated their freedom of expression and participation, guaranteed in the Children's Rights Act.[16] In a 2000 survey conducted by a professor at the University of Kagoshima, out of 450 students who participated, 42.2 percent said they do not feel attached to the national flag and anthem and 7.8 percent confirmed they dislike both, while 27.8 percent felt attached and 21.8 percent didn't have feelings either way.[17] On the question of changing the constitution based on the argument that it was imposed by a foreign power, 53.6 percent opposed a change, while only 11.6 percent supported it.[18]

The belief that younger generations are not supportive or less supportive of the alliance with the United States and its military presence is also misguided. From 1992 to 2001, 65.2 percent (1992) of Japanese age twenty to twenty-nine considered their country's relations with the U.S. as "good," while in 2000, they reached a peak of 82.4 percent in that ten-year period. The older generation held similar views: Among the fifty to fifty-nine group, 66.9 percent in 1992 and 82.6 percent in 2001 considered Japan-U.S. relations to be "good."[19]

Ian Condry has written about the "danger of distortion in the coverage of Japanese nationalism," which could readily apply to South Korea: "It is becoming almost a truism to regard Japan's younger generation as emblematic of a rising Japanese nationalism, but when scholars and reporters highlight such nationalist messages, even when portraying them in a critical light, we risk reinforcing the impression that progressive, or at least alternative voices, are largely absent from youth-oriented media."[20] He found that foreign reporters actively seek out "evidence" of nationalism. For example, "[o]ne British reporter wanted examples of 'right-wing, nationalist Japanese rap.' When I said that most (though not all) Japanese rap tended to espouse progressive politics, the reporter expressed disinterest, saying in effect, 'That's not news.' An American reporter in Tokyo contacted me for comments on right-wing manga, and she too was uninterested in other examples of left-leaning manga."[21]

In Japan, it is the older generation that keeps its eyes, ears, and minds closed to the realities of Japan's war atrocities, while the younger generations are more eager to step up to the historical plate and acknowledge past wrongs, mend old wounds, and forge new friendships with their regional neighbors and the country that dropped the atomic bomb on them. They are the ones busily exchanging views on the internet, working together with regional CSOs, and admiring the cultural products (film, videos, music) imported from their nation's ex-colony, South Korea.

CIVIL-MILITARY RELATIONS

As much as America has received its share of vilification as a militaristic, imperialistic country by many around the world, especially with former President George W. Bush's unilateralist tendencies to use military force, there is another side of the story. American historians like Russell Weigley and political scientists like Samuel Hungtington have emphasized the anti-military effects of having a standing professional military since the days of the Founding Fathers: "From the beginning, career soldiers perceived themselves as occupying a somewhat hostile environment, distrusted by American civilians. . . . The soldiers reciprocated civilian distrust with ill-feeling of their own."[22] One cause for such mutual suspicion was the legacy received from the English tradition of the late seventeenth and eighteenth centuries that the military was an "intrinsic threat to civilian self-government and liberties."[23] Weigley confirms that American colonists "fully accepted the Whig antimilitary tradition and indeed integrated it into American political culture"[24] and that this sentiment "remained a staple of American political discourse through the Jacksonian era and beyond" (despite the creation of a small standing military).[25] Even General George Washington, who was ever faithful to civilian authority even before it was constitutionally codified, was deemed at times with suspicion by the Continental Congress—which had selected him to lead the fight against the British and "supervised the Continental Army with irrational distrust of it, and with irrational apprehension that . . . Washington would turn into another Oliver Cromwell."[26]

The point in raising the American example is twofold: (1) within domestic society, civil-military relations are neither consistent nor stable. There is greater closeness in goals, coordination, and cooperation between civilians and military personnel when common national interests are threatened (e.g., the world wars, Cold War) and when the "civilian government ha[s] bestowed on the military resources sufficient to win overwhelming victories."[27] And they are discordant when clear national security interests or ample resources for the military are lacking and when there are negative civilian views of the legitimacy of the military's presence, purpose, and conduct in war and times of peace. In turn, whether the military feels understood, appreciated, and supported by the civilian population also matters. The United States has gone through peaks and valleys in its own civil-military relations, with the Vietnam War and its aftermath marking the nadir. Andrew Bacevich described the trust/distrust syndrome as the "Vietnam hangover—'You guys betrayed us once, and you could do it again.'"[28] And opinion-makers on the left have commented during the Tailhook and Aberdeen [sex] scandals: "[I]t's hard to imagine why any woman—or any man with a conscience—would want to join the military."[29] If this love-hate dynamic applies to Americans, we can only imagine the more complex relationship in civil-military relations when we consider a foreign military permanently stationed on another country's soil.

In a review of the approaches to understanding civil-military relations within the United States, Deborah Avant summarizes three dominant categories: "(1) the level of military influence on policy; (2) the degree to which the military is representative of society; and (3) the level of civil-military tension."[30] If we apply these criteria to the U.S. troops in Korea, we can begin to imagine why, even without the triggering stressors like the death of the schoolgirls by the U.S. armored vehicle, a low threshold for problematic civil-military relations is built into the political, social, and economic structure of the alliance, especially over the long term. And the possibilities for suspicion and distrust on the part of the civilian host society can flare up quite easily with politically sensitive triggers.

Even when South Korea was overwhelmingly dependent on the United States for economic assistance and military protection, the host society chafed at the presence of such a mighty power and feared its capacity to influence domestic Korean politics. During its period of economic and military dependence on the United States, South Korea, like others in that category (e.g., postwar Japan and the Philippines), had its "initial basing agreement imposed on [it] during a military occupation," which later led to societal challenge of these terms once the dependence decreased and democratization took place.[31] Having a foreign military government and/or a permanent presence on one's territory by definition interferes with domestic sovereignty and governance. Even under deep dependency conditions, Pyong Choon Hahm, the Korean scholar, political advisor, and diplomat, took offense at overhearing "a high-ranking military officer berating the Korean people for their 'mendicant mentality.'"[32] It was less about being ungrateful for American aid but more about the Americans' and the U.S. military's assumption that South Koreans were ineffective in governance and not contributing to American interests. To the contrary, Hahm wrote with gracious sarcasm in *Foreign Affairs:*

> In the course of two decades of mutual effort in fighting Communism, we had been led to believe that the American aid was a token of appreciation and a measure of support for the efforts of an ally in defending this part of the free world against the Communists. . . . We believed that we were defending not only ourselves but Japan, Taiwan, the Philippines, and above all, the interests of the United States in the western Pacific.[33]

This public scolding of American intervention in Korean politics took place in 1964.

Hahm's reproach to the American "high-ranking official" is tantamount to asserting that Korea has its own national and international interests in mind and that U.S. arrogance should not undermine Seoul's own efforts at home and abroad. He also makes it clear that it is not the United States' place to pressure Seoul into normalizing relations with

Tokyo (finalized in 1965): "Especially irksome is the sermonizing attitude of Americans in accusing us of being narrow-minded and spiteful toward the Japanese. They tell us that everyone else has forgiven and forgotten their enmity toward the Japanese, and ask why we cannot do the same." His answer comes down to the "fact . . . that our experience with the Japanese is something no other people can understand."[34] Basically, his message was simple: Mind your own business and don't tell us what to do. This resentment toward U.S. meddling in Korean affairs or lack of appreciation for its own efforts sometimes led Korean leaders, no matter the depth and breadth of the client status of their country, not simply to shut up and roll over to the tune of U.S. policy demands. As Hahm put it in a near proverbial statement, "[t]he fact is that when a nation, however poor, feels that it is assumed to be acting as a beggar, it can hardly be expected to remain a friend."[35]

Distrust of the United States' regard for and long-term intentions in Korea continued into the 1970s, with the Nixon Doctrine and the unilateral withdrawal of about one-third of U.S. forces from Korea and more troops from Asia. Of course, Korean suspicion of the U.S. as a failed friend if not outright foe soared to new heights in the wake of the 1980 Kwangju massacre. The anti-U.S. legacy, forged out of utter disappointment and despair that the U.S. had not come to the "rescue" of the Kwangju people and had "permitted" Chun Doo Hwan's troops to commit such violence on civilians lived on to fuel the anti-American student and democracy movement of the 1980s. That one event marred U.S.-Korean civil-military relations nearly beyond repair. For one, many Koreans interpreted the tragedy as a reflection of how divergent the interests of the U.S. military and the Korean people are; second, many Koreans took the non-intervention of the U.S. military as a form of intervention in Korean politics by siding with the military dictator and his regime.

On the issue of how representative a military is of the society it protects, the disconnect between American service personnel and Korean civilians is blatantly clear. The U.S. military in Korea is not representative of Korean society either in the constitution of personnel or its socioeconomic status and cultural values. During Korea's impoverished postcolonial and pos-war days, even the lowliest GI wielded more material and social power than the great majority of South Koreans. Today the tides have turned, with Korean consumption and spending habits creating an economic environment that has outstripped the personal means of many U.S. troops. And in terms of human capital, the Korean men who perform their compulsory military service in the USFK as Korean Attachments to the U.S. Army (KATUSA) "are the cream of the crop in Korea, from the best universities, with excellent English skills . . . but they are put under the U.S. soldiers who can't even speak English very well." The U.S. Public Affairs official in Korea who had made this observation continued that some KATUSAs come to "hate Americans because they are treated like crap by them [U.S. servicemen]."[36] Humiliating treatment by foreigners, placement in positions that do not reflect their educational and social status within Korean society, and related prejudices against U.S. soldiers who appear (to Koreans) as subpar representatives of the greatest military in the world can abet anti-troop or anti-American sensitivities among some KATUSAs. (During my interview with the bases activist Kim Yonghan, he suggested a new term and affiliation between the two militaries: USATKA, "U.S. Attachments to the Korean Army.")[37]

Additionally, since the 1990s, as evidence accumulated of a rightward shift among U.S. members of the armed services, Korean civilians veered toward the left in civil society organizing and demands on its elected officials after decades of military-authoritarian rule. For example, Ole Holsti discusses the results of the large-scale Triangle Institute Security Studies (TISS) of 1998–99, wherein American military respondents self-identified as having "substantially stronger affinity for conservatism" than American civilian respondents, to the point that "liberals appear to be an endangered species among both the military and active reserves." What is particularly of interest, in contrast to the view of South Korean youth as socially and politically liberal, is that "more than 70 percent of the younger age group [of U.S. service personnel] identified themselves as conservatives," with about one-fifth placing themselves in the most conservative group. [38] Representativeness can be related to trust/distrust between military personnel and civilians. Even among countrymen, it raises questions about common or divergent views of national cohesion, national interest, and the balance between individual and collective priorities, but among people of different nationalities and cultures split by civilian and military identities and roles, the correlation between the lack of representativeness and distrust can be more severe, or at the least, more complicated.

In a 1980 article using numerous examples from Communist societies, David Albright challenged the prevailing acceptance of Samuel Huntington's basic argument that civil-military relations is primarily a function of the effectiveness of civilian control and the level of professionalization of a military. Albright emphasized the inherent difficulty of forging a constructive, mutually supportive relationship between the military and civilian leaders, even in places where the military helped create and build a party, bureaucracy, and state, or defended the values and interests of civilian rulers. [39] Moreover, he distinguished between states and militaries that grow more autonomous versus those that grow dependent on a foreign power, and showed how civil-military relations differ qualitatively between the two types. This is a gap in the general literature on civil-military relations that persists today. Albright highlighted a point that is critical to U.S.-Korea relations and other alliance relationships that require foreign basing: "Heightened dependency [on a foreign power] usually moved civil-military relations out of the domestic realm and into the sphere of foreign policy."[40] If we extrapolate from this observation, then by definition, when a foreign power is involved in the political and military life of another society, civil-military relations can readily become entangled with issues of sovereignty and negotiations over equality of relations and the prerogatives of power between the two countries. Albright does not mention it, but civil-military relations become a twofold matter: first about the domestic military and the civilian society, and second, about the foreign military and the civilian society. Mutual support, loyalty, and trust become ever complex, especially as domestic and foreign policy shifts occur.

Within the U.S.-Korea alliance, there are specific problems related to psychological trust and institutional procedures and communications. Tensions over environmental issues are demonstrative examples. As one USFK official in charge of overseeing environmental issues put it during an interview in the spring of 2002, "It's difficult to say what the real issue" is for the Korean CSOs or other critics. He believed that "[t]here are other issues out there besides the environment," but the CSOs couch them in terms of environmental problems (chapter 3 addresses this tendency in Korea and elsewhere). He often found that "allegations are not valid if you look at the testing and reports," and offered examples. Activists had alleged oil and metal contamination at Story (firing) range that was contaminating drinking water intakes. But when the USFK tested the site and the water, they found no such problem (he added that ongoing testing was to continue). For this official, the issue at Story came down to this: Farmers wanted the U.S. off the range so that they could work the land.[41] On other occasions, Korean organizations, like the People's Solidarity for Participatory Democracy (PSPD), conflated a number of issues as part of their grievance against environmental problems: "From the time of the deployment of U.S. troops in 1945 to the present, environmental pollution has been constant, and the U.S. military has neglected to be concerned about the impact. What all of this shows is that the hegemonic strategies of U.S. militarism stand in the way of Korean reunification, more realistic defense expenditures and sustainable development."[42]

The most widely publicized and contentious case involving the "dumping" of formaldehyde into the Han River was another instance of a crisis based on Korean civilian distrust of the American military and cynicism on the part of USFK personnel toward Korean CSOs. The USFK admitted that about twenty gallons of the chemical were discharged into the sewage system at Yongsan Garrrison, and would have flowed to a waste water treatment center before being released into the river. Amid the public outrage, the USFK investigated the impact of the formaldehyde through the processing plant and found that it had no impact on human health or the environment. The USFK environment officials I interviewed and many other American officials in Seoul with whom I spoke were exasperated by the media coverage, especially of one TV news feature during which a goldfish was dropped into a glass of formaldehyde, demonstrating the "death effect." The USFK held press conferences, released reports, and tried to assure the Korean public that no harm had been inflicted on them, but the environmental officer lamented, "People remember what they see on TV even if technical information is publicly available." He added that "sometimes it doesn't matter what you say," because Koreans will believe only what they want to believe. He was particularly frustrated by the Korean media's tendency to publicize an issue before thoroughly investigating and checking the facts independently (for example, even the conservative, more pro-American *Chosun Ilbo* ran an editorial entitled, "Do They Poison the Potomac?").[43] Even when the USFK had organized a bus tour for members of the Korean media so that they would be able to go around the bases and survey different areas and be briefed about the military's policies and actions regarding environmental protection and cleanup, the USFK official found that the media "wasn't interested in anything positive." As he went around with them for the briefings, "they went off to the side to smoke."[44]

In addition or related to the dynamic of mutual mistrust and skepticism is the fact that the Korean government and the USFK have different standards and procedures for environmental safety, prevention, and cleanup. The USFK makes determinations on specific cases by reviewing its own Overseas Environmental Baseline Guidance Document and the ROK government's environmental laws and then by assessing which side's is more protective. But the USFK environment official I interviewed was quick to emphasize that stringent standards on paper do not necessarily mean more "protective effect." Therefore, the USFK considers if and how the Korean government applies its laws in a uniform manner, including, of course, its own military and civilian facilities. When faced with conflicting standards, the USFK and the Korean government have learned to find a balance. For example, the USFK measures the toxicity level of wastewater on a cumulative basis whereas the ROK government takes spot measurements (which might be higher or lower at a given time than the cumulative approach). What the two sides do, then, is "marry them up" to come up with a common understanding of safety or danger.[45] A particular grievance among the USFK and U.S. Embassy officials I interviewed was that the Korean civic organizations do not scrutinize their own military or corporate entities for environmental problems as vigilantly as they target the U.S. military.

That may be a fair assessment from the perspective of U.S. officials, who felt constantly overscrutinized or held up to higher standards, but from the Korean central government's perspective, civic activism against both Korean corporate and government activities are pervasive, and the government plays multiple roles, as perpetrator of environmental problems, regulator of rules, depository of environmental complaints, collaborator with NGOs, as well as arbitrator among different vested interests. Additionally, major cases like the proposed construction in 2003 of the country's first nuclear waste dump on Wido Islet (Puan County) in Chŏlla Province became a political disaster for the central and local governments. Violent protests by civilians and NGOs opposing the decision by the county head, Kim Jŏnggyu, without the consent of the 70,000 residents, involved the deployment of 8,000 heavily armed police and forced the Ministry of Commerce, Industry, and Energy to withdraw its proposal and search for alternative sites through referenda.[46] The people's protests started in summer 2003, and the withdrawal announcement came in December 2003. When I interviewed MoFAT officials in 2004, they repeated the case of Puan as an example of their fears that domestic environmental issues would have repercussions on unrelated projects and institutions, especially those regarding the U.S. military bases.

The SOFA negotiators added the Memorandum of Special Understandings on Environmental Protection, which was signed on January 18, 2001, by both governments. The memorandum consists mainly of guidelines and procedures for information exchange, periodic review and update of the Environmental Governing Standards, periodic assessment of environmental problems on bases, and planning for how to deal with future problems. Specific details were missing, which upset bases activists who had hoped for stronger rules and procedures. After its ratification, the Korean government offered to provide the USFK more information on developing environmental guidelines and assistance in interpreting Korean laws and standards, while the USFK developed more detailed operating procedures that would enhance clarity and cooperation with the Korean government. Together, they negotiated issues regarding information exchange, survey procedures, and the continued development of environmental standards. [47]

Despite the fact that Korean civic groups and local camp town residents long had complained about lax USFK environmental behavior, the fact is that environmental consciousness and related policymaking are relatively new to both the USFK and the Korean government, when compared with other aspects of alliance management. The U.S. Department of Defense issued its first environmental guideline document in 1991 for overseas facilities,[48] and the USFK drew up its own standards in 1995, which was updated in 1997 as the Final Guideline Standards. The latter document applies to peacetime relations and enumerates general definitions and protocol for dealing with

> environmental standards for air, water (drinking and waste), hazardous waste and materials, solid and medical waste, POL, noise, pesticides, historic and cultural resources, endangered species and natural resources, PCB, asbestos, and spill prevention and response planning. . . . The need or requirement for environmental compliance inspections/audits, environmental coordinator meetings, Host-Nation coordination, existing site condition assessments, and closure plans (camp closure, closure of waste disposal sites, and hazardous waste retrograde closure) is also addressed.[49]

In the meantime, the environment became a full-fledged governmental and policy matter for the Korean government and public only in the 1990s. The Ministry of Environment was formally established in 1990, and in 1994 granted greater power and authority to create and enforce its own rules and policies.

Civil-military relations are generally peripheral to a military's strategic mission and are important insofar as they facilitate that mission. Dealing with local communities, their demographic and cultural composition, economic and political power structures, and such have recently gained acknowledgement as key to the success or failure of military activities in Iraq and Afghanistan. But the longer a military stays on foreign soil, especially under peacetime conditions, the tendency is to take the status quo for granted and not continually invest human, social, economic and political capital into improving civil-military relations. Sporadic efforts are made by the guest military and host government when civil unrest or a serious crime or accident occurs; otherwise neglect is the default policy.

This is what happened in South Korea throughout the decades. In the 1950s and 1960s, individual American soldiers and local Koreans interacted with one another through voluntary activities—for example, the Americans helped build or repair local roads and visited nearby orphanages, held Christmas parties with gifts for the children and other charitable events, or periodically assisted during flooding or road-building, or responded to other local needs. The tendency was to express American humanity through material or technological largesse or time spent playing with parentless children. And between American men and Korean women, the normative relationship was that between soldier and prostitute. In the early 1970s, racial tensions among servicemen and local Koreans' expressions of anger and humiliation at the U.S. base's economic, social, and regulatory hold on their lives erupted into localized public demonstrations. The Camptown Clean-Up Campaign (chapter 2) was developed by both the USFK and the Korean government to establish law and order and improve civil-military relations around the American installations. The SOFA Joint Committee, consisting of representatives from both the Korean government and the USFK, met frequently, as often as once a month with additional subcommittee meetings, to address both mundane procedures and serious problems, including civil-military relations.

In the following decades, civil-military relations took a backseat. The *Korea Herald* reported that "the USFK remained low key in terms of community relations. Despite the unchanging mission and performance in the defense of this nation, the USFK was gradually alienated from Korean lives, with only occasional criminal incidents reminding Koreans of their existence. Media coverage was limited to joint field exercises with the Korean Army, but they too declined in size and frequency."[50] The Joint Committee reduced its meetings to quarterly, then twice annually. My interviews in December 2009 with the USFK officials who oversee and manage the Good Neighbor Program (GNP) unequivocally corroborated that the program was a "reaction to a lack of relationship" between civilian Koreans and U.S. service personnel.[51]

The candlelight vigils, aggressive newspaper coverage, and general criticism of U.S. troop conduct in the 2000s made the USFK keenly aware that civil-military problems were serious and could jeopardize the alliance relationship. Public information aimed at communicating and staying in contact with camp town residents and CSOs would be critical. Like their Korean counterparts, American officials were learning lessons about dealing with a civilian population that was taking advantage of its growing democratic muscles.

In response to the public uproar of the early 2000s, the USFK command, under the leadership of General Leon LaPorte, instituted the Good Neighbor Program in 2003 as a way to "'close the gap' between U.S. soldiers and the host society."[52] Five years later, the commanding general of the USFK, Gen. B. B. Bell, reported before the Senate Armed Services Committee: "The Good Neighbor Program is a USFK hallmark for fostering harmonious relations between our Servicemembers and the Republic of Korea citizenry. . . . [It] will improve the understanding and support of the Korean community for the strategic mission of the USFK and effectively demonstrate the respect of USFK Servicemembers for the laws, history, culture, and customs of the Republic of Korea."[53]

One of the main goals was to help educate USFK personnel about Korean society and sensitivities and to help the Americans interact better with Korean communities. For starters, all arriving service personnel would receive training in Korean culture and history and then have the training reinforced later in their stay.[54] Individual battalions and squadrons were mandated to create programs throughout the year. In response, for example, the Twenty-Ninth Theater Support Command in Taegu developed a version of a program the Army runs in Germany and Japan, called Headstart, to introduce new arrivals to the host society. In late 2009, with the help of faculty and students at Keimyung University, the program included a pre-departure interactive CD about Korea, intensive language instruction, and basic teaching about culture and life in Korea so that soldiers could be prepped before their arrival in Korea. The GNP also developed mandatory three-day training programs in mixed ranks to learn about Korean culture and customs, and other aspects of participating in improved civil-military relations. Additionally, every battalion-sized unit was mandated to interact with a local school, and servicemen and women were encouraged to take tours to Ulsan, Pusan, and the countryside to go on fishing trips and more in order to get off post and get to know the country in which they were residing and working. Many of these trips had Korean corporate sponsorship.[55]

Another aspect of the GNP is to increase outreach and access to the bases by Korean civilians and to increase transparency. For one, USFK staff members are to contact the local mayor's office on a regular basis and exchange information (about military exercises and other activities) that would benefit local residents. Second, the USFK and Koreans formed the Good Neighbor Advisory Council, composed of several mayors, ROK generals, and corporate leaders so that they can interact regularly with USFK commanders.[56] Moreover, there are weekly "windshield tours" to the Yongsan base, where Koreans can visit, tour around the compound, eat with soldiers, and get to know what their work and living conditions are like. One civil-military relations officer I spoke with remarked that often college students and Christian pastors are surprised to see the "real" American base life because they had imagined that U.S. soldiers were "living like kings" in Korea.[57] Other bases sponsor "open houses" for similar purposes.[58] Furthermore, the USFK aims to heighten transparency by loading information onto the USFK website on DUI (driving under the influence of alcohol) and sexual assault cases adjudicated by the office of the Judge Advocate General (JAG).[59] These are ways to dispel mutual ignorance, prevent miscommunication, and decrease distrust on a people-to-people level.

USFK efforts also include programs intended to familiarize the Korean public with the actual presence of troops and to inform them about alliance policies, UN and U.S.-ROK structure, and the contributions of related organizations to security and stability on the peninsula and in the Northeast Asia region. To this effect, the GNP developed the "Young Leaders Program" in 2006, targeting Koreans between thirty and fifty-nine years of age who play some influential role in various sectors of Korean society. For youth, the GNP established the Good Neighbor English Camp in 2005 to "immerse Korean youth in an English-speaking environment" with the hope that they will grow to understand the USFK's mission, policies, and personnel and "become 'goodwill ambassadors' as they relay their experience with friends, families, teachers and classmates."[60]

Perhaps some of the most important aspects of the GNP are the procedures created to facilitate prompt communication and coordination between the USFK and Korean sides when problems occur. A "bilingual hotline" was established so that "complaints from the local community will be received and addressed."[61] And the Korean National Police created "language liaisons"—dispatchers who can communicate in English—with USFK counterparts.[62] And practical measures like systematically cleaning the mud on local streets, left behind after military exercises or the movement of equipment, were implemented for safety reasons and residents' well-being.[63] In 2007 General Bell institutionalized the GNP by creating a Good Neighbor Program Office, "whose mission is to track down all Good Neighbor programs and conduct a comprehensive evaluation of them on a regular basis."[64] Coordination and accountability got a boost from this measure.

In 2009, the USFK Commanding General Walter Sharp declared that the GNP "absolutely" had positive effects on Korean-American civil-military relations: "We can feel a change in the perception Koreans have had toward us. Data from several polls have also shown that Koreans have had a more positive view of the U.S. going back to early 2006," which he attributed in part to the GNP.[65] Koreans have also reached out in turn; for example, Songtan City officials invited U.S. troops to participate in an annual local cultural festival and named it the "Korean-American Friendship Festival."[66]

In addition to the three main aspects of civil-military relations described by Avant earlier in the chapter, James Burk, an expert on American civil-military relations and former editor of *Armed Forces and Society,* emphasizes "institutional presence," which includes the "material and moral integration" of the military "with the larger society."[67] (His findings refer to civil-military relations within the United States but can easily be applied abroad.) Both these factors determine the extent to which (1) the military plays a central or peripheral role in terms of resource claims and contributions (e.g., jobs) and its frequency and directness in social relations with the civilian society so that it "has to be taken into account as an actor in society";[68] and (2) the military is "considered an important actor in the normative order," which he defines as "the understanding of what constitutes a good society."[69] In short, the latter refers to legitimacy of the military institution and its ability to adapt to changing moral expectations, including the "expansion of citizens' rights [civil rights, gay rights, non-discrimination against women, etc., in the U.S. military] and the closely-related interest in building decent or non-humiliating relations between [the military] and the people they serve."[70]

Viewed in this light, the USFK has changed its institutional role as a mainstay of Korean society in economic, security, and cultural terms since the golden age of the 1960s when the U.S. dollar, U.S. firepower, and the global fight against Communism made the United States indispensable as an ally and patron. And in many ways, under decades of domestic authoritarian rule, Koreans aspired morally to emulate the democracy and human rights the United States symbolized. But moral legitimacy in the minds of the Korean people vanished with the 1980 Kwangju period and never has been reconstructed in full. And with democratization and the new publicization of USFK-related crimes against Korean civilians, environmental damage, and so on, Koreans increasingly have come to scrutinize the U.S. forces as reflecting and facilitating or deterring the changing notions of the "good society" in their country. Basic security (protection from the North Korea) and economic and military assistance from the United States had already dropped in salience as constitutive of the "good society" for Koreans starting a couple decades ago, while human rights, civil society activism, and other progressive interests gained salience. Moreover, as inter-Korean relations transformed since the mid- to late 1990s away from Cold War hostility and toward increased empathy for the plight of the North Korean people, South Koreans' notion of the "good society" reflected such changes. With North Korea's economic debacle in the early to mid-1990s and "on the urging of the President Kim Young Sam, South Korea's definition of its security was expanded from the physical protection of the state of ROK (*gukga anbo*) to the preservation of the political and territorial integrity of the entire nation of the Korean people, including both North and South Korea, as well as overseas Koreans (*minjok anbo*)."[71] The U.S. troops were a constant reminder of unfinished war and division, and full sovereignty not yet achieved. If we look at criticisms of the U.S. or anti-Americanism in this light of changing values about what constitutes legitimate norms and aspirations as a society, nationalism does not have to be the sole or primary explanation of worn and torn civil-military relations. Democracy was galvanizing public interest in foreign policy, North Korean power was diminishing, inter-Korean relations took on new importance, and the larger world around the peninsula offered new opportunities for new friends (the policy, or *Nordpolitik,* was initiated by Kim's predecessor, Roh Tae Woo, and continued by Kim).

Additionally, with the phenomenal economic rise of South Korea in the 1980s and after—including the quick recovery from the financial crisis of 1997—the U.S. dollar increasingly lost the power and aura of admiration from Koreans. And Korean companies became the coveted venues of employment for the vast majority of Koreans, whereas in the 1950s through the 1970s, a job on a U.S. compound as a clerk or interpreter was considered valuable and prestigious because of the access to Americans and Americana. And as the South Korean military became a top-notch fighting machine, with Korea's fast-developing information technology to boot, Koreans increasingly questioned the material and moral benefits of the U.S. troops. Especially with the sharp reduction of U.S. troops in Korea in the 2000s, the literal heft of U.S. military power in terms of bodies decreased. And with local empowerment through decentralization, connections with U.S. bases became less important for Korean locals than everyday matters involving local Korean authorities, merchants, residents associations, and development goals. In short, what Burk calls the "social significance"[72] of the USFK in the camp town areas declined.

Burk sides with Morris Janowitz's view (rather than Samuel Huntington's contrasting view) that militaries need to educate and acculturate themselves to the changing social contexts and expectations of civilian society in order to remain effective organizations that would be materially and morally integrated with the society. If they do not, they become alienated by the society and possibly confused about their self-identity and their perception of civilians. Moreover, institutional integration and military effectiveness do not have to be at odds. Based on his study of the U.S. military's relationship with the American society, Burk observes that "the military and society have been morally integrated to the degree that the functional and social imperatives reinforce each other."[73] The interview I conducted with officials in the Office of the Military Attaché of the U.S. Embassy in Seoul reflected this type of understanding. They admitted that dealing with the public had to be an integral part of the military mission and said the military presence "now is not just about warfighting but has to deal with [other] issues in order to get at the military issues."[74] An official in the Public Affairs Office of the U.S. Embassy emphasized the larger point about changes in Korea and the need for U.S. personnel, civilian and military, to adapt: "If you don't know about Korea [today] and all you know is that we saved Korea, then you can't understand the modern situation.[75]

But not all personnel in the USFK and the U.S. Embassy shared this view. There were those who continued to regard bases activism and anti-American sentiment as "endemic to the Korean character—the shrimp [among whales] syndrome," its "aspirations beyond its capacity," and its "tendency toward competition where competition is not necessary."[76] Another official, a very young diplomat, likened Korean civil society's bases activism as a reflection of Korean society's "adolescence," a way "to test the limits of the patron."[77] In another case, a civilian employee of the USFK who managed community (civil-military) relations at the local camp town levels for several decades discussed the numerous changes Korean society underwent since democratization but slipped into calling bases activists "dissidents," as they had been regarded during the authoritarian period. (I made a mental note to myself that in 2002, the more appropriate and accurate term is "dissenter" or "critic," not dissident.)

Furthermore, American reactions to bases activism, candlelight vigils, break-ins at U.S. military compounds, and the criticism of the SOFA negotiations, and the general uproar against U.S. troop conduct in the early 2000s differed depending on the individual official's past experiences with anti-Americanism in Korea, as well as in the other countries in which they had served. For example, to new or young officials, the Koreans' demonstrations and criticisms were more alarming and offensive than they were to their seniors who had earlier served either in Korea or elsewhere where conditions had been worse. Embassy personnel who had witnessed the 1980s radicalization of the student movement, including the conflation of Chun Doo Hwan and Ronald Reagan as the "enemy," the burning of the Pusan Cultural Center, the occupation of the U.S. Information Service office and library, the self-immolation of young activists, and other forms of violence, considered the early 2000s version of protests "to be nothing" in comparison. The officials familiar with alliance politics and domestic Korean politics of the 1980s tended to view the anti-Americanism of that period as "political" but that of the early 2000s as "emotional, knee-jerk" expressions. Such "veterans of anti-Americanism," if they had comparative perspective through tours of duty in places that were more hostile to Americans, saw the public opinion outbursts as part of "pendulum swings" and wondered, as long as the protests were not violent or aggressive, "what's the big deal?"

The other side of civil-military relations is the morale of military personnel. As one Embassy PAO remarked, "The guys put their lives on the line. When they are off duty, they can't move from base to base freely because of anti-American demonstrations. Some bitch about it, but others speak up and say, 'But that's why we're here; so they [Koreans] can do that, to have the right to have demos.'"[78] Even without the heavy activism around the bases, Korea has been one of the least desirable posts for enlisted men and some in the officer corps. Its technical designation as a war zone (in the absence of a peace treaty ending the Korean War), the short tour of duty (TDY)—usually one year and unaccompanied by spouse/family—and the poor living conditions on compounds made Korea less desirable than other allied posts (e.g., Germany, Japan, Italy). General Bell testified before the House Armed Services Committee in 2008 that the military facilities in Korea were "the most dilapidated in the US military, outside of active combat or peace enforcement zones" and emphasized the need for the U.S. Congress to "commit to recapitalizing our facilities and infrastructure."[79]

To remedy a variety of problems—military morale and organizational continuity, strategic flexibility, and the instability of one-year tours that can contribute to civil-military problems—General Bell campaigned for tour normalization in Korea to parallel the TDYs for service in Japan or Europe. While serving as USFK commander, Bell pushed the Pentagon, the U.S. Congress, and the South Korean government to accept and support the extended stay and for Congress to enable the upgrading of living facilities, such as housing, schools, and community centers, on military compounds. The seeds of change began in 2004 when the Defense Department offered the "Assignment Incentive Pay" program to all troops serving in Korea, promising an additional $300 per month if they extended their then current tour of duty by twelve months. Admiral Timothy Keating, commander of the U.S. Pacific Command, offered his support during his tenure, as did Secretary of Defense Robert Gates (while in the George W. Bush administration), stating that "as a matter of principle, I think it [the change] is past time."[80]

On March 2, 2009, the Joint Federal Travel Regulation (JFTR), which establishes the length of military tours, officially sanctioned a three-year tour of duty in Korea (e.g., Pyŏngtaek, Osan, Taegu, Chinhae, and Seoul) and a two-year term for "Area I" facilities, such as Tongduchŏn and Uichŏngbu, close to the DMZ.[81] Both TDYs allow accompanied tours by family and include the $300 monthly incentive pay. General Walter Sharp, who succeeded General Bell in the second half of 2008, emphasized that the "planned transition of operational control of Korean troops during wartime from the United States to South Korea in 2012 and the tour normalization initiative will move U.S. troops beyond this 'crisis mentality'" of perceiving South Korea as an unstable war zone and an unstable alliance.[82] When testifying before the Senate Armed Forces Committee in March 2008, General Bell lamented that in "a modern and vibrant Republic of Korea, the U.S. still rotates servicemembers on one-year unaccompanied assignments as though this remained an active combat zone," and declared, "It is not."[83]

In civil-military terms, the policy change is a way for the United States to reaffirm U.S. commitment to help defend Korea and to ensure a less turbulent long-term presence. In 2008, General Bell criticized the short-term TDY: "Right now, over 90 percent of our servicemembers come to Korea for one-year tours without their families—and that means most of them don't get out and don't really get involved in their communities after work," but with tour normalcy, "American servicemembers could come to Korea . . . with their families—families who will establish life-long connections and friendships with the Korean people."[84] Other USFK officials also stated that the "extended tour length will contribute to further solidifying the Korea-U.S. alliance by forging lifelong friendships at the family level."[85] For decades, Korean and other critics of U.S. troop conduct off duty, such as drunkenness, the patronization of sex clubs, violence against civilians, disregard for Korean laws and customs, or the expression of racial superiority over Koreans, have wondered whether the one-year unaccompanied tour by predominantly young and inexperienced enlistees and lonely soldiers unanchored to families have abetted conduct unbecoming. Normalization of duty, which is slated for completion by the end of this decade (delayed from the 2012 target), would enable about half of the 28,000 force and their families to live more "normally" in Korea and to invest in getting to know the country and people outside the compound gates.

Despite these well-intentioned and long-overdue changes to improve the military's quality of life, readiness, and relationships inside and outside the compound gates in Korea, normalizaton of duty is no guarantee for closing the civil-military gap on the U.S. military's moral and political legitimacy in Korean society. Burk's emphasis on the moral presence, adaptation, and integration of a military in the larger context of a society as a necessary part of its "organizational convergence" or divergence from civilian society needs to be heeded. The "normative order" in Korea now constitutes democracy and civil society activism, and U.S. military actions that appear to accord with or reinforce them versus those that block or contravene them will be interpreted by Koreans as substantively positive or negative respectively.[86]

First, the Kwangju massacre engendered the breach in Koreans' trust in the USFK. Second, when Koreans were suffering from war, poverty, and the sacrifices of reconstruction, American material generosity, from low-cost weaponry to gifts for local orphanages, was gratefully received and helped build social capital with elites and local residents. But current visits to orphanages as part of local outreach efforts or good neighborly gestures are out of sync with the larger Korean society's immense wealth and consumerist tastes compared to the 1950s and 1960s. Third, with the end of the Cold War in Europe and Korea's complex web of diplomatic, economic, and cultural connections with former enemies such as China, Russia, and Vietnam, the political legitimacy of the USFK as the bulwark of the "free world" no longer stands. Fourth, the development of inter-Korean relations and public support of improved relations since the mid- to late 1990s have added more question marks regarding U.S. military and humanitarian policies toward the peninsula. Furthermore, whether and how the USFK has a place in Korea's dynamic and raucous democracy is a big question. The relationship between militaries and democracies (or non-democracies) and democratic transitions has been examined by many scholars, and the American case has been a salient part of the debate. Burk highlights the importance (in American society) of assessing "whether the military and the democracy it protects are supportive of the same normative order,"[87] whether the military is contributory or predatory toward the society it is to protect and promote.[88] These are questions many South Koreans have been asking as their democracy grows and the role of the United States on the peninsula and in East Asia becomes more ambiguous and complex at the same time.

American leaders tout democracy and work to export it abroad, but Americans do not live up to democratic realities in foreign places very well. In some sense, the U.S. likes to take credit for giving birth to democracies, but it does not like the youthful nature of new democracies when they are unruly (disobedient), assertive (nationalistic), unpredictable (emotional), and willing to challenge the power of the U.S. (rebellious and ungrateful). This was the case in the Philippines in the late 1980s and early 1990s and more recently in Korea in the early 2000s. And once Japan, the most established democracy in East Asia, began to define national interests in a way that threatened U.S. economic hegemony, it no longer was treated as the chosen son in Asia. Michael Auslin makes an interesting observation that verges on identifying U.S. hypocrisy or a dual personality disorder:

> As the political and security relationship deepens between the United States and Japan, domestic public opinion plays a correspondingly larger role in alliance relations. U.S. policymakers have for decades sought to increase Japanese roles and upgrade its capabilities in alliance planning, and since the administration of former Prime Minister Junichiro Koizumi (2001–2006), Tokyo has slowly expanded the scope of its international activities. Yet, ironically, at the very moment when Japan has begun to play a larger role on the world stage, foreign observers [i.e., Americans] have openly begun to worry about increased Japanese "nationalism."[89]

Moreover, Thomas Carothers, who has written extensively on democratization and the politics and policies of American democracy promotion abroad, points out the "unquestionably troubled" state of democracy within U.S. borders, while the promoters continue to portray democracy "as a gleaming edifice made up of larger-than-life institutions and structures . . . , characterized as a self-evident truth, with the resulting assumption that democratic values, once properly introduced, will take hold naturally and cement into perpetuity the proper institutional system."[90] His words are cautionary, for the future of American democracy itself, but also for its legitimacy when promoted abroad in a world that no longer regards American democracy as the gleaming, self-evident truth and structure but instead "as taking sides in historical power struggles rather than advancing the abstract principles of democracy."[91] Additionally, the world has grown cynical and filled with "postmodern fatigue with democracy."[92]

In the midst of a decade of U.S. attempts to offer democracy and freedom to cure the ills plaguing Afghan and Iraqi societies, the East Asian alliance partners of the United States serve as timely reminders of what democracy can bring: vibrant civil society activism and local empowerment together with a historical legacy of political and social divisions, stratifications, and authoritarian cultural practices within the civil-society sector. With democracy may come acute challenges to the ability of even pro-U.S. governments to toe the U.S. line. The East Asian cases, especially Korea, also teach the United States to be careful and wary of how it uses its power in the country of occupation, for today's foibles, faux-pas, and slights, let alone severe crimes, by the representatives of the United States can accumulate in the collective memory and become potent sources of mistrust and hostility toward the U.S. well into the future. Outright acts of humiliation and disrespect will bear even more bitter fruits. U.S. national interest can only serve itself when other societies' histories, interests, pride, and perspectives are taken into account. The East Asian cases show that in democracies on the move, people's new democratic identities and interests may end up directing rather than following policies preferred by their own governments or those of the United States.

NOTES

1. Anthony C.Y. Leong, *Korean Cinema: The New Hong Kong* (Victoria, Canada: Trafford Publishing, 2002), 11.

2. Doobo Shim, "The Growth of Korean Cultural Industries and the Korean Wave," in *East Asian Pop Culture: Analysing the Korean Wave*, ed. Chua Beng Huat and Koichi Iwabuchi (Hong Kong: Hong Kong University Press, 2008), 20.

3. Koichi Iwabuchi, *Recentering Globalization: Popular Culture and Japanese Transnationalism* (Durham, NC: Duke University Press, 2002).

4. G. John Ikenberry, "Attacks against the Empire: Anti-Americanism in the Age of Unipolarity," paper presented at the conference "Korean Attitudes

toward the United States: Complexities of an Enduring and Endured Relationship," Georgetown University, January 31–February 1, 2003.

5. Samuel S. Kim, "Northeast Asia in the Local-Regional-Global Nexus: Multiple Challenges and Contending Explanations," in *The International Relations of Northeast Asia,* ed. Samuel S. Kim (Lanham, MD: Rowman & Littlefield, 2004), 27.

6. Larry Diamond, "Promoting Democracy in the 1990s: Actors, Instruments, and Issues," in *Democracy's Victory and Crisis,* ed. Alex Hadenius (Cambridge: Cambridge University Press, 1997), 352.

7. Tony Smith, "National Security Liberalism and American Foreign Policy," in *American Democracy Promotion,* ed. Michael Cox, G. John Ikenberry, and Takashi Inoguchi (New York: Oxford University Press, 2000), 100.

8. Fareed Zakaria, *The Future of Freedom: Illiberal Democracy at Home and Abroad* (New York: W.W. Norton, 2003).

9. Diamond, "Promoting Democracy in the 1990s," 347.

10. *New York Times,* September 16, 1991 (late edition).

11. U.S. National Intelligence Council, "East Asia and the United States: Current Status and Five-Year Outlook Conference Report," September 2000, www.dni.gov/nic/confreports_asiaUSoutlook.html (accessed January 10, 2006).

12. Hinori Sasada, "Youth and Nationalism in Japan," *SAIS Review* 26, no. 2 (summer–fall 2006), 109–122.

13. Center for Strategic and International Studies (CSIS), *Generational Change in Japan: Implications for U.S.-Japan Relations* (Washington, DC: CSIS, October 2002), 40.

14. Ibid., 9.

15. Ibid., 10.

16. Tanaka Nobumasa, "High School Students Struggle against National Anthem Enforcement," December 14, 2002, www.zmag.org/content/print_article.cfm?itemID=2750§ionID=17 (accessed May 12, 2004).

17. "Students' Consciousness regarding the Constitution," *Minami Nippon Shimbun,* www.jca.apc.org/~kenpoweb/articles/oguri112500.html (accessed May 12, 2004). My former research assistant, Chiaki Nishijima, translated the article from Japanese to English. She was able to find only the last names of the survey authors, which were a Professor Koguri and journalist Maeda.

18. Ibid.

19. CSIS, *Generational Change,* 28.

20. Ian Condry, "Youth, Intimacy, and Blood: Media and Nationalism in Contemporary Japan," *Japan Focus: An Asia-Pacific e-journal,* April 8, 2007, www.japanfocus.org/products/topdf/2403 (accessed September 9, 2007).

21. Ibid.

22. Russell F. Weigley, "The American Civil-Military Cultural Gap: A Historical Perspective, Colonial Times to the Present," in *Soldiers and Civilians: The Civil-Military Gap and American National Security,* ed. Peter D. Feaver and Richard H. Kohn (Cambridge, MA: MIT Press, 2001), 215.

23. Ibid., 219.

24. Ibid.

25. Ibid., 223.

26. Ibid., 220.

27. Ibid., 217.

28. Thomas Ricks, "The Military and Society," *Atlantic Monthly*, July 1997, 74.

29. Ibid., 76.

30. Deborah Avant, "Conflicting Indicators of 'Crisis' in American Civil-Military Relations," *Armed Forces and Society*, vol. 24, no. 3 (1998), 375.

31. Alexander Cooley, *Base Politics: Democratic Change and the U.S. Military Overseas* (Ithaca, NY: Cornell University Press, 2008), 20.

32. Pyong Choon Hahm, "Korea's 'Mendicant Mentality,'" *Foreign Affairs* 43, no. 1 (October 1964),167.

33. Ibid., 166.

34. Ibid., 171.

35. Ibid., 167.

36. Author interview, Seoul, winter 2002.

37. Author interview, May 13, 2002.

38. See Ole R. Holsti, "Of Chasms and Convergences: Attitudes and Beliefs of Civilians and Military Elites at the Start of a New Millennium," in *Soldiers and Civilians*, 32–33.

39. David E. Albright, "A Comparative Conceptualization of Civil-Military Relations," *World Politics* 32, no. 4 (1980), 553–576.

40. Ibid., 567.

41. Author interview, USFK, Environment, Seoul, May 20, 2002. See chapter 2 in this volume for a discussion of Mark Gillem's findings on the U.S. military's occupation of land as a major grievance among Koreans.

42. Lee Yujin (Green Korea United), "Forbidden Rights to Pollute the Korean Peninsula: U.S Military Activities and Environmental Disaster," People's Solidarity for Participatory Democracy, January 31, 2003, blog.peoplepower21.org/English/8505 (accessed March 21, 2010).

43. "Do They Poison the Potomac?" *Chosun Ilbo*, English edition, July 15, 2000, www.chosun.com/w21data/html/news/200007/200007140411.html (accessed March 21, 2010). It is also useful to have a basis of comparison: Ole Holsti cites the TISS survey of Americans and American military personnel that found "[o]nly a small minority of civilians believes that the [American] media depict the military in a hostile manner, whereas a much large proportion of the military believes that to be the case" (Holsti, "Of Chasms and Convergences," 66).

44. Author interview, USFK, Environment, Seoul, May 20, 2002. The USFK invited the Korean media onto the bases in the midst of the charge by Korea CSOs that the U.S. military is the source of oil contamination in the underground water and soil at Noksap'yŏng subway station near the base.

45. Ibid.

46. See "100 Protesters, Police Injured at Rally against Nuke Dump Plan," *Seoul Yonhap*, November 20, 2003; Mark Hibbs, "South Korea Concedes Defeat of Ambitious Repository Selection," *Nucleonics Week* (December 18, 2003), 44:51.

47. Author interview, USFK, Environment, Seoul, May 20, 2002.

48. U.S. Department of Defense, DOD Directive 6050.16, "DOD Policy for Establishing and Implementing Environmental Standards at Overseas Installations," September 20, 1991.

49. U.S. Army Headquarters, Combined Forces Command, FC 9518, "ANNEX L to CFC OPLAN (KOREA) 9518X-XX, ENVIRONMENTAL CONSIDERATIONS," Seoul, n.d. ["June 1, 19xx"].

50. "Good Neighbors," *Korea Herald*, March 12, 2003 (accessed July 8, 2009).

51. Author interview with USFK civil-military affairs official, Seoul, December 16, 2009.

52. "Good Neighbors."

53. U.S. Senate, Armed Services Committee, "Statement of General B.B. Bell," April 24, 2007, www.globalsecurity.org/military/library/congress/2007_hr/070424-bell.pdf (accessed July 8, 2009).

54. *Korea Times*, February 25, 2009.

55. Author interview with USFK civil-military affairs official, Seoul, December 16, 2009.

56. Ibid.

57. Ibid.

58. "Gen. LaPorte Seeks Camaraderie with S. Koreans," *Stars and Stripes*, June 20, 2009.

59. Ibid.

60. "US Servicemen Broaden 'Good Neighbors,'" *Korea Times*, May 29, 2008; "Doing Good for Koreans Every Day," *Korea Herald*, May 27, 2008.

61. *Korea Herald*, March 12, 2003.

62. Author interview, USFK civil-military relations officer, Seoul, December 16, 2010.

63. Ibid.

64. *Korea Times*, May 29, 2008.

65. *Korea Times*, February 25, 2009.

66. "Town Invites U.S. Airmen to Party," *Stars and Stripes*, October 10, 2003.

67. James Burk, "The Military's Presence in American Society, 1950–2000," in *Soldiers and Civilians*, 248–249.

68. Ibid., 249–250.

69. Ibid., 250.

70. Ibid., 262–263.

71. Chien-peng Chung, "Democratization in South Korea and Inter-Korea Relations," *Pacific Affairs* 76, no. 1 (spring 2003), 26. Chung refers to the work of Chung-in Moon, "South Korea: Recasting Security Paradigms," in *Asian*

Security Practices—Material and Ideational Influences, ed. Muthiah Alagappa (Stanford: CA: Stanford University Press, 1998).

72. Burk, "The Military's Presence in American Society," 249.

73. Ibid.

74. Author interview, U.S. Embassy, Seoul, winter 2001.

75. Author interview, U.S. Embassy, Seoul, spring 2002.

76. Author interview, U.S. Embassy, Seoul, spring 2002.

77. Ibid.

78. Author interview, U.S. Embassy, Seoul, spring 2002.

79. U.S. Department of Defense, "Statement of General B.B. Bell, Commander, United Nations Command; Commander, Republic of Korea–United States Combined Forces Command; and Commander, United States Forces Korea, before the House Armed Services Committee," March 12, 2008.

80. "Gates, Military Leaders in Korea Advocate Normalized Tours," American Forces Press Service, June 2, 2008, www.defenselink.mil (accessed August 7, 2008).

81. U.S. Army, "Tour Normalization in the Republic of Korea," *Stand-To!,* www.army.mil/standto/archive/2009/05/29 (accessed June 5, 2010).

82. "Tour Normalization to Soften 'Crisis Mentality,'" *Korea Times,* www.koreatimes.co.kr/www/news/nation/2009/11/205_40282.html (accessed August 20, 2010).

83. "Top Commander in Korea Urges Three-Year, Accompanied Tours," American Forces Press Service, www.defenselink.mil (accessed August 7, 2008).

84. "Gates, Military Leaders in Korea Advocate Normalized Tours."

85. Ibid.

86. See Burk, "The Military's Presence," on the "normative order" and substantive judgment as good or bad by civilians, 250.

87. Ibid., 252.

88. Burk includes the British military on the eve of the American revolution and the Indonesian military's occupation of East Timor as examples of predatory institutions (militaries). For other discussions, see Martin C. Needler, "The Latin American Military: Predatory Reactionaries or Modernizing Patriots?" *Journal of Inter-American Studies* 11, no. 2 (April 1969), 237–244; E.A Brett, "Neutralising the Use of Force in Uganda: The Role of the Military in Politics," *The Journal of Modern African Studies* 33, no. 1 (1995), 129–152.

89. Michael R. Auslin, "Japanese Foreign Policy and Domestic Nationalism," American Enterprise Institute, n.d.

90. Thomas Carothers, *Critical Mission: Essays on Democracy Promotion* (Washington, DC: Carnegie Endowment for International Peace, 2004), 148.

91. Ibid., 152.

92. Ibid., 151.

Bibliography

Abramowitz, Morton, and Stephen W. Bosworth. *Chasing the Sun: Rethinking East Asian Policy.* New York: Century Foundation, 2006.

Albright, David E. "A Comparative Conceptualization of Civil-Military Relations." *World Politics* 32, no. 4 (1980), 553–576.

Alexander, M. Jacqui, and Chandra Mohanty. Introduction to *Feminist Genealogies, Colonial Legacies, Democratic Futures,* edited by M. Jacqui Alexander and Chandra Mohanty, xiii–xlii. New York: Routledge, 1997.

Amnesty International. "South Korea: Elderly Farmers Forcibly Evicted for US Army Base." News release, March 17, 2006. www.amnesty.org/en/library/info/ASA25/001/2006.

——. *South Korea: Prisoners Held for National Security Reasons.* New York, NY: Amnesty International U.S.A., 1991.

"Anti-War Protests Begin in Asia-Pacific." National Network to End the War against Iraq. October 15, 2002. Accessed November 19, 2003. www.endthewar.org/features/asiapacific/htm.

Armstrong, Charles. "America's Korea, Korea's Vietnam." *Critical Asian Studies* 33, no. 4 (2001), 527–540.

Asia Partnership for Human Development. *Annual Report 2003.* Bangkok: APHD Secretariat, 4. Accessed November 12, 2008. www.aphd.or.th/annual-report/pdf/aphd-annual-report-2003.pdf.

——. *Mosaic* (magazine). April–August 2004. Accessed December 19, 2008. www.aphd.or.th/mosaic/pdf/mosaic_4.pdf.

Asian Peace Alliance. *Occasional Newsletter,* no. 01-2003 (2003). Accessed November 12, 2008. www.human.mie-u.ac.jp/~peace/APA-03.htm.

Auslin, Michael R. "Japanese Foreign Policy and Domestic Nationalism." American Enterprise Institute, n.d.

Avant, Deborah. "Conflicting Indicators of 'Crisis' in American Civil-Military Relations." *Armed Forces and Society,* vol. 24, no. 3 (1998).

Baek, Jae Hee. "I'm Entertainer, I'm Not Sex Worker." In *Yonggamhan Yŏsŏng-*

dŭl (Women of courage), edited by Magdalena House, 191–228. Seoul: Sam-in Publishing, 2002.

Base21. "Puerto Rican Solidarity with Korean People." http://base21.jinbo.net/show/show.php?p_cd=0&p_dv=0&p_docnbr=21475.

Berger, Thomas U. "Norms, Identity, and National Security in Germany and Japan." In *The Culture of National Security: Norms and Identity in World Politics,* edited by Peter J. Katzenstein, 317–356. New York: Columbia University Press, 1996.

Bleiker, Roland. *Divided Korea toward a Culture of Reconciliation.* Minneapolis, MN: University of Minnesota Press, 2005.

Bong, Youngshik D. *Flashpoints at Sea? Legitimization Strategy and East Asian Island Disputes.* Ph.D. diss., University of Pennsylvania, 2002.

———. "Yongmi: Pragmatic Anti-Americanism in South Korea." *Brown Journal of World Affairs* 10, no. 2 (2004), 153–166.

Bong, Youngshik, and Katharine H.S. Moon. "Rethinking Young Anti-Americanism in South Korea." In *The Anti-American Century,* edited by Ivan Krastev and Alan L. McPherson, 77–108. Budapest and New York: Central European University Press, 2007.

Brett, E.A. "Neutralising the Use of Force in Uganda: The Role of the Military in Politics." *Journal of Modern African Studies* 33, no. 1(1995), 129–152.

Burk, James. "The Military's Presence in American Society, 1950–2000." In *Soldiers and Civilians: The Civil-Military Gap and American National Security,* edited by Peter D. Feaver and Richard H. Kohn, 248–249. Cambridge, MA: MIT Press, 2001.

Carothers, Thomas. *Aiding Democracy Abroad: The Learning Curve.* Washington, DC: Carnegie Endowment for International Peace, 1999.

———. *Critical Mission: Essays on Democracy Promotion.* Washington, DC: Carnegie Endowment for International Peace, 2004.

Center for Strategic and International Studies. *Generational Change in Japan: Implications for U.S.-Japan Relations.* Washington, DC: CSIS, October 2002.

———. *The U.S.–ROK Status of Forces Agreement Revision Process: Path to an Agreement.* Washington, DC: CSIS, 2001.

Centro Internazionale Crocevia. "Rilasciate i contadini coreani subito! Scrivete la vostra indignazione alle autorità coreane" (Release the Korean villagers now! Express your indignation to the Korean authorities). Accessed July 18, 2009. semionline.croceviaterra.it/news/rilasciate-i-contadini-coreani-subito-scrivete-la-vostra-indignazione-alle-autorita-coreane.

Cha, Victor D. "Anti-Americanism and the U.S. Role in Inter-Korean Relations." In *Korean Attitudes toward the United States: Changing Dynamics,* edited by David I. Steinberg, 116–138. Armonk, NY: M.E. Sharpe, 2005.

———. "Focus on the Future, Not the North." *Washington Quarterly* 26, no. 1 (2002), 91–107.

———. "South Korea in 2004: Peninsular Flux." *Asian Survey* 45, no. 1 (2005), 33–40.

Chae, Haesook, Tiffany Carwile, and Scott Damberger. "Understanding Anti-Americanism among South Korean College Students." Paper presented at the annual meeting of the American Political Science Assocation, Chicago, IL, September 2–5, 2004.

Chicago Council on Foreign Relations. *Global Views 2004: Comparing South Korean and American Public Opinion and Foreign Policy.* Chicago: CCFR, 2004.

Cheng, Sea-Ling. *On the Move for Love: Migrant Entertainers and the U.S. Military in South Korea.* Philadelphia: University of Pennsylvania Press, 2010.

Chin, Mikyung. "Self-Governance, Political Participation, and the Feminist Movement in South Korea." In *Democracy and the Status of Women in East Asia,* edited by Rose J. Lee and Cal Clark, 91–104. Boulder, CO: Lynne Rienner, 2000.

Ch'oe, Chaejun. "Miguk, Hanguk, kŭrŏna uri." In Korean House for International Solidarity, special feature: "Do You Know about SOFA?" (Nŏhiga SOFA rŭl Anŭnga?). *Saram i saram ege* (People to people), October-November 2000, 25.

Choi, Chungmoo. "Nationalism and the Construction of Gender in Korea." In *Dangerous Women: Gender and Korean Nationalism,* edited by Elaine H. Kim and Chungmoo Choi. New York: Routledge, 1998.

Chŏn, Ubyŏng. "Pom i onŭn maŭl e saebom ch'atgi" (Finding a new spring in the village of spring). In Chuhan migun munje haegyŏl Undongsa (Korean People's Movement for Solution of U.S. Forces Korea issues), *Nogŭlli esŏ Maehyangni kkaji* (From Nogunri to Maehyangni). Seoul: Dosŏ Publishing, 2000.

Chŏn, Usŏp. "Saraitnŭn ddang, huimang ui ddang" (Land that lives, land of hope). In *Nogŭnri to Maehyangni* (History of the Korean people's movement for solution of U.S. Forces Korea issues). Seoul: Kip'ŭn Chayu Publishing, 2001.

Chŏng, Il-gun. *War in Taech'uri* (documentary film). Purn Productions (available through Third World Newsreel, New York), 2006.

Chŏng, Yujin. "Minjok' ui irŭmŭro sunkyŏlhaejin ddaldŭl" (Daughters who have become pure in the name of the "nation"). *Tangdae Pip'yŏng* 11 (2000).

——. "P'yŏnghwarŭl mandŭn danŭn kŏt" (To make peace). In *Ilsang ui ŏgapkwa sosuja ui inkwŏn* (Daily oppression and the human rights of minorities). Seoul: Saram saeng'gag, 2000.

——. "Okinawa e nŭn woe 'yangki go hom' guho ga ŏbssŭlgga?" (Why in Okinawa is there no "Yankee go home" slogan?). *Tangdae P'ipyŏng* 14 (spring 2001).

Chŏn'guk Yŏnhap. "Paljach'wi" (History). www.nadrk.org/intro/his.html.

Chuhan migun munje haegyŏl undongsa (Korean People's Movement for Solution of U.S. Forces Korea Issues). *Nogunri esŏ Maehyangni kkaji* (From Nogunri to Maehyangni). Seoul: Dosŏ Publishing, 2000.

Chung, Chien-peng. "Democratization in South Korea and Inter-Korea Relations." *Pacific Affairs* 76, no. 1 (spring 2003), 9–35.
Chung, Hyun-back. "Together and Separately: 'The New Women's Movement' after the 1980s in South Korea." *Asian Women* 5 (1997), 19–38.
Chung, Jae Ho. "How America Views China-South Korea Bilateralism." CNAPS working paper. Washington, DC: Brookings Institution, 2003.
——. "From a Special Relationship to a Normal Partnership? Interpreting the 'Garlic Battle' in Sino-South Korean Relations." *Pacific Affairs* 76, no. 4 (winter 2003/2004), 549–568.
——. "The Rise of China and Its Impact on South Korea's Strategic Soul-Searching." Korea Economic Institute, Joint U.S.-Korea Academic Studies, vol. 15 (2005). Accessed February 14, 2007. www.keia.org/Publications/JointAcademicStudies/2005/05JaeHo.pdf.
Citizens' Coalition for Economic Justice. "SOFA Constitutional Review/Claim Request." July 19, 2000.
Condry, Ian. "Youth, Intimacy, and Blood: Media and Nationalism in Contemporary Japan." *Japan Focus,* April 8, 2007. Accessed September 9, 2007. www.japanfocus.org/products/topdf/2403.
Conteris, Andres, Ben Moxham, Herbert Docena, and Wilbert van der Zeijden. "Report of the International Anti-US Bases Conference World Social Forum." Mumbai, India, January 17–20, 2004. Accessed January 16, 2009. www.tni.org/detail_page.phtml?page=acts_wsf4usbases.
Cooley, Alexander. *Base Politics: Democratic Change and the U.S. Military Overseas*. Ithaca, NY: Cornell University Press, 2008.
Cotton, James, and Kim Hyung-a Van Leest. "The New Rich and the New Middle Class in South Korea: The Rise and Fall of the 'Golf Republic.'" In *The New Rich in Asia: Mobile Phones, McDonalds and Middle-Class Revolution,* edited by Richard Robison and David S. G. Goodman, 185–206. London: Routledge, 1996.
Dawson, Jane. *Eco-Nationalism: Anti-Nuclear Activism and National Identity in Russia, Lithuania, and Ukraine*. Durham, NC: Duke University Press, 1996.
Della Porta, Donatella, Massimiliano Andretta, Lorenzo Mosca, and Herbert Reiter. *Globalization from Below: Transnational Activists and Protest Networks*. Minneapolis: University of Minneapolis Press, 2006.
Diamond, Larry. *Developing Democracy toward Consolidation*. Baltimore: Johns Hopkins University Press, 1999.
——. "Promoting Democracy in the 1990s: Actors, Instruments, and Issues." In *Democracy's Victory and Crisis,* edited by Alex Hadenius. Cambridge: Cambridge University Press, 1997.
——. "Rethinking Civil Society: Toward Democratic Consolidation." *Journal of Democracy* 5, no. 3 (1994), 4–17.
"Do They Poison the Potomac?" *Chosun Ilbo,* English edition, July 15, 2000. Accessed March 21, 2010. www.chosun.com/w21data/html/news/200007/200007140411.html.

Dong, Wonmo. "University Students in South Korean Politics: Patterns of Radicalization in the 1980s." *Journal of International Affairs* 40, no. 2 (1987), 233–255.

"East Asia–U.S.–Puerto Rico Women's Network against Militarism." Blog post, People's Solidarity for Participatory Democracy, November 8, 2003. Accessed November 10, 2008. blog.peoplepower21.org/English/7533.

Eberstadt, Nicholas. "Our Other Korea Problem." *The National Interest*, no. 69 (fall 2002), 110–118.

Educational Testing Service (ETS). "TOEFL CBT Total and Section Score Means Table 10, 2003, Rep. no. TOEFL-SUM-0203." TOEFL® Test and Score Data Summary: 2002–2003 Edition. Accessed September 4, 2009. Available at www.ets.org.

Eldridge, Robert D. "The 1996 Okinawa Referendum on US Base Reductions: One Question, Several Answers." *Asian Survey* 37, no. 10 (October 1997), 879–904.

Enloe, Cynthia. *Bananas, Beaches, and Bases: Making Feminist Sense of International Politics*. Berkeley and Los Angeles: University of California Press, 1990.

Frances, Carolyn Bowen. "Women and Military Violence." In *Okinawa: Cold War Island*, edited by Chalmers Johnson, 192–193. Cardiff, CA: Japan Policy Research Institute, 1999.

Friedman, Elisabeth. "Women's Human Rights: The Emergence of a Movement." In *Women's Rights, Human Rights: International Feminist Perspectives*, edited by Julie Peters and Andrea Wolper, 18–35. New York: Routledge, 1995.

Fukumura, Yoko, and Martha Matsuoka. "Redefining Security: Okinawa Women's Resistance to U.S. Militarism." In *Women's Activism and Globalization: Linking Local Struggles and Transnational Politics*, edited by Nancy A. Naples and Manisha Desai, 253. New York: Routledge, 2002.

Fukuyama, Francis. "Women and the Evolution of World Politics," *Foreign Affairs* 77, no. 5 (September/October 1998), 24–40.

Fuller, Graham E. "The Youth Factor: The New Demographics of the Middle East and the Implications for U.S. Policy." Analysis paper #3. Washington, DC: The Saban Center for Middle East Policy, Brookings Institution, June 2003),

Gamson, William. *The Strategy of Social Protest*. Homewood: Dorsey Press, 1975.

"Gates, Military Leaders in Korea Advocate Normalized Tours." American Forces Press Service, June 2, 2008. Accessed August 7, 2008. www.defense link.mil.

"General LaPorte Seeks Camaraderie with S. Koreans." *Stars and Stripes*, June 20, 2009.

George, Terrence. "Local Governance: People Power in the Provinces?" In *Organizing for Democracy: NGOs, Civil Society, and the Philippine State*, edited by G. Sidney Silliman and Lela Garner Noble, 223–253. Honolulu: University of Hawaiʻi Press, 1998.

Gillem, Mark L. *America Town: Building the Outposts of Empire*. Minneapolis, MN: University of Minnesota Press, 2007.

Gleysteen, William H., Jr. *Massive Entanglement, Marginal Influence: Carter and Korea in Crisis*. Washington, DC: Brookings Institution, 1999.

Gregg, Heather S. "Divided They Conquer: The Success of Armenian Ethnic Lobbies in the United States." Working paper no. 13, Inter-University Committee on International Migration, Massachusetts Institute of Technology, 2002.

Green Korea United. "A Korean Environmental Report on the U.S. Bases." June 16, 1999. Accessed July 25, 2001. www.greenkorea.org/A%20Korean%20Environmental%20Report%20on%20the%20U.S.%20Bases.htm.

———. "Do Not Trust the US Military." October 2, 2000. Accessed April 12, 2007. www.greenkorea.org/zb/print_innerHTM.php.

———. "Petition Statement to the ROK Ministry of Defense." August 8, 2000. Accessed August 8, 2001. www.greenkorea.org/sub_board/way-board.cgi?db=eng_statement&j=v&no=2&pg=1.

———. "Protest Statement." August 8, 2000. Accessed August 8, 2001. www.greenkorea.org/sub_board/way-board.cgi?db=engl_statement&j=v&no=3&pg=1.

———. "Report on Land Readjustment Plan." Accessed March 5, 2002. www.greenkorea.org/english.

Grinker, Roy Richard. *Korea and Its Futures: Unification and the Unfinished War*. New York: St. Martin's Press, 1998.

Hahm, Chaibong. "Anti-Americanism, Korean-Style." In *Korean Attitudes toward the United States: Changing Dynamics*, edited by David I. Steinberg, 220–230. Armonk, NY: M. E. Sharpe, 2005.

Hahm, Pyoung Choon. "Korea's 'Mendicant Mentality.'" *Foreign Affairs* 43, no. 1 (October 1964), 165–174.

Halloran, Richard. "The Rising East: Anti-Americanism Brews Quietly in Asian Societies Allied to U.S." *Honolulu Star-Bulletin*, February 24, 2002. Accessed May 23, 2006. www.archives.starbulletin.com/2002/02/24/editorial/halloran.html.

Hathaway, Will, and David S. Meyer. "Competition and Cooperation in Movement Coalitions: Lobbying for Peace in the 1980s." In *Coalitions and Political Movements: The Lessons of the Nuclear Freeze*, edited by Thomas R. Rochon and David S. Meyer, 61–80. Boulder, CO: Lynne Rienner, 1997.

Heng, Geraldine. "'A Great Way to Fly': Nationalism, the State, and the Varieties of Third-World Feminism." In *Feminist Genealogies, Colonial Legacies, Democratic Futures*, edited by M. Jacqui Alexander and Chandra Mohanty, 30–45. NY: Routledge, 1997.

Hibbs, Mark. "South Korea Concedes Defeat of Ambitious Repository Selection." *Nucleonics Week*, December 18, 2003, 44:51.

Hollander, Paul. *Anti-Americanism: Irrational and Rational.* Somerset, NJ: Transaction Publishers, 2003.

Holsti, Ole R. "Of Chasms and Convergences: Attitudes and Beliefs of Civilians and Military Elites at the Start of a New Millennium." In *Soldiers and Civilians: The Civil-Military Gap and American National Security,* edited by Peter D. Feaver and Richard H. Kohn, 15–100. Cambridge, MA: MIT Press, 2001.

Hwang, Kyŏngsu. "Kulyok hyŏbsang hanŭni ch'arari Kunsan konghang p'aesoehaja" (Rather than submit to negotiations, better to get rid of the Kunsan airport). *Mal chi* (Mal magazine), January 1998.

Hyde, Henry J. Letter to President Roh Moo Hyun from Henry J. Hyde, chairman, U S House of Representatives Committee on International Relations. Sept. 15, 2005. Accessed July 25, 2009. www.icasinc.org/2005/2005l/2005lh2h.html.

Hyman, Sidney. *Youth in Politics: Expectations and Realities.* New York: Basic Books, 1972.

Ikenberry, G. John. "Attacks against the Empire: Anti-Americanism in the Age of Unipolarity." Paper presented at the conference "Korean Attitudes toward the United States: Complexities of an Enduring and Endured Relationship." Georgetown University, January 31–February 1, 2003.

Inoguchi, Takashi. "Three Frameworks in Search of a Policy: U.S. Democracy Promotion in Asia-Pacific." In *American Democracy Promotion : Impulses, Strategies, and Impacts,* edited by Michael Cox, G. John Ikenberry, and Takashi Inoguchi, 267–286. New York: Oxford University Press, 2000.

"International Grassroots Summit on Military Base Cleanup: A Healthy Environment Is a Human Right." Report on conference, Trinity College, Washington, DC, October 25–29, 1999. Accessed April 27, 2006. www.webcom.com/ncecd/basecleanup.htm.

Iwabuchi, Koichi. *Recentering Globalization: Popular Culture and Japanese Transnationalism.* Durham, NC: Duke University Press, 2002.

Jager, Sheila Miyoshi. *Narratives of Nation Building in Korea: A Genealogy of Patriotism.* Armonk, NY: M.E. Sharpe, 2003.

Japan Ministry of Foreign Affairs. "Japan-U.S. Special Action Committee (SACO) Interim Report." April 15, 1996. Accessed July 13, 2009. www.mofa.go.jp/region/n-america/us/security/seco.html.

Jaquette, Jane. "Women and Democracy: Regional Differences and Contrasting Views." *Journal of Democracy* 12, no. 3 (2001), 111–125.

Jung, Jai Kwan. "Growing Supranational Identities in a Globalizing World? A Multilevel Analysis of the World Values Survey." Unpublished paper, Department of Government, Cornell University.

Jung, Shin-mook, Ae-rahn Kim, and Hyun-sun Kim. "The Sisters' Position on the Special Law against Sex Trafficking." In *Sex Trafficking Eradication Project: Networking against the Asian Sex Industry and Promoting Anti Sex Trafficking Legislation.* Conference report, Seoul: Saewoomtuh for Prostituted Women and Their Children/Human Rights Solidarity for Women and Migration in Korea, October 9–11, 2001, 77–86.

Kang, Sang-Won. "The Korean Anti-Base Peace Movement, Focused on P'yŏngt'aek." Global Network against Weapons and Nuclear Power in Space. April 17, 2009. www.space4peace.org/actions/gnconf_09/focus%20on%20pyeongtaek.htm.

Keck, Margaret E., and Kathryn Sikkink. *Activists Beyond Borders: Advocacy Networks in International Politics.* Ithaca, NY: Cornell University Press, 1998.

Kempadoo, Kamala, and Jo Doezema, eds. *Global Sex Workers: Rights, Resistance, and Redefinition.* New York: Routledge, 1998.

Kim, Hyuk-Rae. "The State and Civil Society in Transition: The Role of Non-Governmental Organizations in South Korea." *Pacific Review* 13, no. 4 (2000), 595–613.

Kim, Hyun Sook. "Korea's 'Vietnam Question': War Atrocities, National Identity, and Reconciliation in Asia." *Positions* 9, no. 3 (2001), 621–635.

Kim, Hyunsook Lee. "So'pa kaejŏng, muŏtsi munje inga? Yŏsŏng e kwanjŏm esŏ" (SOFA revision, what are the problems? Women's perspectives). Statement. Seoul, February 8, 2001.

Kim, Hyunsun. "Juhan migun kwa yŏsŏng in'kwŏn" (The U.S. military in Korea and women's human rights). Paper presented at the Jeju Academic Conference on Human Rights, 2001.

Kim, Ilpyong J., and Eun Sung Chung. "Establishing Democratic Rule in South Korea: Local Autonomy and Democracy." *In Depth* 3, no. 1 (1993).

Kim, Jinwung. "Recent Anti-Americanism in South Korea." *Asian Survey* 29, no. 8 (August 1989), 749–763.

Kim, Myongsob, and Jun Young Choi. "Can We Trust America? An Empirical Analysis of Anti-Americanism in South Korea." Paper presented at the Northeastern Political Science Association meeting, Boston, MA, November 11–13, 2004.

Kim, Myongsob, Suzanne Parker, and Jun Choi. "Increasing Distrust of the USA in South Korea." *International Political Science Review* 27, no. 4 (2006), 427–445.

Kim, Myung-hee. "Saewoomtuh for Prostituted Women and Their Children." In *Sex Trafficking Eradication Project: Networking against the Asian Sex Industry and Promoting Anti Sex Trafficking Legislation.* Conference report, Seoul: Saewoomtuh for Prostituted Women and Their Children/Human Rights Solidarity for Women and Migration in Korea, October 9–11, 2001.

Kim, Samuel S. "Northeast Asia in the Local-Regional-Global Nexus: Multiple Challenges and Contending Explanations." In *The International Relations of Northeast Asia,* edited by Samuel S. Kim, 3–64. Lanham, MD: Rowman & Littlefield, 2004.

Kim, Seung-Hwan. "Anti-Americanism in Korea." *The Washington Quarterly* 26, no. 1 (2002), 109–122.

Kim, Sunhyuk, "Civil Society in South Korea: From Grand Democracy Movement to Petty Interest Groups?" *Journal of Northeast Asian Studies* 15, no. 2 (1996), 81–97.

——. *The Politics of Democratization in South Korea: The Role of Civil Society.* Pittsburgh: University of Pittsburgh Press (2000).

——. "State and Civil Society in South Korea's Democratic Consolidation: Is the Battle Really Over?" *Asian Survey* 37, no. 12 (1997), 1135–1144.

Kim, Yi-seon. "Measures to Support Children of Multicultural Families." *Gender Review* (autumn 2009). www.koreafocus.or.kr/design2/layout/content_print.asp?group_id=102827.

Kim, Yonghan. "Okinawa migun kiji panhwan undong e sŏ paeunda" (Learning from the return of U.S. military base movement in Okinawa). *Wŏlgan Mal* (Monthly Mal magazine), September 1996.

Kim, Yŏnja. *Amerika t'aun wang ŏnni* (The King Sister of America town). Seoul: Sam-in Publishing, 2005.

Kirk, Donald. *Korean Crisis: Unraveling of the Miracle in the IMF Era.* New York: St. Martin's Press, 1999.

Korea Church Women United (KCWU). "Women and Tourism: International Seminar Report." Seoul: KCWU, April 20–23, 1988.

Korea Federation of Environmental Movements. "About Us." Accessed March 23, 2007. english.kfem.or.kr/aboutus/aboutus1.htm.

Korean House for International Solidarity. *SOFA Inducement.* Seoul: n.d.

——. *Saram i saram ege* (People to people), April–May 2000.

——. Special feature: "Do You Know about SOFA?" (Nŏhiga SOFA rŭl anŭnga?). *Saram i saram ege* (People to people), October–November 2000.

Kwon, Insook. "Militarism in My Heart: Women's Militarized Consciousness and Culture in South Korea." Ph.D. diss., Clark University, 2000.

Land Research Action Network. "South Korea: US Military Expansion Plan Threatens the Right to Food of 200 Rice Farmers, Taech'uri, P'yŏngt'aek, Kyŏnggi-do Province." Accessed June 20, 2009. www.landaction.org/display.php?article=435.

Lane, Max. "Philippines: Asian Peace Alliance Formed." *Green Left Online,* September 11, 2002. Accessed December 3, 2008. www.greenleft.org.au/2002/508/27508.

Lee, Jae-kyoung. "Anti-Americanism in South Korea: The Media and the Politics of Signification." Ph.D. diss., University of Iowa, 1993.

Lee, Jong Soo. "The Politics of Decentralization in Korea." *Local Government Studies* 22, no. 3 (autumn 1996), 60–71.

Lee, Jung-Hoon. "Globalization, Nationalism, and Security Options for South Korea." In *Democratization and Globalization in Korea: Assessments and Prospects,* edited by Chung-in Moon and Jongryn Mo, 227–246. Seoul: Yonsei University Press, 1999.

Lee, Namhee. "Anti-Communism, North Korea, and Human Rights in South Korea: 'Orientalist' Discourse and Construction of South Korean Identity." In *Truth Claims: Representation and Human Rights,* edited by Mark

Bradley and Patrice Petro, 43–72. New Brunswick, NJ: Rutgers University Press, 2002.

——. *The Making of Minjung: Democracy and the Politics of Representation in South Korea*. Ithaca, NY: Cornell University Press, 2007.

——. "The South Korean Student Movement: Undongkwŏn as a Counterpublic Sphere." In *Korean Society: Civil Society, Democracy, and the State*, edited by Charles K. Armstrong. New York: Routledge, 2006.

Lee, Rose. "Democratic Consolidation and Gender Politics in South Korea." In *Democracy and the Status of Women in East Asia*, edited by Rose J. Lee and Cal Clark, 123–141. Boulder, CO: Lynne Rienner, 2000.

Lee, Seok-woo, and Sung-ha Yoo. "An Issue of Conscience: Conscientious Objection to Military Service in Korea from a Religious and International Viewpoint." Unpublished manuscript, 2005.

Lee, Sook-Jong. "Allying with the U.S.: Changing South Korean Attitudes." *The Korean Journal of Defense Analysis* 17, no. 1 (spring 2005), 81–104.

——. "Anti-Americanism in Korean Society: A Survey-Based Analysis." *The United States and South Korea: Reinvigorating the Partnership* 14, 183–204. Washington, DC: Korea Economic Institute, June 30, 2004.

——. "The Assertive Nationalism of South Korean Youth: Cultural Dynamism and Political Activism." *SAIS Review* 26, no. 2 (2006), 123–132.

——. The Rise of Korean Youth as a Political Force: Implications for the U.S.-Korea Alliance." Paper presentation, Center for Northeast Asia Policy Studies, Brookings Institution, Washington, DC, June 16, 2004. Accessed July 5, 2004. www.brookings.edu/fp/cnaps/events/20040616.htm.

Lee, Su-Hoon. "Korea's Environmental Movement." In *Asia's Environmental Movements: Comparative Perspectives*, edited by Yok-shiu F. Lee and Alvin Y. So, 90–119. Armonk, NY: M. E. Sharpe, 1999.

Lee, Su-Hoon, Hsin-Huang Michael Hsiao, and Hwa-Jen Liu, et al. "The Impact of Democratization on Environmental Movements." In *Asia's Environmental Movements: Comparative Perspectives*, edited by Yok-shiu F. Lee and Alvin Y. So, 230–251. Armonk, NY: M. E. Sharpe, 1999.

Lee, Yean-Ju, Dong-Hoon Seol, and Sung-Nam Cho. "International Marriages in South Korea: The Significance of Nationality and Ethnicity." *Journal of Population Research* 23, no. 2 (2006), 165–182.

Lee, Yok-shiu F., and Alvin Y. So. Introduction to *Asia's Environmental Movements: Comparative Perspectives*, edited by Yok-shiu F. Lee and Alvin Y. So, 5–11. Armonk, NY: M. E. Sharpe, 1999.

Lee, Yoonkyung. "Migration, Migrants, and Contested Ethno-Nationalism in Korea." *Critical Asian Studies* 41, no. 3 (2009), 363–380.

Lee, Yujin (Green Korea United). "Forbidden Rights to Pollute the Korean Peninsula: U.S. Military Activities and Environmental Disaster." People's Solidarity for Participatory Democracy. January 31, 2003. Accessed January 15, 2009. blog.peoplepower21.org/English/8505.

LeeAn, Jiyoung. "Resistance to 'Integration' by Marriage Migrants." *AALA*

Newsletter 7, Friends of Asia (December 2008). www.arenaonline.org/xe/?document_srl=254.

Leong, Anthony C. Y. *Korean Cinema: The New Hong Kong.* Victoria, Canada: Trafford Publishing, 2002.

Lewis, Linda Sue. *Laying Claim to the Memory of May: A Look Back at the 1980 Kwangju Uprising*. Honolulu: University of Hawai'i Press, 2002.

Lindsay-Poland, John, and Nick Morgan. "Overseas Military Bases and Environment." *Foreign Policy in Focus* 3, no. 15 (June 1998). Accessed January 28, 2006. www.fpif.org/briefs/vol3/v3n15mil_body.html.

Ling, Lily H. M. "The Limits of Democratization for Women in East Asia." In *Democracy and the Status of Women in East Asia,* edited by Rose J. Lee and Cal Clark, 169–182. Boulder, CO: Lynne Rienner, 2000.

Linz, Juan J., and Alfred Stepan. "Toward Consolidated Democracies." *Journalof Democracy* 7, no. 2 (1996), 14–33.

Magno, Francisco A. "Environmental Movements in the Philippines" In *Asia's Environmental Movements: Comparative Perspectives,* edited by Yok-shiu F. Lee and Alvin Y. So, 143–178. New York: M. E. Sharpe, 1999.

McAdam, Doug. "Legacies of Anti-Americanism: A Sociological Perspective." In *Anti-Americanisms in World Politics,* edited by Peter J. Katzenstein and Robert O. Keohane, 251–272. Ithaca, NY: Cornell University Press, 2007.

McCarthy, John D. "Velcro Triangles: Elite Mobilization of Local Antidrug Issue Coalitions." In *Routing the Opposition: Social Movements, Public Policy, and Democracy,* edited by David S. Meyer, Valerie Jenness, and Helen Ingram, 87–116. Indianapolis: University of Minnesota Press, 2005.

McCarthy, John D., and Mayer N. Zald. "Resource Mobilization and Social Movements: A Partial Theory." *American Journal of Sociology* 82, no. 6 (May 1977), 1212–1241.

———. "Social Movement Industries: Competition and Cooperation among Movement Organizations." In *Research in Social Movements, Conflicts, and Change,* vol. 3, edited by Louis Kriesberg. Greenwich, CT: JAI Press, 1980.

McReynolds, John A. "Community Relations Advisory Council (CRAC), Bupyong (ASCOM)." Memorandum, U.S. Forces Korea, November 1, 1968.

Mendel, Douglas H. "Japanese Views of the American Alliance." *Public Opinion Quarterly* 23, no. 3 (1959), 326–342.

Mitchell, Derek J., ed. *Strategy and Sentiment: South Korean Views of the United States and the U.S.-ROK Alliance.* Washington, DC: Center for Strategic and International Studies, 2004.

Mo, Jongryn. "Political Learning, Democratic Consolidation, and Politics of Labor Reform in South Korea." In *Democratic Consolidation and Globalization in Korea: Assessments and Prospect,* edited by Chung-in Moon and Jongryn Mo, 303–326. Seoul: Yonsei University Press, 1999.

Mochizuki, Mike M. "A New Bargain for a Stronger Alliance." In *Toward a True Alliance: Restructuring U.S.-Japan Security Relations,* edited by Mike M. Mochizuki, 5–42. Washington, DC: Brookings Institution, 1997.

Moon, Chung-in. "Changing South Korean Perception of the United States since September 11." Paper presented at the annual meeting of the Japan Association for Asian Studies, Tokyo, November 8, 2003.

———. "Globalization: Challenges and Strategies." *Korea Focus* 3, no. 3 (May/June 1995), 62–77.

———. "South Korea: Recasting Security Paradigms." In *Asian Security Practices: Material and Ideational Influences,* edited by Muthiah Alagappa, 264–287. Stanford: CA: Stanford University Press, 1998.

———. "South Korea in 2008: From Crisis to Crisis" *Asian Survey* 49, no. 1 (2009), 120–128.

Moon, Katharine H.S. "Citizen Power in Korean-American Relations." In *Korean Attitudes toward the United States: Changing Dynamics,* edited by David I. Steinberg, 233–246. Armonk, NY: M.E. Sharpe, 2005.

———. "Civil Society Organizations and Alliance Politics." In *Strategy and Sentiment: South Korean Popular Opinion and the U.S.-ROK Alliance,* edited by Derek Mitchell. Washington DC: Center for Strategic and International Studies, 2004.

———. "Korean Nationalism, Anti-Americanism and Democratic Consolidation." In *Korea's Democratization,* edited by Samuel S. Kim, 135–158. New York: Cambridge University Press, 2003.

———. "Migrant Workers' Movements in Movements in Japan and South Korea." In *Egalitarian Politics in the Age of Globalization,* edited by Craig N. Murphy, 174–204. London: Palgrave, 2002.

———. *Sex among Allies: Military Prostitution in U.S.-Korea Relations.* New York: Columbia University Press, 1997.

———. "South Korean Movements against Militarized Sexual Labor." *Asian Survey* 39, no. 2 (March-April 1999), 310–327.

———. "South Korea–U.S. Relations." *Asian Perspective* 28, no. 4 (2004), 39–61.

———. "Strangers in the Midst of Globalization: Migrant Workers and Korean Nationalism." In *Korea's Globalization,* edited by Samuel S. Kim, 147–169. New York: Cambridge University Press, 2000.

Moon, Seungsook. "Carving Out Space: Civil Society and the Women's Movement in South Korea." *Journal of Asian Studies* 61, no. 2 (2002), 473–500.

———. *Militarized Modernity and Gendered Citizenship in South Korea.* Durham, NC: Duke University Press, 2005.

———. "Overcome by Globalization: The Rise of a Women's Policy in South Korea." In *Korea's Globalization,* edited by Samuel S. Kim, 126–146. New York: Cambridge University Press, 2000.

———. "A Reflection on 'Multiculturalism' and Migrant Workers in South Korea." *AALA Newsletter* 7, Friends of Asia (December 2008).

Nam, Chang-hee. "Relocating the U.S. Forces in South Korea: Strained Alliance, Emerging Partnership in the Changing Defense Posture." *Asian Survey* 46, no. 4 (2006), 615–631.

National Campaign for the Eradication of Crime by U.S. Troops in Korea.

"Migun changabch'a e ŭihae sumjin tu yŏjungsaeng e chugŭm ŭl aedohamyŏ" (Statement of condolence over the death of the two school girls killed by the U.S. armored vehicle). July 14, 2002. Accessed September 24, 2002. www.usacrime.or.kr.

Needler, Martin C. "The Latin American Military: Predatory Reactionaries or Modernizing Patriots?" *Journal of Inter-American Studies* 11, no. 2 (April 1969), 237–244.

Nelson, Laura C. *Measured Excess: Status, Gender, and Consumer Nationalism in South Korea*. New York: Columbia University Press, 2000.

Neumann, A. Lin. "Hospitality Girls in the Philippines." *Southeast Asia Chronicle*, no. 66 (January–February 1979), 18–23.

Nitta, Keith A. "Paradigms." In *U.S.-Japan Relations in a Changing World*, edited by Steven K. Vogel, 63–93. Washington, DC: Brookings Institution Press, 2002.

Norris, Pippa, and Ronald Inglehart. "Women and Democracy. Cultural Obstacles to Equal Representation." *Journal of Democracy* 12, no. 3 (2001), 126-140.

Nye, Joseph S. "The Case for Deep Engagement." *Foreign Affairs* 74 (July–August 1995), 90–102.

Oh, John Kie-chiang. "Anti-Americanism and Anti-Authoritarian Politics in Korea." In *Two Koreas in Transition: Implications for U.S. Policy*, edited by Ilpyong J. Kim, 245–262. Rockville, MD: In Depth Books, 1998.

Oh, Kyung-Taek. "Transnational Cooperation of NGOs in Northeast Asia: Campaign against Shipment of Taiwanese Nuclear Waste to North Korea." Paper presented at the annual meeting of the American Political Science Association, August 29–September 1, 2002.

O'Neil, Andrew. "The 2000 Inter-Korean Summit: The Road to Reconciliation?" *Australian Journal of International Affairs* 55, no. 1 (April 1, 2001), 55–63.

Ota, Masahide. "Governor Ota at the Supreme Court of Japan." In *Okinawa: Cold War Island*, edited by Chalmers A. Johnson. Cardiff, CA: Japan Policy Research Institute, 1999.

Park, Heh-Rahn. "Narratives of Migration: From the Formation of Korean Chinese Nationality in the PRC to the Emergence of Korean Chinese Migrants in South Korea." Ph.D. diss., University of Washington, 1996.

Peace Boat. "Japanese-Korean Historic Peace Voyage Marks 60 Years since World War II." April 26, 2005. Accessed December 12, 2008. www.peaceboat.org/english/nwps/pr/arc/050426/index.html.

——. "Regional Voyage 2007." October 28, 2007. Accessed December 12, 2008. www.peaceboat.org/english/voyg/61/index.html.

People's Solidarity for Participatory Democracy. *Ch'amyŏ sahoe* (Participatory society). April 2002.

——. "Forbidden Rights to Pollute the Korean Peninsula: U.S Military Activities and Environmental Disaster." January 31, 2003. Accessed March 21, 2010. blog.peoplepower21.org/English/8505.

Perpinan, Sister Mary Soledad, R.G.S. "Confronting Prostitution Tourism." *Canadian Women's Studies* 7, nos. 1–2 (1986), 125–129.

Pew Global Attitudes Project. *Views of a Changing World.* Washington, DC: Pew Research Center for the People and the Press, 2003.

———. "American Character Gets Mixed Reviews: U.S. Image Up Slightly, But Still Negative." Survey report, June 23, 2005. pewglobal.org/2005/06/23/us-image-up-slightly-but-still-negative.

Pew Research Center. *Trends 2005*. Washington, DC: Pew Research Center, 2005. pewresearch.org/assets/files/trends2005.pdf.

Pew Research Center for the People and the Press. *What the World Thinks in 2002. How Global Publics View: Their Lives, Their Countries, The World, America.* Washington, DC: Pew Research Center, 2002. www.people-press.org/2002/12/04/what-the-world-thinks-in-2002/.

"Philippine Public Opinion Is Mixed on Presence of U.S. Troops." *Stars and Stripes.* March 1, 2002. Accessed November 19, 2003. www.globalsecurity.org/military/library/news/2002/03/mil-020301-ss02.htm.

Pinguel, Bal, Herbert Docena, and Wilbert van der Zeijden. "No Bases." *Report on the Strategy Meetings of the International Network against Foreign Military Bases.* World Social Forum 2005, Brazil, January 27, 31, 2005. Accessed December 12, 2008. www.tni.org/acts/wsf5bases.pdf.

Putnam, Robert D. "Bowling Alone: America's Declining Social Capital." *Journal of Democracy* 6, no. 1 (January 1995), 65–78.

———. *Making Democracy Work: Civic Traditions in Modern Italy.* Princeton: Princeton University Press, 1993.

Rainbow Center (Flushing, NY). *Rainbow Newsletter* no. 3 (1994).

Reel, Monte, and Manny Fernandez. "More than 100,000 March in Washington, DC: Antiwar Protest Largest Since '60s." *Washington Post.* October 27, 2002. www.commondreams.org/headlines02/1027-07.htm.

Republic of Korea Ministry of Environment. "Local Agenda 21 in Korea." October 17, 2003. Accessed January 20, 2009. eng.me.go.kr/docs/news/hotissue/hotissue_view.html?topmenu=E&cat=520&seq=19&page=4.

Republic of Korea Ministry of Foreign Affairs and Trade, North America Division. "Sŏlmyŏng charyo-LPP hyŏbjŏng palhyo" (Materials for explaining the LPP agreement). October 31, 2002. Accessed November 24, 2002. www.mofat.go.kr/main/index.jsp.

Ricks, Thomas. "The Military and Society." *Atlantic Monthly,* July 1997.

Riley, Thomas R., and Steven A. Raho III. "Engagement and Enlargement in Korea." U.S. Army War College Fellowship research project, U.S. Army War College, Carlisle Barracks, PA, April 1996.

Rose, Fred. *Coalitions across the Class Divide: Lessons from the Labor, Peace, and Environmental Movements.* Ithaca, NY: Cornell University Press, 2000.

Saewoomtuh Counseling Center. "SOFA kaejŏng e daehan uri e ipjang" (Our position on the SOFA revision). July 27, 2000.

Santos, Aida. "Gathering the Dust: The Bases Issue in the Philippines." In *Let the Good Times Roll,* edited by Saundra Sturdevant and Brenda Stolzfus. New York: New Press, 1992.

Sasada, Hironori. "Youth and Nationalism in Japan." *SAIS Review* 26, no. 2 (summer–fall 2006), 109–122.

Schreurs, Miranda A. *Environmental Politics in Japan, Germany, and the United States.* New York: Cambridge University Press, 2002.

Schwartz, Gary. *Beyond Conformity or Rebellion: Youth and Authority in America.* Chicago: University of Chicago Press, 1987.

Seong, Kyoung-Ryung. "Civil Society and Democratic Consolidation in South Korea: Great Achievements and Remaining Problems." In *Consolidating Democracy in South Korea,* edited by Larry Diamond and Byung-Kook Kim, 87–109. Boulder, CO: Lynne Rienner, 2000.

———. "Delayed Decentralization and Incomplete Democratic Consolidation." In *Institutional Reform and Democratic Consolidation in Korea,* edited by Larry Diamond and Doh Chull Shin, 1271–1248. Stanford: Hoover Institution Press, 2000.

Shim, Doobo. "The Growth of Korean Cultural Industries and the Korean Wave." In *East Asian Pop Culture: Analysing the Korean Wave,* edited by Chua Beng Huat and Koichi Iwabuchi. Hong Kong: Hong Kong University Press, 2008.

Shin, Gi-Wook. *Ethnic Nationalism in Korea: Genealogy, Politics, and Legacy.* Stanford, CA: Stanford University Press, 2006.

———. "Marxism, Anti-Americanism, and Democracy in South Korea: An Examination of Nationalist Intellectual Discourse." *Positions* 3, no. 2 (1995), 510–536.

———. "South Korean Anti-Americanism: A Comparative Perspective." *Asian Survey* 36, no. 8 (August 1996), 787–803.

Shin, Gi-Wook, and Kyung Moon Hwang, eds. *Contentious Kwangju: The May 18 Uprising in Korea's Past and Present.* Lanham, MD: Rowman & Littlefield, 2003.

Shin, Gi-Wook, James Freda, and Gihong Yi. "The Politics of Ethnic Nationalism in Divided Korea." *Nations and Nationalism* 5, no. 4 (October 1999), 465–484.

Shorrock, Tim. "The Struggle for Democracy in South Korea in the 1980s and the Rise of Anti-Americanism." *Third World Quarterly* 8, no. 4 (October 1986), 1195–1218.

Singerman, Diane. "The Economic Imperatives of Marriage: Emerging Practices and Identities among Youth in the Middle East." Working paper (Middle East Youth Initiative) no. 6. Washington, DC: Wolfensohn Center for Development, Brookings Institution, September 2007.

Sison, Marites. "Philippine Reaction to the Return of U.S. Troops: 'Welcome Back, GI Joe.'" February 19, 2002. Accessed November 19, 2003. www.worldpress.org/article_model.cfm?article_id=501&dont=yes.

Smith, Jackie. "Exploring Connections between Global Integration and Political Mobilization." *Journal of World-Systems Research* 10 (2004), 255–285.

Smith, Sheila A. "Challenging National Authority: Okinawa Prefecture and the U.S. Military Bases." In *Local Voices, National Issues: The Impact of Local Initiative in Japanese Policy-Making,* edited by Sheila A. Smith, 101–103. Ann Arbor, MI: University of Michigan Press, 2000.

———. *Shifting Terrain: The Domestic Politics of the U.S. Military Presence in Asia*. Honolulu: East-West Center, 2006.

Smith, Tony. "National Security Liberalism and American Foreign Policy." In *American Democracy Promotion,* edited by Michael Cox, G. John Ikenberry, and Takashi Inoguchi, 85–103. New York: Oxford University Press, 2000.

Snow, David A., E. Burke Rochford, Jr., Steven K. Worden, and Robert D. Benford. "Frame Alignment Processes, Micromobilization, and Movement Participation." *American Sociological Review* 51 (August 1986), 464–481.

Sohn, Bong-Scuk, and Chung-Si Ahn, "Citizen Participation in Local Governance in South Korea." Paper presented at the conference "New Developments in Local Democracy in Asia: Appraising a Decade of Experience, Problems, and Prospects." Seoul: Seoul National University, April 8–9, 2002.

Song, Ho-Keun. "Local Government and Social Development: Leadership, Development, and Participation." Paper presented at the conference "New Developments in Local Democracy in Asia: Appraising a Decade of Experience, Problems, and Prospects." Seoul: Seoul National University, April 8–9, 2002.

Song, Jin. *Financial Crisis in Korea: Implications for US-Korea Relations.* Occasional paper. Honolulu: Asia-Pacific Center for Security Studies, May 1998. Accessed May 16, 2001. www.apcss.org/Publications/Ocasional%20Papers/OPKorea.html.

"South Korea's Filmmakers Roll Into Action to Protect Foreign-Movie Quota." *International Herald Tribune,* December 11, 1998. Accessed April 2, 2008. www.iht.com/articles/1998/12/11/seoul.t_0.php.

Staggenborg, Suzanne. "Coalition Work in the Pro-Choice Movement: Organizational and Environmental Opportunities and Obstacles." *Social Problems* 33, no. 5 (June 1986), 374–390.

"Statement of the Japan Environment Lawyers Federation Regarding the Dugong Population of Okinawa." Japan Environmental Lawyers Federation. August 1, 2001. Accessed November 13, 2003. jca.apc.org/JELF/English/JELFstateD.html.

"Students' Consciousness regarding the Constitution." *Minami Nippon Shimbun*. Accessed May 12, 2004. www.jca.apc.org/~kenpoweb/articles/oguri112500.html.

Sturdevant, Saundra, and Brenda Stolzfus. "Disparate Threads of the Whole: An Interpretive Essay." In *Let the Good Times Roll,* edited by Saundra Sturdevant and Brenda Stolzfus. New York: New Press, 1992.

"Survey and Preservation of the Dugongs and Habitat in Okinawa and a Message for World Peace." Love Dugong Network. 2nd ed. March 11, 2000.

Accessed November 12, 2003. www.okinawa-u.ac.jp/~tsuchida/Save-Dugong/love/messageE.html.

Tanaka, Nobumasa. "High School Students Struggle against National Anthem Enforcement." December 14, 2002. Accessed May 12, 2004. www.zmag.org/content/print_article.cfm?itemID=2750§ionID=17.

Tarrow, Sidney G. *The New Transnational Activism.* New York: Cambridge University Press, 2005.

———. *Power in Movement: Social Movements and Contentious Politics.* New York: Cambridge University Press, 1998.

Thompson, W. Scott. "Anti-Americanism and the U.S. Government." In *Annals of the American Academy of Political and Social Science* 497, edited by Thomas Perry Thornton, 20–34. 1988.

"Top Commander in Korea Urges Three-Year, Accompanied Tours." American Forces Press Service, March 11, 2008. Accessed August 7, 2008. www.defenselink.mil.

"Town Invites U.S. Airmen to Party." *Stars and Stripes,* October 10, 2003.

Tripp, Aili Mari. "Women and Democracy: The New Political Activism in Africa." *Journal of Democracy* 12, no. 3 (2001), 141–155.

Truong, Thanh-dam. *Sex, Money, and Morality: Prostitution and Tourism in Southeast Asia.* Atlantic Highlands, NJ: Zed Books, 1990.

UNESCAP (United Nations Economic and Social Commission for Asia and the Pacific), Human Settlements section. "Country Paper: Republic of Korea." In *Local Government in Asia and the Pacific: A Comparative Analysis of Fifteen Countries* (n.d.). Accessed March 24, 2009. www.unescap.org/huset/lgstudy/country/korea/korea.html.

United Nations Environment Program. "The Programme for the Development and Periodic Review of Environmental Law for the First Decade of the Twenty-First Century." Decision 21/23 of the Governing Council of 9, February 16–17, 2001. Accessed January 16, 2009. www.unep.org/law/PDF/GC22_2_3_add2_Montevideo%20III.pdf.

U.S. Army. "Tour Normalization in the Republic of Korea." *Stand-To!* Accessed June 5, 2010. www.army.mil/standto/archive/2009/05/29.

U.S. Army Headquarters. Combined Forces Command. FC 9518. "ANNEX L to CFC OPLAN (KOREA) 9518X-XX, ENVIRONMENTAL CONSIDERATIONS." Seoul, n.d. ["June 1, 19xx"].

U.S. Department of the Air Force. District 45 (AFOSI). Report of Investigation. File #7745D6-206. August 5, 1977.

U.S. Department of Defense. DOD Directive 6050.16. "DOD Policy for Establishing and Implementing Environmental Standards at Overseas Installations." September 20, 1991.

———. "Statement of General B.B. Bell, Commander, United Nations Command; Commander, Republic of Korea–United States Combined Forces Command; and Commander, United States Forces Korea, before the House Armed Services Committee." March 12, 2008. www.dod.gov/dodgc/olc/docs/testBell080312.pdf.

U.S. Department of State, Office of Research. "Trends in South Korean Opinion of the U.S." Opinion analysis M-42-03, April 9, 2003.

U.S. General Accounting Office. Report to Congressional Requesters. "Military Base Closures: U.S. Financial Obligations in the Philippines." Washington, DC: January 1992.

U.S. National Intelligence Council. "East Asia and the United States: Current Status and Five-Year Outlook Conference Report." September 2000. Accessed January 10, 2006. www.dni.gov/nic/confreports_asiaUSoutlook.html.

U.S. Senate Armed Services Committee. *Department of Defense Authorization for Appropriations for Fiscal Year 2002: Hearings on S. 1416*. 107th Cong. 1st sess. March 27, 2001. Available at www.gpo.gov.

U.S. Senate. Armed Services Committee. "Statement of General B. B. Bell." April 24, 2007. Accessed July 8, 2009. www.globalsecurity.org/military/library/congress/2007_hr/070424-bell.pdf.

"US Servicemen Broaden 'Good Neighbors.'" *Korea Times*, May 29, 2008.

Veterans For Peace. *Report of the VFP Delegation to South Korea*. October 5, 2006. Accessed July 18, 2009. www.veteransforpeace.org/File/pdf/Korea%20Delegation%20Report.pdf.

Tikhonov, Vladimir (Pak Noja). "South Korea—An Inverted Pyramid?" *AALA Newsletter* 7, Friends of Asia (December 2008).

Waylen, Georgina. "Women and Democratization: Conceptualizing Gender Relations in Transition Politics." *World Politics* 46 (1994).

Weigley, Russell F. "The American Civil-Military Cultural Gap: A Historical Perspective, Colonial Times to the Present." In *Soldiers and Civilians: The Civil-Military Gap and American National Security*, edited by Peter D. Feaver and Richard H. Kohn, 215–246. Cambridge, MA: MIT Press, 2001.

Wells, Kenneth M. "The Price of Legitimacy: Women and the Kŭnuhoe Movement, 1927–1931." In *Colonial Modernity in Korea*, edited by Gi-Wook Shin and Michael Robinson, 191–220. Cambridge, MA: Harvard University Press, 1999.

Wickam, John A. *Korea on the Brink: A Memoir of Political Intrigue and Military Crisis*. Dulles, VA: Brassey's Inc., 2000.

Wiest, Dawn, and Jackie Smith. "Regional Institutional Contexts and Patterns of Transnational Social Movement Organization." *Korea Observer* 37, no. 1 (spring 2006).

Yamamoto, Tadashi. *Deciding the Public Good: Governance and Civil Society in Japan*. Tokyo: Japan Center for International Exchange, 1999.

Yang, Gi-Yong. "Attitudes, Issues and Agenda for New Relationship between Local Communities and the USFK." Working paper, Pukyong National University, November 5, 2004.

Yi, Kyochŏng. "Chuhan migun ui Yun Kŭmi-ssi salhae sa'gŏn kwa Tongduch'ŏn simindŭl ui tujaeng" (The case of the USFK murder of Yun Kŭmi and Tongduch'ŏn citizens' struggle). September 17, 2002.

Yi, Pyŏnggil. "Pup'yŏng migun kiji twich'atgi wa chiyŏk undong" (Pup'yŏng return of land and regional movement). In Chu han migun munje haegyŏl Undongsa (Korean People's Movement for Solution of U.S. Forces Korea Issues), *Nogŭlli esŏ Maehyangni kkaji* (From Nogunri to Maehyangri). Seoul: Dosŏ Publishing, 2000.

Yoshida, Shin'ichi. "Rethinking the Public Interest in Japan: Civil Society in the Making." In *Deciding the Public Good: Governance and Civil Society in Japan*, edited by Tadashi Yamamoto, 13–50. Japan Center for International Exchange, 1999.

Zakaria, Fareed. *The Future of Freedom: Illiberal Democracy at Home and Abroad*. New York: W. W. Norton, 2003.

Index

www.ingramcontent.com/pod-product-compliance
Lightning Source LLC
Chambersburg PA
CBHW020342270326
41926CB00007B/281

* 9 7 8 0 5 2 0 2 8 9 8 1 9 *